MIND
FOR MINDFUL PARENTING

A No-Fluff Daily Guide to Parenting Gen Beta with Love and Science (0–5 Years)

SHRADHA MAHESHWARI

Disclaimer

This book is intended for informational and educational purposes only and should not be considered a substitute for medical, developmental, or professional advice. While the activities and recommendations are based on scientific research and best practices, every child is unique, and their growth and development may vary.

Parents and caregivers should use their own discretion and consult with a paediatrician, child development specialist, or healthcare provider before implementing any activities, especially if a child has specific medical or developmental needs. The author and publisher assume no liability for any outcomes resulting from the use of this book.

Use your intuition, not just information.

Dedication

This book is dedicated to all the parents, caregivers, and educators who devote themselves to nurturing the limitless potential of young minds. Your unwavering dedication shapes the future in ways words alone cannot express.

To my family and friends - your steadfast support fuels my ambition, and your belief in me has been my greatest strength. To my husband, Sourabh—thank you for standing by me through every late night, every doubt, and every dream. This book carries your quiet strength in every page.

And to the fellow moms who generously shared their journeys — your stories bring heart, honesty, and hope to these pages. This book is as much yours as it is mine.

And to **Samarth**, who gifted me the profound journey of motherhood, teaching me the true essence of presence, patience, and purpose. You have shown me that with awareness and the right tools, a mother can navigate the delicate balance between parenting and pursuing her dreams, without the weight of guilt.

With love and gratitude, this book is for you.

Table of Contents

A Moment that Changed Everything

I still remember the night I sat by Samarth's crib, completely overwhelmed. The house was quiet, but my mind was racing. I had a to-do list a mile long, parenting books stacked by the bed, and an anxious voice whispering: Am I doing enough?

Then he looked up at me, just a few months old, his tiny hand wrapping around my finger, his eyes locking into mine with pure trust - like I was his whole world.

And in that instant, everything shifted.

It wasn't about being the "perfect" parent.

It wasn't about the play gym mat we had set up or organic flashcards.

It was about this connection — raw, real, and powerful.

That night, I let go of the pressure to perform and embraced the power of presence. I stopped worrying if I was doing "enough," and started trusting that I was enough — and so was Samarth.

Because when we become fully present, we don't just raise a child- we awaken their genius.

That's the moment I became a mindful parent.

And what followed was magical.

Samarth began engaging more, smiling more, exploring his world with fearless curiosity. I saw how the smallest moments, a shared giggle, a story at bedtime, a song during bath, were building the strongest foundations for his future.

This book was born from that shift. It's a guide to the everyday magic of mindful parenting - where brain development meets love, play, and presence. A soul-deep reminder that you are exactly what your child needs.

Let's raise brilliant little humans with intention, love, and presence.

One mindful moment at a time.

Dear Parent,

Congratulations on beginning this incredible journey with your child. The early years, especially from birth to five, is the most powerful and magical window for brain development. But here's the beautiful truth:

You don't need to pressure, drill, or rush your child to learn.

What they need is **you** - your time, your voice, your playful spirit, and your love. That's what builds the strongest, smartest, and happiest brains.

This book is not about pushing your child to "get ahead." It's about giving them the **right kind of experiences at the right time** - through play, connection, and everyday moments.

What This Book Offers

This book doesn't just *tell* you what matters, it *shows* you how to do it: step-by-step, every day.

- **A science-backed, stage-by-stage roadmap** to unlock your child's brain potential from birth to age 5

- **Joyful, easy-to-do activities** that build brain connections while feeling like play

No pressure. No screens. No perfection needed.

It's not school at home — it's parenting with intention, guided by research.

Why It Works

Your child's brain develops fastest in these early years.

Every time you read a story, stack blocks, sing a song, or play peek-a-boo, you're actually **building the brain's wiring** for language, thinking, movement, math, focus, and empathy.

And because it all happens through love and play, your child learns **with joy, not fear**.

From One Parent to Another

Whether you follow the plan daily or a few times a week, you are making a difference. You're helping your child become not just smarter but **more curious, confident, and connected**.

With heart,

– Shradha Maheshwari

Parent. Love-Giver. Joy-bringer.

CHAPTER 1

Introduction

Why the First Five Years Matter Most

Did you know that by the age of five, your child's brain will have built nearly 90% of its neural connections? Every experience, every interaction, and every moment of play shapes the foundation for their future intelligence, emotional resilience, and social skills. Harvard University's Centre on the Developing Child reports that a baby's brain forms **more than 1 million new neural connections every second** during the first few years of life. These connections form the foundation for learning, memory, emotional regulation, and social skills.

There are **critical windows** in early development:

- **Language** – 80% of language skills are established by age 3.

- **Emotional Regulation** – Empathy and self-control circuits form early.

- **Motor & Sensory Skills** – Coordination and sensory processing peak before age 5.

But with parenting advice coming from every direction - community, blogs, forums, reels - it's easy to feel overwhelmed.

That's where this book comes in. It's a research-backed, practical roadmap to support your child's development in a joyful, natural way, one day at a time

The Role of Mindful Parenting

Your child's brain is built not just through time, it's built through **presence.**

Mindful parenting means being aware, intentional, and emotionally available. It's about enriching your child's world through everyday moments, talking, playing, reading, bonding - not expensive tools or rigid schedules.

When you engage mindfully:

- You build neural pathways that support critical thinking and emotional intelligence
- You foster creativity and resilience
- You create a secure environment where your child thrives

Conversely, disengagement or overexposure to screens can hinder healthy brain wiring, leading to emotional or cognitive delays. With mindful parenting, you're not just managing the day, you're *shaping a future.*

As a parent or caregiver, you have an extraordinary opportunity to influence your child's future. This book is your daily tool for turning ordinary moments into rich developmental experiences and building a brain that is wired for success - academically, socially, and emotionally.

At the heart of this book is the **M.I.N.D. Framework** — a simple yet powerful model for turning mindful parenting into meaningful daily action.

Each letter stands for a core principle that guides this journey from birth to age five:

M - Moments That Matter

- *Be present in the small things - they're the building blocks of your child's brain.*

- Prioritize presence over perfection. Every interaction is a chance to connect and grow.

I - Intentional Interaction

- *It doesn't take more time - just more attention.*

- Thoughtfully designed, brain-building play fuels development in natural, joyful ways.

N - Nurture Through Love

- *Love isn't extra - it's essential wiring.*

- Responsive, emotionally secure parenting lays the foundation for resilience, empathy, and trust.

D - Daily Growth

- *Each day matters. Small actions, done consistently, create lifelong impact.*

- With age-appropriate guidance and everyday tools, your child flourishes, one moment, one milestone at a time.

This framework will ground you in what truly matters: **connection over perfection, presence over pressure,** and science-backed parenting that's **done with love, not overwhelm.**

Why This Book?

In a world overflowing with parenting content, it's hard to know what to trust

Many well-known parenting books explain *why* early brain development matters and once I understood the theory, I wanted a joyful, grounded plan I could follow in real life during playtime, bath time, or even a meltdown.

This book is that plan. A no-fluff, daily companion to help you nurture your child's growing brain with love, presence, and science-backed actions.

And more importantly—**this book is designed for today's child.**

We're not raising the children we once were—we're raising Generation Alpha and beyond, the first true children of the future. They will grow up in a world more complex, more digital, and more demanding than we can predict. The parenting methods of the past don't fit this new world. What Gen Alpha needs is not pressure, but presence. Not rote learning, but resilience. Not perfect parents, but connected ones.

It's time for a shift : toward mindful, connected parenting that nurtures the whole child and equips them to thrive in a future we can't fully predict. This book is your clear, science-backed guide, offering:

- A complete developmental plan - cognitive, emotional, motor, sensory, and physical
- Month-by-month, week-by-week, and day-by-day breakdowns
- Age-wise activities using everyday items - no fancy toys required
- A screen-free approach focused on connection, not consumption
- Expert insights from top child development research globally

It's not just a book, it's your daily tool for confident, connected parenting.

Raising a genius doesn't require expensive toys. It takes the right strategies, meaningful interactions, and age-appropriate activities. This book shows you how simple, everyday objects can be even more powerful than high-end educational gadgets.

With this book, your coffee table companion, you'll:

- Have a trusted guide to support development
- Reduce parenting stress and decision fatigue
- Feel confident that you're doing "enough" every single day

And for those moments when you wonder *"What should I do with my toddler today?"* this book has your back.

Who Is This Book For?

- **Parents & Caregivers** seeking a structured plan to enhance their child's early brain development.
- **Educators** looking for engaging, activity-based learning tools.
- **Paediatricians & Child Development Professionals** who wish to recommend evidence-based strategies to families.

How This Book Is Designed

To ensure holistic development, this book focuses on **7 core areas**:

- **Cognitive Development** – Problem-solving, memory, attention
- **Motor Development** – Fine/gross motor skills, hand-eye coordination
- **Language & Communication** – Speech, comprehension, vocabulary
- **Sensory Development** – Exploring textures, sounds, and environments

- **Social-Emotional Growth** – Bonding, empathy, self-regulation

- **Physical Development** – Strength, posture, mobility

- **Creative Exploration** – Imagination, play, and artistic expression

Each chapter breaks down the first five years into age-appropriate stages. The plan moves month-by-month, week-by-week, and day-by-day. Every activity is tailored to support these 7 core developmental areas without overwhelming you.

This structure means you won't need multiple resources or scattered ideas. Just open to your child's age and begin.

How to Use This Book

You don't need hours. You just need **intentional moments**.

Here's how:

- Follow the structured plan for your child's age

- Choose from curated daily and weekly activities

- Track progress with milestone checklists

- Use the Parent Toolkit for extra ideas and tips

- Be flexible - if today's activity doesn't work, try again later

- Don't stress if your child isn't "getting it" right away, each child grows at their own pace

- Avoid comparison - your child's journey is uniquely beautiful

- Enjoy the process - focus on connection, not perfection

- Make it a habit - keep this book nearby and use it often

- Repeat what works - repetition reinforces learning

With this guide, you'll always have a plan. No second-guessing. No overwhelm.

Unlock Your Child's Full Potential

By following this science-backed developmental plan, you'll raise a child who is confident, curious, and well-rounded.

This book is your companion in creating joyful, meaningful early childhood experiences—laying the foundation for a lifetime of learning and success.

Let's begin this beautiful journey together. One Mindful moment at a time.

CHAPTER 2

Year 1: The Foundation Year

Sensory Growth & Emotional Bonding

Quote

"The way we talk to our children becomes their inner voice."

— Peggy O'Mara

Mantra

I am my child's safe place. Every cuddle, every gaze, is shaping a beautiful brain.

M.I.N.D. for Year 1

Moments That Matter

Be present in the small things - they're the building blocks of your baby's brain.

Intentional Interaction

Every cuddle, coo, and lullaby is a brain-building gift.

Nurture Through Love

Your calm, warm responses build emotional safety and trust.

Daily Growth

Tiny milestones today lay the foundation for a lifetime of learning.

Welcome to Year 1: The Foundation Year

The first year of your baby's life is filled with quiet milestones and powerful brain development. Every coo, cuddle, and glance is helping build over a million neural connections every second. But this year is foundational not just for your baby — it's for you, too.

You're learning how to tune in, how to trust your instincts, and how to turn ordinary moments into meaningful ones. This year is not about doing more — it's about noticing more. With just a little awareness, everyday moments become brain-building, heart-strengthening, and deeply connective.

Let's begin.

How to Use This Guide in Year 1

This guide is designed to support you without overwhelming you. You don't need special toys, a perfect routine, or a checklist to chase. You just need intention, consistency, and presence.

Here's how to use it:

- Follow the same daily structure: 7 short activities a week, with 2–3 expanded Mindful Moments for depth and insight.

- Each month includes milestones, a unique Reflect & Recharge, and a supportive "What If..." section and a relatable parent story.

- Start small. Do what you can each day. One mindful moment is more powerful than a perfect schedule.

- Repeat freely. Babies love repetition. If something sparks joy or connection, return to it often.

- Trust the rhythm. Each month builds gently on the last — no pressure, no deadlines.

- Flip to your baby's current month and begin from there. This is your anchor, not your to-do list.

You've already started the most important work — showing up with love. This guide simply shows you how to build on that, one mindful day at a time.

Let this be your *daily anchor* — not your to-do list.

Month 1: Mindful Beginnings

Focus: Bonding, sensory awakening, and early trust-building

Milestones to Watch For

Common Range (Birth to 1 Month):

- Responds to familiar voices

- Makes brief eye contact

- Lifts head briefly when on tummy

- Makes small jerky movements of arms and legs

Emerging Milestones (Up to 2 Months)

- Begins to follow objects with eyes

- Coos or makes soft sounds

- Starts to bring hands to mouth

- Opens and closes hands

These are general developmental signs. Every baby is unique, some may do these sooner, others later.

Week 1: Early Sensory Engagement

Day 1: Skin-to-Skin Contact & Gentle Rocking

Mindful moment

Hold your baby close against your chest for 10–15 minutes, wrapped in a blanket. Sway gently or sit still together.

Why it matters

Regulates your baby's body and builds a strong emotional bond.

Try this

Make it a quiet daily ritual after feeding or bath time.

Day 2: Sing-Song Talking

Speak in a melodic tone while dressing baby. Narrate your actions with warmth.

Day 3: Visual Stimulation

Show bold, black-and-white images after feeding. Move them slowly for baby to track.

Day 4: Music & Movement

Gently bounce baby to soft music. Let your voice guide the rhythm.

Day 5: Tummy Time

Mindful moment

Lay baby on their tummy for few seconds post-nap. Use a rolled towel under their chest and position yourself face-to-face.

Why it matters

Tummy time helps babies build core strength and start exploring how their body moves—foundational for crawling and sitting later on.

Tip

Sing or talk gently to hold their attention. Even short sessions make a big difference.

Day 6: Infant Massage

Massage baby's arms and legs in circular strokes after bath.

Day 7: Nature Sounds

Play calming rain or forest sounds before nap to relax baby's senses.

Parent hack of the week

Turn diaper time into talk time.

Instead of rushing, slow down just a little. Smile, connect, and say:

"Let's wipe your tiny toes... one toe, two toes, squiggle squiggle!"

You're not just cleaning - you're creating connection and language foundations.

Week 2: Visual & Auditory Stimulation

Day 1: Eye Contact Game

Hold baby close and blink slowly. Smile when they respond.

Day 2: Texture Discovery

Let baby touch a soft cloth or bumpy teether during alert time.

Day 3: Reading Time

Mindful moment

Choose a black-and-white baby book and read slowly, pausing at each page.

Why it matters

Stimulates visual attention and encourages word exposure.

Try this

Repeat the same book each day this week.

Day 4: Mirror Time

Place baby in front of a mirror during tummy time. Describe what you both see.

Day 5: Leg Pedals

Bicycle baby's legs after a diaper change. Smile and narrate the motion.

Day 6: Lullaby Cues

Sing the same lullaby each evening while holding baby gently.

Day 7: Sound Chase

Shake a rattle on one side, then the other. Wait for baby to turn their head.

Parent hack of the week

Turn your diaper setup into a mini connection corner.

Tape up bold black-and-white images, and during changes say things like:

"Look who's here again... Hello, Mr. Stripey!"

It's not just clean-up - it's visual stimulation and social play, wrapped in love.

Week 3: Motor & Social Development

Day 1: Grasp & Let Go

Offer your finger or a soft toy. Let baby grip and release.

Day 2: Floor Freedom

Lay baby on a soft mat and let them wiggle. Talk gently while nearby.

Day 3: Expressive Face Play

Mindful moment

Make big, animated expressions. Pause for baby to study your face.

Why it matters

Builds emotional connection and recognition.

Tip

Add gentle sound effects with each expression.

Day 4: Tummy Toy Reach

Place a bright toy just out of reach to encourage head lifting.

Day 5: Sound Conversations

Mindful moment

Respond to baby's coos with your own. Use soft tones and smiles.

Why it matters

Encourages communication and social turn-taking.

Tip

Pause to give baby time to "talk back."

Day 6: Bath Splash

Encourage baby to kick and splash in the water during bath.

Day 7: Temperature Touch

Let baby feel a cool spoon and a warm cloth. Describe the sensations.

Parent hack of the week

When tummy time is tough, change the view.

Lay baby on your chest as you recline. Smile and say,

"Can you see Mama's face? You're doing it!"

It's core work and bonding rolled into one.

Week 4: Enhanced Sensory Exploration

Day 1: Texture Basket

Let baby explore safe household textures while you describe them.

Day 2: Toy Tracking

Move a bright toy side to side during alert time. Pause to let baby refocus.

Day 3: Rattle Time

Let baby hold a rattle with your help. Encourage shaking.

Day 4: Funny Sounds

Make playful sounds with your mouth. Observe baby's reactions.

Day 5: Rolling Practice

Mindful moment

Help baby roll gently from side to back. Smile and cheer their effort.

Why it matters

Builds early coordination and strengthens muscles.

Try this

Use your voice to guide their direction.

Day 6: Voice Play

Talk in whispers, then louder tones. See which voice baby prefers.

Day 7: Palm Play

Open and close baby's hand around a soft object. Say "open... close."

Parent hack of the week

Create a mini "touch tour" during the day.

Carry baby to the window curtain, the couch, and the mirror. Let them touch and hear,

"This is smooth... This one is crinkly... Oh! This one's cool."

You're building vocabulary and trust, one texture at a time.

Reflect & Recharge: End of Month 1
Parent story: The power of one small shift

"I was unsure at first. But one evening, while we did our usual tummy time, my baby lifted her head, locked eyes with me, and smiled. That tiny moment made me feel like I was exactly what she needed."

— *Ria, mom of a 1-month-old*

What if my baby isn't doing this yet?

- New-borns often spend more time observing than doing, quiet stillness is not a delay.

- Tummy time can be hard at first. Try it on your chest or across your lap if the floor feels too big.

- Responses like eye contact or cooing may take time. Stay consistent, and trust that connection is building beneath the surface.

Mindful Reminder

In these earliest weeks, there's no right pace - only your presence. The quiet moments, the gentle touches, the way you hold their gaze... that's where trust is forming. You're not just feeding and soothing, you're laying the emotional foundation for a lifetime.

Month 2: Growing Awareness

Focus: Strengthening sensory processing, early motor skills, and responsive interaction

Milestones to Watch For:
Common Range (1 to 2 Months)

- Lifts head more steadily during tummy time

- Begins to smile in response to familiar faces

- Follows objects with eyes more smoothly

- Makes cooing or gurgling sounds

Emerging Milestones (Up to 3 Months)

- Starts reaching toward objects

- Recognizes caregiver voices and turns toward them

- Begins to open and close hands with intention

- Kicks legs actively when excited

Development unfolds at its own pace. Look for connection over perfection.

Week 1: Building Head Control

Day 1: Lap Tummy Time

Lay baby across your thighs on their tummy. Gently rub their back and hum.

Day 2: Upright Hold & Head Watch

Carry baby upright against your shoulder. Let them look around the room.

Day 3: Mirror Motivation

Mindful moment

Prop baby on a tummy-time cushion facing a mirror. Sit behind and talk gently.

Why it matters

Helps strengthen neck muscles while encouraging visual attention.

Try this

Make silly faces in the mirror to keep them curious.

Day 4: Side Lying Play

Place baby on their side with a rolled blanket behind them. Offer a soft toy.

Day 5: Face-to-Face Tummy Time

Lie down facing your baby during tummy time. Cheer them on as they lift their head.

Day 6: Gentle Rocking

Rock baby in your arms while supporting their neck. Sing or hum a slow tune.

Day 7: Visual Scarf Sweep

Sweep a lightweight scarf gently across their field of vision during alert time.

Parent hack of the week

Turn your walk into a tiny adventure.

Before stepping out, whisper: "Let's go explore." As you walk, point out trees, wind, or a bird's sound.

Even a five-minute stroll becomes a story—told heart to heart.

Week 2: Sound Awareness & Vocal Interaction

Day 1: Talking Through the Day

Narrate your routines—feeding, changing, bathing—like a gentle play-by-play.

Day 2: Sound Mimicry Game

Mindful moment

When baby coos, pause and mimic the sound with the same tone. Wait, then respond again.

Why it matters

Encourages back-and-forth communication and emotional connection.

Tip

Watch for their eye contact or smile—it's baby's version of "I hear you."

Day 3: Rhythmic Tapping

Tap gently on a soft surface near baby while singing or chanting slowly.

Day 4: Whisper Time

Whisper simple sentences close to baby's ear. Repeat with warmth.

Day 5: Lullaby with Gentle Strokes

Sing a favourite lullaby while slowly tracing baby's arms or cheeks.

Day 6: Rattle Follow

Shake a rattle and move it around baby's head. Wait for their eyes to track.

Day 7: Listening Pause

Turn off everything and listen to one natural sound together—birds, a fan, a breeze.

Parent hack of the week

Turn feeding into a rhythm moment.

While baby feeds, gently tap or stroke their back in rhythm with your words. Say,

"You're doing so well... sip, sip, sigh."

It calms them—and deepens your bond.

Week 3: Exploring Hands

Day 1: Finger Grasp Play

Let baby wrap their fingers around yours. Gently guide open and close.

Day 2: Fabric Touch Time

Offer baby a small square of soft or crinkly fabric to feel.

Day 3: Hand-to-Hand Game

Mindful moment

Gently bring baby's hands together and separate them slowly.

Why it matters

Builds body awareness and coordination.

Try this

Narrate the movement: "Together... and open!"

Day 4: Soft Rattle Grip

Place a soft rattle in baby's hand and help them grasp and move it.

Day 5: High-Contrast Tummy Play

Place a black-and-white object under baby's hands during tummy time.

Day 6: Guided Texture Tour

Touch baby's hands to textured items—bumpy ball, wooden spoon, soft towel.

Day 7: Splash and Grab

During bath, let baby reach for floating toys or water drops.

Parent hack of the week

Make a "finger story" at bedtime.

Take baby's fingers and narrate:

"This little finger feels soft... this one feels cool."

It's language, touch, and calm—all in one gentle ritual.

Week 4: Visual Focus & Tracking

Day 1: Scarf Float

Float a colourful scarf above baby's face. Watch their eyes follow.

Day 2: Side-to-Side Toy Track

Move a bright toy slowly left to right. Pause and smile mid-way.

Day 3: Mobile Gaze

Mindful moment

Hang a black-and-white or simple mobile above baby's resting spot. Let them watch it move.

Why it matters

Builds visual focus and spatial awareness.

Try this

Change its position slightly each week to renew curiosity.

Day 4: Mirror Talk

Hold baby in front of a mirror and talk about what they see.

Day 5: Light Play

Sit near a window. Let baby watch light shift across the wall.

Day 6: Peekaboo Reveal

Hide and reveal a toy under a soft cloth. Pause for anticipation.

Day 7: Picture Book Scan

Read a bold-image book slowly. Let baby glance at each page.

Parent hack of the week

Make diaper time a visual moment.

Place a new image or photo above the changing area each week.

Say: "Let's see who's up there today!"

It turns a routine into curiosity and comfort.

Reflect & Recharge: End of Month 2
Parent story: A quiet shift

"I wasn't sure any of this was working, until one day, I mimicked my son's coo and he cooed right back. It felt like our first real conversation. A tiny back-and-forth that made everything feel worth it."

— Mateo, father of a 2-month-old

What if my baby isn't doing this yet?

- If your baby isn't cooing yet, they may still be soaking in sound. Keep talking, they're listening.

- Some babies smile or track later than others. Familiar faces and repeated moments help those skills bloom.

- Don't rush interaction. Quiet alertness is part of early learning too.

> ### Mindful reminder
>
> You don't need to entertain or stimulate constantly. Simply noticing your baby and responding gently is enough. The rhythm you're building together, talk, pause, smile - is the beginning of their sense of connection to the world.

Month 3: Emerging Curiosity

Focus: Social engagement, early reaching, and visual-motor coordination

**Milestones to Watch For
Common Range (2 to 3 Months)**

- Smiles spontaneously, especially at people

- Holds head up more during tummy time

- Brings hands to mouth more often

- Tracks objects across midline with eyes

Emerging Milestones (Up to 4 Months)

- Begins to reach toward toys

- Makes vowel-like sounds ("ah," "oh")

- Recognizes familiar faces from a distance

- Pushes down legs when feet are placed on a surface

Development isn't a race - it's a relationship. Stay curious with your baby, not ahead of them.

Week 1: Social Smiles & Face Connection

Day 1: Morning Smile Exchange

After waking, lean in slowly and smile. Pause and let baby "respond."

Day 2: Close-Up Talking

Talk to baby at close range. Watch for coos, smiles, or widened eyes.

Day 3: Emotion Imitation

Mindful Moment

Sit face-to-face and copy baby's expressions - whether it's wide-eyed surprise or lip smacking.

Why it matters

Mirrors help babies recognize patterns and social cues, forming the base of emotional intelligence.

Try this

Add a soft "oooh!" or "wow!" to highlight expressions. You're building social language.

Day 4: Familiar Face Photo Tour

Show baby simple photos of close family. Point and say names warmly.

Day 5: Peek & Smile

Pop out from behind a cloth or pillow with a big grin. Pause for baby's delight.

Day 6: Rhythm Talk

Repeat baby's sounds back with rhythm and a gentle beat.

Day 7: Story Faces

Tell a one-minute story with facial drama - raise eyebrows, open mouth wide, whisper and smile.

Parent Hack of the Week – The Mirror Pause

Try this during tummy time or after feeding - place a mirror beside baby and gently lean in from the side. Whisper, "Who's that?" When your baby sees both your face and their own, you get two smiles in one. It's a surprise game that builds recognition and joy.

Week 2: Reaching, Touch, and Movement

Day 1: Gentle Reach Practice

Hold a soft toy above baby's chest. Let them stretch or swipe.

Day 2: Sensory Playtime on Lap

Mindful Moment

Lay baby on your lap facing you. Offer a textured scarf or teether to explore with hands.

Why it matters

Lap positioning gives both body support and clear social access - perfect for touch, communication, and reach.

Tip

Use your voice to guide exploration: "This is soft... this one's bumpy."

Day 3: Kick & Touch

During diaper change, hold a textured cloth to baby's feet. Let them kick it.

Day 4: Floating Object Gaze

Hang a ribbon or soft item within view. Let baby follow its sway.

Day 5: Finger Count Song

Hold baby's hand and sing while gently tapping each finger.

Day 6: Elbow Time

Let baby lie with arms free near their face. Watch how they explore their hands.

Day 7: Bat-at Toy

Dangle a toy within swatting distance. Celebrate when baby connects.

Parent Hack of the Week – The Elbow Picnic

Take a few minutes in a sunlit spot with your baby in just a diaper. Let them lie with elbows free to move and explore. No toys - just light, voice, and touch. It's a mini sensory picnic that helps body awareness bloom.

Week 3: Visual Exploration & Attention

Day 1: High-Contrast Pattern Cards

Place black-and-white cards around baby's play area. Let them explore with their eyes.

Day 2: Side-Switch Toy Watch

Move a toy across baby's field of vision from left to right.

Day 3: Light & Shadow Show

Mindful Moment

Sit near a window in the morning or evening. Let baby watch shifting shadows or filtered light.

Why it matters

Natural light movement strengthens visual tracking and depth awareness.

Try this

Gently talk about what they see—"That's a tree... it's waving hello."

Day 4: Mirror Angles

Place a mirror at a diagonal beside baby during play. Observe reactions.

Day 5: Book Peek

Read a high-contrast baby book. Let baby look; pause on favourite pages.

Day 6: Light Chase

Use a flashlight on the ceiling. Move it slowly, then stop—let baby "find" it again.

Day 7: Tummy-Time Window Watch

Lay baby near a window during tummy time. Point to clouds, trees, or cars.

Parent Hack of the Week – Shadow Play

Use a curtain, plant, or even your fingers to cast gentle shadows across the wall during quiet time. Say softly, "Look, the tree is dancing..." You're turning everyday light into a visual tracking game—and a moment of calm curiosity.

Week 4: Sounds, Silliness & Sensory Memory

Day 1: Silly Sound Day

Make funny sounds—pops, squeaks, soft raspberries—and pause for reactions.

Day 2: Touch-and-Tell

Let baby feel soft and crinkly objects. Say what each one is.

Day 3: Scented Connection

Mindful Moment

Hold baby close while holding a safe natural homemade scent at safe distance (lavender sachet, lemon peel).

Why it matters

Familiar scents create comforting sensory memory and early emotional links.

Try this

Use the same calming scent during bedtime to build gentle routine cues.

Day 4: Water Drip Surprise

Let a few drops of warm water fall onto baby's feet or tummy during bath. Narrate the sensation.

Day 5: Shake & Pause

Shake a soft rattle, then stop suddenly. Watch baby's expression.

Day 6: Whisper a Song

Whisper a lullaby at different times of day—not just bedtime. Watch how baby responds.

Day 7: Smile-Sigh Stretch

Gently stretch baby's arms out wide. Say "smiiile," then bring them in: "sigh." Make it playful.

Parent Hack of the Week – The Lemon Cue

Try this calm-down ritual before naps: hold a lemon peel near your baby's nose during cuddles. Say, "Mmm, that's fresh." Over time, that scent becomes a gentle cue for slowing down, soothing, and settling into sleep.

Reflect & Recharge: End of Month 3
Parent Story – The First Reach

One afternoon, my daughter reached for a crinkly scarf on my lap, just barely, just once. I didn't even expect it. But when her tiny hand landed and crinkled it, her eyes lit up. It was like she had *made* something happen. That moment? It felt like the start of her becoming *her*.

— *Amina, mom of a 3-month-old*

What if my baby isn't doing this yet?

- Rolling and reaching often come in waves—one day, everything clicks.

- If your baby isn't babbling or tracking yet, focus on building consistent routines and playful repetition.

- Social smiles and vocal play take time. Your expressions and sounds are their invitation—keep sending them.

> ## Mindful Reminder
>
> This month isn't about "doing more" - it's about seeing more. That sparkle in their eyes when they follow your voice or reach for your face? That's growth. That's connection. You're not just keeping up— you're already showing up , one moment at a time!

Month 4: Exploring Movement

Focus: Building body awareness, reaching, rolling, and social curiosity

Milestones to Watch For
Common Range (3 to 4 Months)

- Pushes up on forearms during tummy time

- Smiles more consistently at people

- Bats at toys with hands

- Brings hands together

Emerging Milestones (Up to 5 Months)

- Rolls from tummy to back

- Reaches for and grasps objects

- Begins to laugh

- Turns toward voices

Milestones are guideposts, not scorecards. Your baby's pace is just right for them.

Week 1: Reaching & Grasping

Day 1: Toy Above Chest

Hold a bright toy 8–10 inches above baby's chest. Let them swipe and try to grasp.

Day 2: Hand-to-Hand Practice

Bring baby's hands together and apart while saying "Together… open!"

Day 3: Grasp and Pull

Mindful Moment

Offer a soft cloth for baby to grab. Gently pull while they hold on.

Why it matters

This builds grip strength and introduces simple cause-effect.

Try this

Narrate playfully: "Hold tight! Whoooosh!"

Day 4: Side Lying Reach

Place baby on their side with a toy just in reach. Encourage swiping.

Day 5: Supported Sitting

Prop baby in a sitting position briefly (with pillows or your legs). Offer a toy to track.

Day 6: Rattle Hold

Help baby grasp a rattle. Let them feel it and explore with movement.

Day 7: Wrist Toy Wiggle

Secure a soft toy to baby's wrist or ankle and let them watch it move.

Parent Hack of the Week – The Sock Game

Pull a crinkly sock halfway over baby's hand or foot. Say, "Where's that sound coming from?" When they wiggle and hear it, it's like they've discovered their own magic trick—repetition builds wonder.

Week 2: Tummy Time & Core Strength

Day 1: Forearm Push-Up

During tummy time, gently place your hand under baby's chest to encourage lifting.

Day 2: Tummy Toy Slide

Slide a toy in a slow arc just above their eyeline. Watch for neck movement.

Day 3: Face-to-Face Cheerleader

Mindful Moment

Lie face-to-face during tummy time and cheer baby's efforts. Smile, clap softly, and say "You're doing it!"

Why it matters

Social encouragement during motor work activates reward systems in the brain.

Try this

Use a silly cheer voice to boost attention and make it fun.

Day 4: Elbow Rock

Rock baby gently side to side on their tummy with your hands under their arms.

Day 5: High-Contrast Tummy Prop

Place a black-and-white card in front of baby during tummy time.

Day 6: Mirror Belly Time

Put a mirror on the floor in front of baby. Let them "meet" their reflection.

Day 7: Chest-to-Knee Push

Let baby push their feet against your hands while lying on their back. Say "Push, push!"

Parent Hack of the Week – The Couch Lift

Use the edge of the couch as a tummy time prop. Place baby so their arms are on the cushion and you're at eye level on the floor. Suddenly, tummy time becomes a social game, not a chore.

Week 3: Rolling & Side-to-Side Movement

Day 1: Side Tummy Roll

Lay baby on their side and gently help them roll to tummy.

Day 2: Blanket Tug

Lay baby on a soft blanket. Gently tug one side to roll them halfway.

Day 3: Tummy-to-Back Twist

Mindful Moment

Help baby roll from tummy to back by guiding their hips. Smile and cheer!

Why it matters

Rolling supports coordination, muscle strength, and spatial awareness.

Try this

Say "Over we go!" in the same tone each time—it becomes a cue.

Day 4: Hip Wiggle Dance

Hold baby upright and gently sway side to side while singing.

Day 5: Leg Lift Play

Lay baby down and slowly lift their legs like a mini bicycle ride.

Day 6: Side-by-Side Chat

Lie next to baby on their side. Copy their movements and sounds.

Day 7: Rolling Toy Reach

Place a toy just out of reach on baby's side and let them lean toward it.

Parent Hack of the Week – The Blanket Roll

Lay baby on a soft blanket. Slowly roll them from one side to the other, saying, "Wheee!" It's part stretch, part surprise—and it helps them learn the rhythm of rolling without pressure.

Week 4: Social Play & Body Awareness

Day 1: Mirror Nose Kiss

Bring baby to the mirror and kiss your reflection. Then kiss theirs!

Day 2: Baby See, Baby Do

Make silly faces and copy baby's expressions right back.

Day 3: Foot Discovery Game

Mindful Moment

Gently bring baby's feet toward their hands and let them hold or kick.

Why it matters

Builds body awareness and early coordination.

Try this

Say, "These are your feet! Kick, kick!" and giggle together.

Day 4: Finger Wiggle Song

Sing a nursery rhyme while wiggling baby's fingers to the beat.

Day 5: Body Label Play

Touch different body parts gently and name them aloud.

Day 6: Belly Button Peek

Lift baby's shirt gently, say "Belly button!" and give a soft kiss.

Day 7: Puppet Talk

Use a soft puppet to "talk" to baby and play peekaboo.

Parent Hack of the Week – The Mirror Game 2.0

Instead of just looking, try acting in the mirror. Bounce baby while saying, "Look at us!" or do slow spins. Seeing themselves move is magic—it makes mirrors come alive.

Reflect & Recharge: End of Month 4
Parent Story – The Surprise Laugh

I was making silly faces after lunch - just to keep her distracted while cleaning her hands. Suddenly, she let out this tiny laugh. I stopped and did it again. Another laugh. It was the first time I heard it and I teared up. Something so small, and it cracked open something big.

— *Naomi, mom of a 4-month-old*

What if my baby isn't doing this yet?

- Some babies prefer stillness over rolling at first—this is part of learning body control.

- Laughing out loud may come later, especially if your baby is more serious or observant.

- Focus on responding warmly, not performing milestones. Your attunement is the real goal.

> ### Mindful Reminder
>
> The world is opening up for your baby—one roll, one giggle, one gaze at a mirror at a time. They don't need perfect performance. They need your presence, your play, and your joy in the little things. One Moment at a time!

Month 5: Awakening Awareness

Focus: Visual focus, body control, playful interaction, and sensory curiosity

Milestones to Watch For
Common Range (4 to 5 Months):

- Rolls from tummy to back (and possibly back to tummy)
- Reaches out with more control
- Pushes up onto hands during tummy time
- Turns head to follow voices

Emerging Milestones (Up to 6 Months)

- Begins to sit with support
- Laughs out loud
- Passes toys from one hand to the other
- Recognizes their name

Development looks like practice, not perfection. Repetition is your baby's favourite teacher.

Week 1: Visual Curiosity & Focus

Day 1: Window Light Watch

Sit near a window and let baby track shifting light or trees.

Day 2: Scarf Float

Float a light scarf above baby's face and pause mid-air for eye contact.

Day 3: Picture Peek Book Time

Mindful Moment

Read a baby book with colourful faces or animals. Pause on each page and name what you see.

Why it matters

Sharpens visual attention and strengthens word-image pairing.

Try this

Repeat the same book daily this week — familiarity boosts focus.

Day 4: Mirror Playtime

Place a mirror beside baby and let them watch movement.

Day 5: Toy Tracking Game

Move a toy in slow curves. Let baby follow and reach toward it.

Day 6: Mobile View

Hang a lightweight mobile near tummy time space. Let baby watch it spin.

Day 7: Flashlight Adventure

In a dim room, point a flashlight toward a wall or toy. Slowly move and pause.

Parent Hack of the Week – The Light Dance

Right after a feed, I took my phone's flashlight and aimed it at the ceiling fan. The spinning shadows fascinated my baby — and gave me five quiet minutes to breathe. Light + movement = instant magic.

Week 2: Building Body Control

Day 1: Supported Sit & Play

Sit baby with support between your legs. Offer a toy to hold or track.

Day 2: Chest Push-Ups

During tummy time, place a toy just ahead to encourage baby to push up on hands.

Day 3: Side Roll Boost

Mindful Moment

Gently help baby roll from back to side, then side to tummy. Narrate the move: "We're rolling over!"

Why it matters

Builds muscle coordination and spatial sense.

Try this

Use the same playful tone to signal the movement each time.

Day 4: Wobble Practice

Sit baby upright (with support), then gently rock them side to side.

Day 5: Mirror Sit

Sit baby in front of a mirror in your lap. Watch their reaction to upright reflections.

Day 6: Towel Tunnel

Create a mini tunnel with a rolled towel. Let baby push through during tummy time.

Day 7: Leg Kick Count

Lie baby on their back. Gently count out leg kicks with rhythm.

Parent Hack of the Week – The Sit & See

I sat cross-legged and leaned my baby against my legs, hands supporting her chest. We faced the window—and suddenly she was "sitting" and seeing the world. Add a soft toy, and it's a new perspective, safely framed by you.

Week 3: Interactive Play & Laughter

Day 1: Silly Sound Face

Make unexpected sounds (raspberries, "oooh!") with animated expressions.

Day 2: Tickle Cue Game

Use the same phrase - "Here comes the tickle!" - before gently tickling baby's tummy or toes.

Day 3: Coo & Pause Conversation

Mindful Moment

Respond to baby's sounds with your own. Wait for their turn—then go again.

Why it matters

This teaches social rhythm and builds vocal confidence.

Try this

Make your responses rhythmic or musical to keep it fun.

Day 4: Puppet Surprise

Use a simple sock or puppet for peekaboo and talking fun.

Day 5: Peekaboo Echo

Hide your face behind a cloth. Say a word, then reveal your smile.

Day 6: Belly Bounce

Lay baby on your knees and bounce gently while singing.

Day 7: Big Laugh Replay

Do something silly that made baby laugh earlier - yes, again!

Parent Hack of the Week – The Repeat Giggle

One morning, I blew a raspberry on my baby's belly and she laughed out loud. I did it again, same laugh. And again. Turns out, babies don't get bored of joy. When something delights them, repeat it. You're teaching cause-effect and how joy feels.

Week 4: Touch, Texture & Sensory Play

Day 1: Texture Tour

Offer baby safe items: soft washcloth, crinkly paper, smooth spoon. Narrate each feel.

Day 2: Hand-to-Object

Help baby grasp a textured toy, then guide it to their cheek or chest.

Day 3: Scent & Cuddle Routine

Mindful Moment

Use the same natural scent during calm time (lavender cloth, lemon zest nearby). Cuddle quietly.

Why it matters

Repeated sensory cues create emotional safety and routine memory.

Try this

Use the scent before nap or bedtime to help baby associate it with calm.

Day 4: Feet Touch Game

Touch baby's feet to soft or cool objects. Name each sensation.

Day 5: Bath time Sensory Talk

During bath, narrate what baby is feeling: "Warm water… slippery hands…"

Day 6: Palm to Palm

Open and close baby's hand around a soft object. Whisper "open… close…"

Day 7: Gentle Hairbrush Feel

Lightly stroke baby's arm with a soft baby brush. Pause for reaction.

Parent Hack of the Week – The Scent Signal

Each night, I gently stroked a natural lavender-scented cloth under my baby's chin before lullaby time. Now, the scent alone makes her eyelids flutter. Scent isn't just soothing—it's a signal. Soft repetition becomes trust.

Reflect & Recharge: End of Month 5
Parent Story – The "I Know You" Smile

We were in a room full of people, and someone else picked him up. He looked around, then saw me and grinned. Like, full recognition. That "I know you" smile? It floored me. It was the first time I felt known, not just needed.

— *Surbhi, mom of a 5-month-old*

What if my baby isn't doing this yet?

- If your baby isn't sitting yet, keep building core strength with floor play and supported upright time.

- Passing toys or transferring between hands develops with practice—use light, easy-to-grasp objects.

- Awareness and interaction might look like stillness or staring—that's attention at work..

Mindful Reminder

This month is about awakening—not rushing. Every glance, stretch, and coo is part of your baby waking up to the world. Let them unfold slowly. You're not just showing them life—you're showing them you. One moment at a time.

Month 6: Confidence in Motion

Focus: Rolling, sitting with support, playful communication, and exploring cause and effect

Milestones to Watch For
Common Range (5 to 6 Months):

- Rolls from back to tummy and tummy to back
- Pushes up fully on arms during tummy time
- Laughs spontaneously
- Grabs and mouths toys with control

Emerging Milestones (Up to 7 Months):

- Sits with less support
- Begins to bounce when held upright
- Transfers toys between hands
- Responds to name and tone of voice

Your baby is learning how to move with intention. They're not just exploring the world—they're figuring out how to act on it.

Week 1: Strengthening Core for Sitting

Day 1: Upright Window Sit

Sit baby with support near a window. Narrate what you see together.

Day 2: Pillow Circle

Mindful Moment

Surround baby with soft pillows in a sitting position and let them wobble and catch themselves with your gentle support.

Why it matters

Balancing—even briefly—activates core and side muscles, helping baby learn how to control their own posture.

Try this

Let them tip gently, then catch themselves. Say, "Wobble, wobble... whoa!" to make it playful.

Day 3: Sit-to-Lie Practice

Let baby start in a sitting position, then slowly lower them back and lift again like a mini sit-up.

Day 4: Chest Push-Ups

During tummy time, place a toy just ahead to promote lifting and shifting weight.

Day 5: Mirror Sit & Smile

Place baby in your lap facing a mirror. Make faces and narrate reactions.

Day 6: Side-to-Side Rock

Gently rock baby in a sitting position. Hold their hands for balance.

Day 7: Supported Sit & Reach

Mindful Moment

While baby is sitting supported, place toys just out of reach. Encourage a slow lean and reach.

Why it matters

Encourages trunk control, reaching coordination, and spatial awareness.

Try this

Use soft toys that are easy to grasp and praise effort more than result.

Parent Hack of the Week – The Laundry Basket Lounge

Place a folded blanket in a clean laundry basket and sit baby inside with a few soft toys. It creates a cosy, supported space for upright sitting—and lets them explore hands-free from a brand-new view.

Week 2: Rolling Mastery & Full-Body Movement

Day 1: Diagonal Toy Reach

Place a toy diagonally to one side during tummy time to encourage rolling.

Day 2: Leg Over Assist

Help baby bring one leg across their body gently to initiate a roll.

Day 3: Rolling Cheer Game

Mindful Moment

Guide baby through a slow roll and cheer each part: "Lift… reach… roll!"

Why it matters

Supports coordination, sequencing, and builds trust during new movements.

Try this

Use the same cheer words consistently—predictable cues build motor memory.

Day 4: Back-to-Tummy Countdown

Say "1-2-3… Roll!" and gently help baby from back to tummy with your hands at hips and shoulders.

Day 5: Blanket Swoop

Lift one side of a soft blanket gently to help baby roll from one side to the other.

Day 6: Toy Across Chest

Encourage baby to bring hands together at midline with a toy placed between them.

Day 7: Elbow-to-Tummy Time

During tummy time, help baby tuck one arm forward for better weight shifting.

Parent Hack of the Week – The Blanket Bumper Roll

Use a rolled towel or blanket beside baby's body to gently encourage rolling. A soft side nudge plus your voice saying, "We're going over!" helps turn practice into play.

Week 3: Cause, Effect & Playful Sounds

Day 1: Rattle & Pause

Shake a rattle, then hold still. Wait for baby to move or vocalize—then repeat.

Day 2: Sound Echoes

Mimic baby's sounds, then add one of your own. Pause to see if they follow.

Day 3: Tactile Cause & Effect

Mindful Moment

Tape crinkly paper to the floor or table. Let baby press and explore.

Why it matters

Builds sensory feedback loops—what they touch creates sound!

Try this

Say "You did that!" each time they crinkle to build confidence.

Day 4: Toy Toss & Retrieve

Let baby drop a soft toy from your lap. Pick it up and say, "You dropped it!"

Day 5: Spoons and Surfaces

Let baby bang a spoon on different surfaces (towel, tray, crinkly mat). Narrate sounds.

Day 6: Peekaboo Response

Cover your face with a scarf, say baby's name, then peek and smile.

Day 7: Voice Call & Turn

From behind, call your baby's name and wait to see if they turn.

Parent Hack of the Week – The Spoon Song

Give your baby a spoon and let them bang it on different surfaces—a tray, cloth, or your palm. Match their rhythm and add a beat: "Tap tap taaap." It's music, play, and connection in one.

Week 4: Exploring Hands & Object Control

Day 1: Hand-to-Hand Toy Transfer

Give baby a toy in one hand and guide it toward the other.

Day 2: Rolling Ball Reach

Roll a soft ball near baby. Let them reach and try to stop it.

Day 3: Grab & Feel Basket

Mindful Moment

Create a small basket with soft, textured toys. Let baby explore with both hands.

Why it matters

Supports bilateral coordination, texture exploration, and focused attention.

Try this

Narrate what they're touching—"That's bumpy… This one's squishy!"

Day 4: Wrist Rattle Dance

Mindful Moment

Secure a soft rattle around baby's wrist or ankle. Watch as they notice the sound comes from their own movement.

Why it matters

Builds self-awareness, hand-eye coordination, and cause-effect learning.

Try this

Gently shake their hand and say, "You made that sound!" Then pause and let them try.

Day 5: Block Bang

Give baby two soft blocks. Let them bang them together.

Day 6: Crinkle & Chew

Offer a crinkly-safe toy that's also safe to mouth. Watch the multitasking begin!

Day 7: Ball Tap & Roll

Let baby push a soft ball on the floor. Cheer when it rolls.

Parent Hack of the Week – The Treasure Sock

Hide a crinkly toy or soft rattle inside a long baby sock and hand it to your baby. Tug, pull, and surprise—what comes out? It's baby's first peek into problem-solving and discovery.

Reflect & Recharge: End of Month 6
Parent Story – The First Sound Game

We were playing peekaboo with a scarf when he suddenly shouted, "Ahh!"—not crying, just *saying* it. I froze, smiled, and said "Ahh!" back. We kept it going: Ahh. Ahh! AH! It felt like the first real game *he* started. Like he had something to say—and knew I'd listen.

— *Lin, dad of a 6-month-old*

What if my baby isn't doing this yet?

- Some babies roll or sit early; others are content watching the world for a little longer. Both are valid.

- New skills may suddenly "click" after weeks of quiet attempts. Keep offering time and space.

- Encourage exploration, not performance. Your baby is building confidence—not a checklist.

> ### Mindful Reminder
>
> This month brings movement, sound, and spark. But what your baby really needs is still the same—your steady, encouraging presence. You are the rhythm to their unfolding story. Keep showing up. They feel it, every time. One Moment at a time !

Month 7: Exploring Independence

Focus: Sitting stability, hand-to-hand control, object play, early vocal imitation

Milestones to Watch For
Common Range (6 to 7 Months):

- Sits without support for short periods

- Uses hands to push up and reach in multiple directions

- Babbles with consonant sounds (ba, da, ma)

- Begins to explore toys with more intention (bangs, drops, transfers)

Emerging Milestones (Up to 8 Months):

- Moves from tummy to sitting with assistance

- Begins to imitate sounds and facial expressions

- Uses hand to rake or scoop objects
- Responds to name consistently

Every skill builds on the last. Your baby is now connecting movement with intention, and sound with response.

Week 1: Sitting Confidence & Balance

Day 1: Sit & Reach Game

Place a toy slightly out of reach to one side. Let baby lean to grab it while seated.

Day 2: Pillow-Free Sit Time

Let baby sit on a firm mat with you close by. Count how long they balance.

Day 3: Sit and Stretch

Mindful Moment

Place baby in a seated position and guide them through gentle leaning (left, right, forward). Keep it slow and playful.

Why it matters

Lateral movement improves core control and builds safe reflexes for when baby tips.

Try this

Narrate each stretch: "Leeeean left... and up! Now forward!"

Day 4: Mirror Sit and Smile

Sit baby facing a mirror. Make silly faces and name emotions.

Day 5: Side-to-Side Tap

Gently tap a toy on baby's right, then left. Let them shift to follow it.

Day 6: Towel Roll Support

Place a rolled towel behind baby's hips to help with balance during free play.

Day 7: Book Balance

Read a board book while baby sits in your lap, upright and steady.

Parent Hack of the Week – The Sit-Spot Switch

Use two safe sitting spots at home (like a mat and a high chair with toys) to change the view and posture. Variety keeps balance practice fun and reduces frustration.

Week 2: Hand Skills & Two-Handed Play

Day 1: Hand Transfer Toy

Give baby a toy in one hand and watch them move it to the other.

Day 2: Two-Hand Tap

Offer a soft block for baby to bang between hands.

Day 3: Treasure Basket Exploration

Mindful Moment

Fill a shallow basket with safe, textured household items. Let baby explore using both hands.

Why it matters

Encourages bilateral coordination, curiosity, and fine motor experimentation.

Try this

Sit across and name what they touch: "That one's cool... squishy... rough."

Day 4: Stack & Smash

Stack two blocks. Let baby knock them down. Repeat.

Day 5: Wrist Rattle Time

Put a soft rattle on baby's wrist. Watch the self-made sound spark curiosity.

Day 6: Crinkle Toy Pass

Give baby a crinkly toy and encourage them to pass it hand to hand.

Day 7: Finger Puppet Reach

Wiggle a puppet on your finger and let baby grab it with both hands.

Parent Hack of the Week – The Basket Reset

Keep a small bin of toys with different feels—smooth, bumpy, cold, soft. When baby gets fussy, swap in a new texture. One touch can re-engage attention.

Week 3: Early Imitation & Vocal Play

Day 1: Face-to-Face Babble

Talk back when baby babbles. Use similar tones.

Day 2: Sound + Gesture Game

Wave while saying "hi" or clap with "yay!"

Day 3: Echo Play

Mindful Moment

Repeat baby's sounds exactly, then add one syllable of your own. Pause to let them respond.

Why it matters

This builds turn-taking, language rhythm, and confidence.

Try this

Keep your voice light and animated—baby will mimic tone before words.

Day 4: Sing-Along Face Time

Sing simple songs with hand gestures: "If You're Happy..."

Day 5: Tongue Show

Stick out your tongue slowly. Wait. Does baby try too?

Day 6: Consonant Call-Out

Emphasize a consonant sound: "Ba-ba! Ma-ma!"

Day 7: Name and Touch

Say baby's name, then gently touch their chest or hand.

Parent Hack of the Week – The Silly Sound Mirror

Sit in front of a mirror with your baby. Make silly sounds and watch their reaction. Seeing your face + hearing the sound = double engagement. Bonus if they try to copy!

Week 4: Cause & Effect through Object Play

Day 1: Toy Drop Game

Let baby drop a toy from highchair. Say "Uh-oh!" and return it.

Day 2: Lid Tap

Offer a container and a spoon. Let baby tap and listen.

Day 3: Light Switch Exploration

Mindful Moment

Hold baby and gently guide their hand to flip a switch. Say "on!" and "off!"

Why it matters

Repetitive action with a visible result teaches control and predictability.

Try this

Let baby try the switch in a few different rooms or lamps.

Day 4: Ball Push

Roll a ball slightly away. Encourage baby to push it back.

Day 5: Pop Toy Fun

Use a baby-safe pop-up toy. Celebrate each "pop!"

Day 6: Door Knock Game

Hold baby's hand to gently knock on a door. Say "Knock, knock!"

Day 7: Sound Box Play

Shake or open a container with a small object. Let baby mimic the action.

Parent Hack of the Week – The Uh-Oh Echo

Turn dropping into learning. Each time baby drops something, say "Uh-oh!" then pause. Over time, they may say it too. It becomes their first game of action-and-response.

Reflect & Recharge: End of Month 7
Parent Story – The Babble Breakthrough

She had been babbling for weeks, but one afternoon, she looked at me and clearly said "ba-ba" while holding out her hand. I said it back, and she beamed. It wasn't just a sound—it was a word *to me*. We had started our first real conversation.

— *Sofia, mom of a 7-month-old*

What if my baby isn't doing this yet?

- Your baby may focus more on movement or observation this month. Vocal play might come next.

- Sitting independently takes core strength and practice. Short, repeated tries help.

Progress isn't always visible Day-to-Day. Often it shows up in sudden leaps.

> ### Mindful Reminder
>
> Your baby is no longer just reacting to the world—they're trying to *interact* with it. Every wobble, drop, sound, and smile is an invitation. Keep responding. You're building connection in every little moment.

Month 8: Engaged Exploration

Focus: Active play, early crawling motions, imitation, and sensory communication

**Milestones to Watch For
Common Range (7 to 8 Months):**

- Sits steadily without support
- Begins to rock on hands and knees or scoot
- Bangs toys together or shakes objects with purpose
- Responds to own name and familiar voices

Emerging Milestones (Up to 9 Months):

- Crawls or moves forward in some way
- Uses voice to express joy or frustration
- Shows interest in mirror reflections and gestures
- Begins to understand "no" or simple instructions

Your baby is ready to go—literally. They're learning how their body moves and how their voice connects with you.

Week 1: Early Crawling & Movement

Day 1: Tummy Rock Practice

Place baby on hands and knees. Gently rock their hips forward and back.

Day 2: Crawl-Over Obstacle

Lay a rolled towel on the floor. Let baby try to scoot or roll over it.

Day 3: Reach-and-Crawl Game

Mindful Moment

Place a favourite toy just beyond reach while baby is on their tummy. Cheer as they try to move toward it.

Why it matters

Builds motivation, strengthens upper body, and encourages coordinated movement.

Try this

Use your voice like a beacon: "Almost there... you got it!"

Day 4: Barefoot Floor Time

Let baby explore on a soft surface without socks. Notice their foot movement.

Day 5: Mirror Crawl

Prop a mirror at floor level. Encourage baby to approach their reflection.

Day 6: Lap Sit Bounce

Sit baby in your lap and gently bounce. Say, "Ready, set... bounce!"

Day 7: Open Space Play

Give baby room to scoot, roll, or pivot. Stay nearby and narrate their moves.

Parent Hack of the Week – The Sock Slide

Place baby in socks on a smooth floor and gently help them slide as they rock. That tiny bit of slipperiness builds balance awareness and motion control in a fun, giggly way.

Week 2: Two-Handed Play & Grip Strength

Day 1: Toy Bang

Give baby two soft toys to bang together. Show them how first.

Day 2: Textured Ball Hold

Offer a soft, textured ball to grasp and explore.

Day 3: Cup & Drop Exploration

Mindful Moment

Place a few small toys in a plastic cup. Let baby pull them out one at a time.

Why it matters

Builds pincer grasp, hand strength, and problem-solving skills.

Try this

Say, "What's inside?" to build curiosity before each grab.

Day 4: Highchair Tray Tap

Place toys on baby's tray and let them bang, slide, or drop them.

Day 5: Spoon Pull Game

Offer a spoon. Gently tug as baby holds it tight.

Day 6: Crinkle Paper Fold

Let baby crumple or fold crinkly paper with both hands.

Day 7: Stuffed Toy Push

Place a soft toy in front of baby during tummy time. Let them push it forward.

Parent Hack of the Week – The Cup Grab Trick

Use a light plastic cup and place a safe toy inside. Baby's curiosity will spark action. Once they figure out "grab and dump," it becomes their favourite kind of mess-making.

Week 3: Sound, Gesture & Vocal Imitation

Day 1: Hand Clap Song

Clap baby's hands to a simple beat. Sing while doing it.

Day 2: Babble Repeats

Repeat baby's sounds. Add gentle changes: "Ba-ba" becomes "Ba-ba-BOOM!"

Day 3: Gesture Match Game

Mindful Moment

Do simple gestures (clap, wave, shake head) and wait. See if baby imitates.

Why it matters

Strengthens imitation, memory, and communication through body cues.

Try this

Pair gestures with sound: "No-no" with head shake, "Hi-hi" with wave.

Day 4: Vocal Play in Mirror

Look in mirror together and say sounds: "Da-da," "Ooo," "Ba!"

Day 5: Tap & Talk

Tap gently on different surfaces. Say, "tap-tap-tap!" Baby may join.

Day 6: Bubble Pop Sound Game

Blow bubbles. Say "Pop!" with each burst. Encourage vocal response.

Day 7: Name Echo

Say baby's name with excitement. Pause and wait for vocal response.

Parent Hack of the Week – The Clap-and-Pause Game

Start clapping while singing "Clap your hands!" then suddenly stop and freeze. Babies love the surprise—and they often initiate the clap again. That's turn-taking in action.

Week 4: Sensory Curiosity & Interactive Play

Day 1: Cold Spoon Surprise

Let baby hold a cool metal spoon. Watch their expression change.

Day 2: Texture Crawl Path

Create a short path with towels, rubber mats, or bubble wrap. Let baby explore.

Day 3: Water Play Touch

Mindful Moment

Let baby sit with a shallow water bowl and splash with hands.

Why it matters

Introduces temperature, resistance, and movement all in one sensory-rich experience.

Try this

Add one floating toy. Say, "Can you splash Mr. Duck?"

Day 4: Towel Peekaboo

Cover baby lightly with a towel and say "Where's baby?" Pause before reveal.

Day 5: Natural Light Play

Sit by a sunny window. Let baby notice light and shadow shifts.

Day 6: Container Tap

Place a lid on a container and let baby tap, pat, or try to open it.

Day 7: Gentle Feather Touch

Brush baby's hand or cheek with a soft feather or cloth.

Parent Hack of the Week – The Sink Splash Setup

Place baby at the kitchen sink (held securely or in a high chair) and let water trickle from the tap. Splashing fingers under running water is simple, safe, and endlessly engaging.

Reflect & Recharge: End of Month 8
Parent Story – The Mirror Moment

I was folding laundry when I saw Anaya staring at herself in the mirror. She smiled, touched her head, then looked back at me like she'd discovered someone new. I joined her on the floor and we spent 10 minutes just smiling at ourselves. It wasn't just a reflection—it was recognition.

— *Leena, mom of an 8-month-old*

What if my baby isn't doing this yet?

- Some babies rock for weeks before they crawl—it's still movement prep.

- Not imitating yet? Keep gestures playful and repeat often. Imitation builds through repetition.

- Your baby may be absorbing more than they're showing. Growth is still happening—even in silence.

Mindful Reminder

Your baby's curiosity is blooming. They're not just moving for movement's sake—they're experimenting, connecting, and expressing. Every "pop," crawl, and giggle is proof that the world is opening up, one moment at a time.

Month 9: Smart Interactions

Focus: Object exploration, memory building, gestures, and emerging problem-solving

Milestones to Watch For
Common Range (8 to 9 Months):

- Crawls or scoots with control
- Begins to pull up to stand with support
- Uses gestures like waving or clapping
- Looks for dropped objects (early object permanence)

Emerging Milestones (Up to 10 Months):

- Stands while holding furniture
- Uses finger to point or poke
- Begins to understand simple words like "bye-bye" or "no"
- Repeats sounds or gestures to get attention

Your baby is starting to test ideas, recall experiences, and communicate with purpose. Interaction is now a full-body, full-brain adventure.

Week 1: Pulling Up & Stability

Day 1: Supported Stand

Hold baby under their arms and let their feet press against the floor.

Day 2: Couch Cruise

Let baby stand holding the couch edge. Cheer their balance.

Day 3: Rise & Reach Game

Mindful Moment

Place a toy slightly above baby's seated level. Support them as they reach and try to pull up.

Why it matters

Builds leg strength, visual-motor coordination, and spatial planning.

Try this

Say "Up, up, up!" as they reach to connect movement with direction.

Day 4: Knee Bounce Play

Sit baby on your lap and gently bounce to a rhyme or chant.

Day 5: Push-to-Stand Wall

Use a firm cushion or low table for baby to push against while rising.

Day 6: Floor Sit Retrieval

Place a toy nearby and encourage baby to go from standing back to sitting to pick it up.

Day 7: Mirror Stand

Prop a mirror at standing height. Let baby admire their progress.

Parent Hack of the Week – The Cushion Wedge Trick

Tuck a firm pillow under the edge of the couch so baby has a slanted surface to practice pulling up. It's safer than hard furniture and gives them just the right push.

Week 2: Object Permanence & Memory

Day 1: Hidden Toy Peekaboo

Hide a toy under a cloth. Ask, "Where did it go?"

Day 2: Behind-the-Back Reveal

Hide a rattle behind your back. Show it again with surprise.

Day 3: Box Discovery Game

Mindful Moment

Place several toys in a soft box or bag. Let baby pull each out and explore.

Why it matters

Builds recall, cause-effect understanding, and focused play.

Try this

Narrate: "You found the duck! What's next?" Encourage slow, curious pulls.

Day 4: Lid Pop-Off

Give baby a small plastic container with a lid to remove and inspect.

Day 5: Look-and-Find

Put a favourite toy in view, then gently cover part of it with a cloth.

Day 6: Watch and Wait

Drop a ball into a clear container. Pause and let baby anticipate the bounce.

Day 7: Puzzle Piece Pull

Let baby tug a large piece out of a simple wooden puzzle.

Parent Hack of the Week – The Bag of Wonders

Stuff a small tote with safe random items (spoon, crinkly paper, sock). Baby pulls each one out like magic. Refill weekly—it turns memory and motor skills into a surprise show.

Week 3: Gestures, Sounds & Communication

Day 1: Waving Practice

Wave "hi" and "bye" consistently with greetings.

Day 2: Action + Word

Pair gestures with words: clap with "yay," point with "look!"

Day 3: Sound Copy Fun

Mindful Moment

Make a fun sound (like "oooh" or "ba!"). Wait for baby to mimic, then repeat.

Why it matters

Strengthens auditory memory, social exchange, and vocal curiosity.

Try this

Use different pitches and faces to keep them engaged.

Day 4: Clap-to-Rhythm

Clap a rhythm and pause. See if baby tries to repeat it.

Day 5: Finger Point Game

Point at pictures in a book. Say, "Where's the cat?" and then point again.

Day 6: Shake-to-Get-Attention

Give baby a toy that makes noise when shaken. Say, "You made that sound!"

Day 7: Name & Response

Call baby's name from across the room. Celebrate if they turn toward you.

Parent Hack of the Week – The Echo Voice Trick

Say a single word in a fun voice—"Hello!"—then repeat it in a whisper, then a giggle. Changing tone helps baby tune in, and they'll start listening for the switch.

Week 4: Simple Problem Solving & Play Sequences

Day 1: Block Tower Topple

Stack two blocks. Let baby knock them over with purpose.

Day 2: Push-Pull Tray Game

Use a shallow tray with toys. Encourage baby to slide or push them off.

Day 3: Cause & Try Again Game

Mindful Moment

Place a toy in a container that's tricky to open. Watch baby try to solve it.

Why it matters

Encourages persistence, observation, and early trial-and-error thinking.

Try this

Give gentle hints without doing it for them. Celebrate effort, not success.

Day 4: Ball in a Cup

Drop a ball in a wide cup. Let baby turn it over and retrieve it.

Day 5: Velcro Tab Practice

Use soft fabric books or toys with Velcro to open and close flaps.

Day 6: Pop-up Surprise

Use a jack-in-the-box or spring toy. Help baby trigger the surprise.

Day 7: Snack in Reach

Place a safe snack in a container with a loose lid. Let baby work to get it.

Parent Hack of the Week – The Sock-in-a-Cup Game

Roll up a baby sock and stuff it into a plastic cup. Show baby how to dig it out. Add a second one and make it a puzzle. It's soft, safe, and satisfying to solve.

Reflect & Recharge: End of Month 9
Parent Story – The Surprise Wave

We were at the elevator when a neighbour waved. I said, "Say hi, Avishi," expecting nothing. But she raised her little hand and waved back—grinning. My heart leapt. It was the first time she joined a social moment instead of just watching.

— Amrita, mom of a 9-month-old

What if my baby isn't doing this yet?

- Pulling up takes strength *and* confidence. Keep offering sturdy, low surfaces to practice.

- Some babies gesture before crawling; others focus on movement first—both are fine.

- Not mimicking yet? Repetition and exaggerated expression help build recognition.

Mindful Reminder

This month is full of attempts—some successful, some not. Every pull, point, wave, and peek shows your baby's desire to connect, explore, and solve. You don't need to guide each step—just make space, cheer often, and keep showing up.

Month 10: Intentional Play

Focus: Standing strength, imitation, simple problem-solving, and social gestures

Milestones to Watch For
Common Range (9 to 10 Months):

- Pulls to stand and may cruise along furniture

- Picks up small objects using fingers

- Waves or claps on their own

- Understands simple commands like "come here" or "no"

Emerging Milestones (Up to 11 Months):

- Tries to squat down from standing

- Points at things to show interest

- Begins to combine sounds with gestures
- Stacks, inserts, or purposefully places objects

Your baby is using movement, memory, and mimicry to interact more intentionally with the world—and with you.

Week 1: Standing Strength & Movement

Day 1: Push-to-Stand Game

Let baby push against a stable surface to rise to stand.

Day 2: Furniture Cruise

Encourage baby to move sideways along the couch while holding on.

Day 3: Kneel-and-Pull Play

Mindful Moment

Place a toy just above baby's eye level. Encourage them to kneel, then pull up to get it.

Why it matters

Strengthens legs and core, and introduces problem-solving through position shifting.

Try this

Use a toy that lights up or makes noise to keep their interest.

Day 4: Assisted Squat

Hold baby's hands while they squat to pick up a toy and stand back up.

Day 5: Wall Tap

Place a toy against the wall at standing height. Tap it and encourage baby to do the same.

Day 6: Barefoot Balance

Let baby stand barefoot on different surfaces—mat, carpet, hard floor.

Day 7: Lap Stand Bounce

Hold baby upright on your lap and gently bounce to music.

Parent Hack of the Week – The Couch Gap Challenge

Leave a small space between the couch and a sturdy object. Let baby try to cruise from one to the other. You're building problem-solving and balance—one tiny step at a time.

Week 2: Fine Motor & Precision Play

Day 1: Finger Food Pickup

Offer small soft foods (banana bits, peas) and let baby grasp with fingers.

Day 2: Lid Lift Practice

Place a toy under a light plastic lid and let baby remove it.

Day 3: Drop & Retrieve Basket

Mindful Moment

Place a small basket next to baby and give them objects to drop in and retrieve.

Why it matters

Strengthens hand-eye coordination, memory, and repetition-based learning.

Try this

Say "In!" and "Out!" as baby repeats the action.

Day 4: Poke-the-Dough

Make soft dough and let baby poke with fingers or small tools.

Day 5: Peg & Hole Toy

Let baby insert pegs into large-holed toys or containers.

Day 6: Cup Stack Knock

Stack two cups and let baby pull or push them apart.

Day 7: Ribbon Pull Game

Place ribbons through holes in a lid. Let baby pull them one by one.

Parent Hack of the Week – The Lid Line-up

Line up different-sized plastic lids on baby's tray. They'll explore spinning, banging, flipping—and you'll have a quiet 10-minute stretch while they build coordination.

Week 3: Imitation & Simple Words

Day 1: Mimic Sound Play

Make simple sounds: "buh-buh," "la-la," and wait for baby's echo.

Day 2: Gesture Combo

Wave while saying "bye," clap with "yay," nod with "yes."

Day 3: Copy Me Game

Mindful Moment

Do a 3-step action: clap, smile, touch your head. Pause to let baby try.

Why it matters

Boosts memory, pattern recognition, and attention span.

Try this

Celebrate every partial success—even just one step copied is a big win.

Day 4: Book Point-Along

Point to objects in a book. Encourage baby to point too.

Day 5: Word with Gesture

Say "milk" while pointing to the cup or "up" with outstretched arms.

Day 6: Action Mirror

Face a mirror and make silly expressions. Watch for baby's response.

Day 7: Toy Voice Match

Pick up a toy and say a unique sound for each. Repeat the same sound for the same toy each time.

Parent Hack of the Week – The Sound Signal Game

Assign a silly sound to a toy—"moo" for the cow, "vroom" for the car. Use the sound before offering the toy. Over time, baby will reach for the toy based on sound alone—early language magic.

Week 4: Early Problem Solving & Cause-Effect

Day 1: Toy Under Cup

Hide a toy under one of two cups. Say, "Where is it?"

Day 2: Door Open Peek

Let baby open a cupboard door (safe, of course!) to find a toy inside.

Day 3: Soft Obstacle Crawl

Mindful Moment

Make a crawling path using pillows or blankets. Place toys across it.

Why it matters

Builds spatial awareness, problem-solving, and movement coordination.

Try this

Encourage from the other side—"Come get it!"—without helping too quickly.

Day 4: Push-to-Light

Use a toy that lights up when pressed. Say "Push!" and watch for repeat attempts.

Day 5: Fabric Pull

Tuck a small cloth inside a larger one. Let baby pull to reveal.

Day 6: Stacking Rings

Place rings in a small pile. Let baby try to stack or bang them.

Day 7: "How Does It Work?" Toy

Offer a toy with a button, flap, or slider. Let baby try freely.

Parent Hack of the Week – The Pillow Trap

Hide a toy under a couch cushion and say, "Hmm… where did it go?" Baby will push, lift, dig—solving a puzzle and building strength without even knowing it.

Reflect & Recharge: End of Month 10
Parent Story – The Little Helper

I dropped a spoon and said, "Oops!" Before I could reach, Maya crawled over, picked it up, and handed it to me—grinning. It was the first time she saw a need and responded. I didn't teach it. She *noticed*.

— Nora, mom of a 10-month-old

What if my baby isn't doing this yet?

- Pulling to stand often happens after cruising. Let your baby take their own route.

- Precision play comes with repetition. Just having small things to poke and grab helps.

- Imitation grows from consistency—do your routines the same way and they'll join when ready.

> **Mindful Reminder**
>
> This month, you may notice your baby trying to help, copy, respond—or just surprise you. These aren't "milestones" as much as moments of awareness. Keep inviting them in. They're watching more than you know.

Month 11: Brave Beginnings

Focus: Independent movement, basic problem-solving, social games, and first steps in self-expression

Milestones to Watch For
Common Range (10 to 11 Months)

- Cruises confidently along furniture
- Stands briefly without support
- Drops objects on purpose and watches the result
- Repeats sounds or gestures to get attention

Emerging Milestones (Up to 12 Months)

- Takes first independent steps
- Imitates play (like stirring or brushing)
- Uses gestures like pointing or nodding
- Understands short, simple phrases

Your baby is not just exploring spaces—they're learning to own them. This month is about beginnings: of movement, play, and bold little acts of independence.

Week 1: Cruising, Standing & First Steps

Day 1: Couch-to-Table Move

Encourage baby to cruise from couch to nearby table.

Day 2: Squat and Grab

Place a toy low. Let baby squat from standing to pick it up.

Day 3: Open Space Stand

Mindful Moment

Stand baby in a safe, open space and let go briefly while supporting nearby.

Why it matters

Builds balance confidence and helps baby feel the shift from leaning to standing alone.

Try this

Smile, clap, or hold out your hands to encourage a step—even if they just sway.

Day 4: Walking While Holding

Let baby hold your fingers and walk across the room.

Day 5: Pull-Up Practice

Set toys just above reach to encourage pull-to-stand.

Day 6: Soft Landing Path

Place cushions or a folded blanket on the floor where baby can "fall" gently while trying to move.

Day 7: Mirror Walk

Hold baby while they walk toward their reflection in a full-length mirror.

Parent Hack of the Week – The Laundry Line Runway

Tie a scarf or soft rope along the length of a hallway at baby's chest height. They'll walk while holding it like a balance bar—early steps, but on their terms.

Week 2: Cause & Effect with Purpose

Day 1: Container Dump

Fill a plastic tub with small safe toys. Let baby dump and refill.

Day 2: Push-to-Move Toy

Use a rolling toy that moves when pushed.

Day 3: Light-Up Discovery

Mindful Moment

Offer a light-up or button toy with cause-effect feedback. Let baby explore freely.

Why it matters

Encourages intentional action, builds memory of "what happens when…"

Try this

Say "You did it!" every time they press a button to connect action and outcome.

Day 4: Drop Game with Sounds

Drop a ball in a tin or container. Let baby repeat and listen.

Day 5: Lid Flip

Place a small object under a lid or cup and let baby uncover it.

Day 6: Bang & Pause

Let baby bang two objects. Then stop and wait—do they continue?

Day 7: Zip Bag Peek

Fill a clear zip bag with safe items. Let baby press, poke, and open.

Parent Hack of the Week – The Water Bottle Spinner

Fill a clear plastic bottle with dry beans, glitter, or beads. Seal it tight. Show baby how to roll it—watch them chase, spin, and learn what motion does.

Week 3: Gestures, Play Imitation & Expression

Day 1: Bye-Bye Practice

Wave and say goodbye as you leave the room briefly.

Day 2: Clap and Copy

Clap in a pattern. Pause. Watch for a mimic.

Day 3: Pretend Play Start

Mindful Moment

Hand baby a brush or cup and model "pretending"—brushing hair or sipping.

Why it matters

Builds symbolic thinking and social understanding.

Try this

Narrate what you're doing: "I'm brushing hair... want to try?"

Day 4: Emotion Faces

Make happy, sad, surprised faces. See which one baby mirrors.

Day 5: Gesture Sound Pair

Use a consistent sign (like "all done" or "more") while saying the word.

Day 6: Look & Laugh

Play peekaboo with exaggerated laughter. Watch for baby's response.

Day 7: Object Exchange

Offer a toy, then open your hand for baby to return it.

Parent Hack of the Week – The Sock Sip

Hand baby a clean sock and say "Drink?" while pretending it's a cup. They'll giggle—and often try it too. You're teaching pretend play, not just silliness.

Week 4: Independent Play & Little Choices

Day 1: Two Toy Pick

Hold out two toys. Let baby choose one.

Day 2: Open Shelf Moment

Place 2–3 toys on a low shelf. Let baby go to them freely.

Day 3: "Your Turn" Game

Mindful Moment

Roll a ball or push a car and say, "Your turn!" Wait without prompting.

Why it matters

Introduces turn-taking, patience, and social play rhythm.

Try this

Smile and clap when they engage—even just reaching is progress.

Day 4: Snack Self-Feed

Offer small pieces of soft food. Let baby grab and eat.

Day 5: Toy Toss Basket

Place a soft basket near baby. Let them toss toys in.

Day 6: Book Flip Freedom

Let baby hold and flip through a sturdy book on their own.

Day 7: Music Pause

Play a short song. Pause mid-way. Wait to see if baby reacts or moves.

Parent Hack of the Week – The Snack Choice Trick

Offer two small snacks in each hand and ask, "Which one?" When baby points or reaches, name their choice. A simple yes builds early decision-making.

Reflect & Recharge: End of Month 11
Parent Story – The First Choice

Luca was fussing, so I knelt down and held out two toys: a car and a spoon. He looked at both, then grabbed the car with a big grin. It was the first time he picked what *he* wanted. I didn't realize how empowering that could be—for both of us.

— *Ayaka, mom of an 11-month-old*

What if my baby isn't doing this yet?

- Not walking yet? Many babies walk closer to 13–14 months. Cruising counts too.

- Pretend play may look like mouthing or banging at first. That's still exploration.

- Simple choices can start small—what matters is offering the chance.

Mindful Reminder

You don't need to make every moment count—you just need to make room for moments to happen. Whether it's a wobbly step, a giggle, or a glance, your baby is building confidence—on their time, with your trust.

Month 12: Bold Explorers

Focus: First steps, object use, early understanding of routines, and playful independence

Milestones to Watch For
Common Range (11 to 12 Months):

- Stands independently
- Takes a few steps alone
- Points to objects of interest
- Uses gestures and some words to express wants

Emerging Milestones (Up to 13 Months)
Imitates everyday activities (wiping, talking, feeding)

- Brings items when asked
- Begins to follow simple one-step commands
- Shows preferences or makes basic choices

This month marks a major shift: your baby is now not just observing the world—they're participating in it.

Week 1: First Steps & Movement Control

Day 1: Step & Catch

Stand a short distance away and encourage baby to walk toward you.

Day 2: Cruise and Pivot

Let baby cruise along furniture, then pivot to another object nearby.

Day 3: Standing Pause Practice

Mindful Moment

Support baby to stand on their own, then let go for a few seconds. Count together.

Why it matters

Builds balance, confidence, and body awareness needed for walking.

Try this

Smile and count aloud: "One… two… three!" before catching them.

Day 4: Walk-and-Hold

Let baby walk while holding one of your hands—not both.

Day 5: Rug Path Crawl

Set up a trail of soft mats or blankets for crawling and scooting.

Day 6: Push Toy Parade

Offer a push walker or toy cart to practice forward motion.

Day 7: Toe Tap Dance

Dance with baby, tapping their feet gently to rhythm.

Parent Hack of the Week – The Pillow Path

Line up floor cushions or pillows in a zigzag pattern. Baby will step, crawl, cruise, or climb their way through. Every surface change adds balance fun.

Week 2: Object Use & Everyday Tools

Day 1: Baby Brush Play

Offer a soft brush and model brushing your hair.

Day 2: Spoon Scoop Time

Give baby a spoon and bowl with soft food or dry cereal.

Day 3: Pretend Feed a Toy

Mindful Moment

Hand baby a cup or spoon and a stuffed toy. Model feeding the toy.

Why it matters

Supports imitation, empathy, and symbolic thinking.

Try this

Narrate: "Teddy's hungry… you're feeding him. Yum yum!"

Day 4: Cloth Clean Game

Give baby a soft cloth and model wiping the table or floor.

Day 5: Sock Stuff & Pull

Stuff socks into a soft container. Let baby pull them out and repeat.

Day 6: Toy Phone Chat

Use a pretend phone and say "Hello!" Hand it to baby and wait.

Day 7: Lid Match

Offer containers with matching lids. Let baby try to pair them.

Parent Hack of the Week – The Daily Helper Trick

Let baby "help" during chores—holding a sponge, moving a sock, "stirring" an empty bowl. Their imitation builds identity: "I'm part of this world."

Week 3: Words, Gestures & Simple Commands

Day 1: Point & Label

Point to objects and name them clearly.

Day 2: "Give it to me"

Ask baby to hand you a toy. Smile and thank them when they do.

Day 3: Gesture-and-Word Match

Mindful Moment

Pair familiar words with gestures: "Up?" with arms lifted, "No" with head shake.

Why it matters

Builds connection between movement and meaning—key to early language.

Try this

Repeat the same word/gesture combo several times in the Day.

Day 4: Favourite Word Hunt

Say a familiar word ("ball" or "dog") and wait for baby to look or point.

Day 5: Name It Game

Ask, "Where's your nose?" or "Where's the light?" and wait for a response.

Day 6: Talk to the Mirror

Look into the mirror and say baby's name with a smile.

Day 7: Say + Pause

Say a phrase like "All done!" and pause to let baby repeat or react.

Parent Hack of the Week – The Point & Wait

Point to a bird, toy, or object and pause. Let baby track it before you speak. That wait builds anticipation—and trains them to watch for meaning.

Week 4: Routines, Choices & Independent Play

Day 1: "Pick One" Moment

Offer two toys or books. Let baby choose with hand or eyes.

Day 2: Shoe Time Participation

Invite baby to bring you shoes when getting ready to go out.

Day 3: Step-by-Step Snack

Mindful Moment

Offer a few bites of snack, then pause and ask "More?" with gesture. Wait for a sign.

Why it matters

Encourages turn-taking, communication, and routine cues.

Try this

Use the same word and gesture every time—consistency helps memory.

Day 4: Clean-Up Fun

Model putting toys in a bin and invite baby to join.

Day 5: Water Pour

Give two cups and a small amount of water. Let baby pour back and forth.

Day 6: Pyjama Pull

Let baby help pull arms through sleeves or lift feet during dressing.

Day 7: Free Book Flip

Place a few board books within reach. Let baby turn pages at their own pace.

Parent Hack of the Week – The Goodbye Signal

Start waving "bye" when turning off lights, ending play, or finishing bath. It becomes a closing signal—and helps baby predict what's next.

Reflect & Recharge: End of Month 12
Parent Story – The First Helper

I dropped a sock while folding laundry. Without asking, Isla toddled over, picked it up, and dropped it in the basket. It felt tiny, but it hit me—she understood what I was doing and wanted to help. It wasn't just a task. It was our rhythm.

— Clara, mom of a 12-month-old

What if my baby isn't doing this yet?

- Walking may come this month—or in the next few. Cruising still counts as mobility.

- If baby isn't imitating yet, keep routines simple and repeatable. They learn through rhythm.

- Offering choices helps them practice—even if they choose with just a glance.

Mindful Reminder

One year in, and everything is starting to feel more interactive. Don't worry about keeping up, just keep connecting. You're not raising a checklist. You're raising a person.

Year 1: Congratulations on an Incredible First Year!

You did it! The first year of your child's life has been an extraordinary journey filled with love, learning, and growth. Every smile, every little milestone, and every new discovery is a testament to your dedication as a parent. Through all the sleepless nights, joyful moments, and challenges, you have given your child the best start in life. **You are doing an amazing job!**

Now, as you wrap up this first year, take a moment to celebrate how far both you and your child have come. Parenthood is a continuous learning experience, and your efforts, no matter how big or small, are making a lasting impact. Use the **Milestone Tracker** to review progress and rate key achievements. This will help you reflect on your baby's strengths and areas that may need more support..

Trust yourself, and keep going! Each stage of growth comes with new challenges and exciting opportunities. Stay patient, stay engaged, and most importantly, cherish the precious moments ahead.

You've got this! Congratulations once again on completing Year 1. Your love, dedication, and hard work are shaping a bright and beautiful future for your child.

Understanding Your Child's Developmental Tracker

Every child develops at their own pace. These trackers are designed to provide a structured way to observe and support your child's growth, but they should not be seen as rigid timelines. It's completely normal for some children to excel in certain areas while taking more time in others.

How to Use the Tracker

- **Rate on a scale of 0-5** based on your child's current abilities in each category.

- **No need to rush or compare!** Some children might be more advanced in speech but take longer with motor skills, and that's completely fine.

- **Use it as a guide**, not a test. If your child isn't yet meeting certain milestones, observe their progress over time instead of worrying.

- **Celebrate small wins!** Any progress, no matter how small, is valuable.

What If My Child is Behind in Some Areas?

- **Variability is normal** – Development is not linear, and children often leap ahead in some skills while taking more time in others.

- **Support their growth** through interactive play, reading, conversations, and hands-on activities that align with their interests.

- **Patience is key** – Keep engaging them in activities without pressure or comparisons.

- **Seek guidance if necessary** – If you have concerns, consulting a paediatrician or child development expert can provide reassurance and strategies for support.

Remember: Progress over perfection! ✻

Category	Activity	Rating(0-5)
Sensory & Cognitive Growth	Tactile exploration: grasping, reaching, mouthing objects	
Sensory & Cognitive Growth	Visual tracking, recognizing faces, and responding to stimuli	
Sensory & Cognitive Growth	Simple problem-solving: object permanence, cause-effect play	
Language & Communication Development	Recognizing sounds, responding to voices, and cooing/babbling	
Language & Communication Development	Building early vocabulary (simple words like mama, dada, bye-bye)	
Language & Communication Development	Understanding gestures and simple instructions	
Motor Skills & Physical Development	Gross motor: rolling, sitting, crawling, standing with support	
Motor Skills & Physical Development	Fine motor: grasping objects, finger-feeding, transferring items between hands	

Motor Skills & Physical Development	Hand-eye coordination through object manipulation	
Social & Emotional Foundation	Attachment and bonding with caregivers	
Social & Emotional Foundation	Recognizing emotions and responding to social cues	
Social & Emotional Foundation	Developing early trust, comfort, and self-soothing behaviours	

As you wrap up this first precious year, take a quiet moment to honour every cuddle, cry, and coo.

Each tiny milestone was a giant leap in love and connection.

Growth isn't just in firsts — it's in the bond you've built together.

This chapter ends, but the journey of becoming continues, hand in hand.

What's Next?

Year 2 isn't a new race, it's a gentle continuation. The connection you've built is still the foundation. Keep following your child's lead, one small step at a time.

Year 2: The Explorer Year

Mobility, Language, and Discovery

Quote

"Play is the highest form of research."

— *Albert Einstein*

Mantra

I follow their wonder. I guide with love. I grow with them.

M.I.N.D. for Year 2

Moments That Matter

Let curiosity lead the way - it's how toddlers connect and learn.

Intentional Interaction

Use playtime to fuel movement, language, and bonding.

Nurture Through Love

Stay patient through big emotions - they're still learning how to feel.

Daily Growth

Repetition and routine anchor growth in their fast-changing world.

Welcome to Year 2

The Journey From Babyhood to Toddlerhood

"Your child isn't just growing - they're becoming."

Year 2 is a beautiful blend of boldness and tenderness. Your baby is now on the move—exploring, expressing, and experimenting with the world in brand-new ways. And you? You've grown, too. You've learned to read their cues, trust your instincts, and celebrate every little moment. Now, it's time to deepen the connection.

This year is all about **supporting independence** while **anchoring emotional safety**—offering room to roam, with your presence still steady and close.

What's New This Year

- Activities will gently shift toward **autonomy, language, imitation, emotional regulation**, and **social awareness**.

- You'll notice more moments that include **choices, role play, gentle discipline**, and **collaboration**—skills toddlers are wired to practice.

- Your presence, language, and consistency remain their strongest tools for brain-building.

How to Use This Guide in Year 2

Follow the same **daily structure**: *7 short activities a week, with 2–3 expanded Mindful Moments for depth and insight.*

- Each week still includes a fresh, **Parent Hack**, a unique **Reflect & Recharge**, and a supportive **"What If..."** section.

- Activities stay short and realistic—but now with more focus on **choices, routine-building, emotional labelling**, and **movement-based learning**.

Milestones to Watch in Year 2
Emerging Skills (13–18 months)

- Walks independently or with minimal support

- Uses gestures like pointing, waving, or clapping

- Tries to imitate words or familiar sounds

- Understands simple requests ("Come here," "Give me the ball")

- Begins pretend play (feeding doll, talking on toy phone)

- Shows interest in helping with daily routines

Expanding Skills (19–24 months)

- Runs, climbs, and moves with more confidence

- Uses 10–50+ words and begins two-word combinations

- Shows preferences and makes simple choices

- Understands and follows one-step instructions

- Begins expressing feelings with sounds or gestures

- Demonstrates early problem-solving (stacking, cause-effect toys)

These are ranges, not rules. Your toddler's timeline is unique. Growth isn't a checklist. It's a story unfolding, one moment at a time.

Month 13: Confident Explorers Focus: Walking, early problem-solving, gesture communication, and everyday independence

Week 1: Walking, Climbing & Gross Motor Play

Day 1: Cushion Trail

Line up soft cushions or folded blankets and let your toddler step, crawl, or walk across.

Day 2: Climb & Descend

Offer a low, safe step or sturdy box for practicing stepping up and down with help.

Day 3: Toy Push Parade

Mindful Moment

Give your toddler a push toy or empty laundry basket to push around the room.

Why it matters

Builds balance, coordination, and direction control as walking becomes purposeful.

Try this

Narrate where they're going: "You're taking Bunny to the kitchen!"

Day 4: Sidewalk Explorer

Go outside and let your toddler walk on different surfaces: pavement, grass, gravel.

Day 5: Step-Over Game

Lay down a rolled towel or small pillow and invite them to step over with help.

Day 6: Rolling Ball Chase

Roll a soft ball and encourage your toddler to chase and retrieve it.

Day 7: Lap Bounces

Sit your toddler on your lap and bounce to a rhythm: "Up, up, down!"

Parent Hack of the Week – The Furniture Course

Set up a mini obstacle course using sofa cushions, chairs to walk around, or a tunnel of boxes. It's a safe indoor adventure that builds balance and confidence—and gives you 20 minutes of free play.

Week 2: Gesture Play, Language Rhythm & Social Sharing

Day 1: Clap Game

Clap slowly and see if your toddler joins in. Add a rhythm like "clap-clap-pause."

Day 2: Point and Talk

During book time, point to pictures and name them. Pause to let your toddler point.

Day 3: Action + Word

Mindful Moment

Use a clear gesture alongside a word: wave and say "bye," shake head and say "no."

Why it matters

Gestures paired with words help toddlers make connections before speech fully develops.

Try this

Repeat your gestures consistently during routines—soon your toddler will join in.

Day 4: Simple Sign Use

Model simple baby signs for "more," "all done," or "milk."

Day 5: Mirror Mimicry

Stand with your toddler in front of a mirror. Wave, clap, touch your nose.

Day 6: Toy Exchange

Offer one toy and wait for your toddler to hand you another. Say "Thank you!"

Day 7: Dance Freeze

Play music and dance together. Pause suddenly. Freeze and smile.

Parent Hack of the Week – The Echo Basket

Place a few familiar objects in a basket. Name each slowly, adding a playful tone: "Spoon! Ball! Sock!" Your toddler will start repeating sounds or grabbing the right item. Language starts here.

Week 3: Everyday Tools & Imitation Play

Day 1: Spoon Practice

Let your toddler try feeding themselves with a soft-tipped spoon.

Day 2: Shoe Helper Time

Hold out their shoe and say, "Foot in!" Let them try to push it in.

Day 3: Little Helper Moment

Mindful Moment

Give your toddler a dry cloth and invite them to wipe a surface with you.

Why it matters

Imitation of household routines builds independence, motor coordination, and pride.

Try this

Narrate your joint task: "We're wiping the table clean!"

Day 4: Pretend Feed

Hand them a toy cup or spoon. Watch as they "feed" a stuffed animal or you.

Day 5: Lid-On Challenge

Offer containers with lids. Let them try opening and closing.

Day 6: Brush Hair Together

Offer a baby brush and let them try brushing their hair after watching you.

Day 7: Water Pouring Game

With supervision, give two cups and let your toddler pour water between them.

Can you pour water for your teddy? Pretend it's tea time!

Parent Hack of the Week – The Clean-Up Song Trick

Make a short jingle for tidying up: "Put the toys away, hooray!" Use it every time. The song creates a cue—and soon your toddler will dance while helping.

Week 4: Problem Solving, Curiosity & Attention Span

Day 1: Peekaboo Box

Hide a toy under a scarf and watch your toddler find it.

Day 2: Puzzle Match Time

Use a simple shape puzzle and guide them to match 1–2 pieces.

Day 3: Drawer Discovery

Mindful Moment

Create a safe drawer or low shelf just for your toddler to explore.

Why it matters

Encourages independent discovery and supports memory and object permanence.

Try this

Rotate a few safe objects weekly to renew curiosity.

Day 4: Stack & Knock

Stack soft blocks and let them knock it down.

Day 5: Tap & Listen

Tap different surfaces with a spoon and name the sound: "Clink! Thud!"

Day 6: Cause & Response Toy

Offer a pop-up or button toy they can activate.

Day 7: Book Hide-and-Seek

Ask, "Where's the dog?" while reading. Pause for toddler to find it.

Parent Hack of the Week – The Drawer of Wonders

Pick one kitchen drawer and fill it with safe, interesting items: measuring cups, plastic bowls, a soft brush. Let your toddler explore freely while you cook. It's independent learning, disguised as play.

Reflect & Recharge: End of Month 13
Parent Story – The First Helper

I was folding clothes when Anika toddled over, picked up a sock, and dropped it in the basket. Then she looked up, grinning. She knew she helped. My little girl—walking, watching, joining in. It felt like a new chapter had started.

— Priya, mom of a 13-month-old

What if my toddler isn't walking yet?

- Cruising, scooting, or pulling up still count as progress.

- Every child develops their gross motor skills in their own rhythm.

- Keep giving floor time, sturdy surfaces, and encouragement—they'll get there.

> ## Mindful Reminder
>
> Your toddler is more than their milestones. Their wonder, joy, and effort tell the real story. Keep celebrating small steps—you're building a curious, confident explorer, one moment at a time.

Month 14: Everyday Explorers

Focus: Problem-solving, early independence, imitation, and social connection

Week 1: Object Use & Cause-Effect Play

Day 1: Lid Pull Game

Offer a small container with a loose lid. Let your toddler open and close it freely.

Day 2: Scoop and Drop

Use a spoon and dry cereal or pom-poms. Show scooping and dropping into a bowl.

Day 3: Scoop & Pour Exploration

Mindful Moment

Give your toddler two small cups and something to scoop (like oats or small blocks). Let them pour back and forth. Warm-Weather Twist: Try scooping with sand or soil outdoors.

Why it matters

Encourages hand-eye coordination, planning, and repetition.

Try this

Place a tray underneath to contain the mess and let the play unfold.

Day 4: Push-Button Toy

Provide a toy with pop-ups or buttons to activate.

Day 5: Water Cup Test

Offer two cups and a bit of water. Let your toddler pour or spill.

Day 6: Ball Roll Bounce

Roll a ball down a folded pillow ramp. Invite them to copy you.

Day 7: Velcro Strap Fun

Use baby shoes or toys with Velcro and guide opening/closing together.

Parent Hack of the Week – The Mystery Pouch

Fill a cloth pouch or old pencil case with small safe objects. Say, "What's inside?" and watch your toddler pull each out with surprise. It's cause-effect magic + fine motor fun in one.

Week 2: Gesture Play & Social Communication

Day 1: Mirror Play Faces

Make happy, sad, and surprised faces in the mirror. Let them mimic you.

Day 2: "Where's It?" Book Game

Point to objects in a book: "Where's the ball?" Pause and let them respond.

Day 3: Gesture + Word Combo

Mindful Moment

Use familiar gestures like waving "bye" or shaking head "no" paired with words.

Why it matters

Toddlers understand gestures before speech—this builds both pathways.

Try this

Use gesture-word pairs consistently during transitions like mealtime or bath.

Day 4: Dance and Freeze

Play music and dance. Pause and say, "Freeze!"

Day 5: Point-and-Name Hunt

Walk around the house pointing at objects and naming them slowly.

Day 6: Sign Language Start

Model 1–2 baby signs (like "more" or "milk") during routines.

Day 7: Sharing Game

Offer a toy, then hold your hand out and say, "Your turn?" Encourage back-and-forth.

Parent Hack of the Week – The Mirror Mimic Trick

Sit with your toddler in front of a mirror and make silly faces or peek behind them. When they copy or laugh, you've built a mini-feedback loop of social learning—with joy!

Week 3: Imitation & Daily Helper Routines

Day 1: Sock Stuff Game

Hand your toddler a sock and a soft toy. Show how to "hide" it inside.

Day 2: Spoon-to-Doll Feed

Offer a small spoon and let them pretend-feed a doll or you.

Day 3: Little Helper Routine

Mindful Moment

Hand your toddler a wipe or cloth and invite them to clean the table with you.

Why it matters

Strengthens imitation, confidence, and pride in contributing.

Try this

Narrate with "We're cleaning together!" to reinforce teamwork.

Day 4: Shoe Setup

Hand them a shoe and encourage "foot in!" even if they don't get it yet.

Day 5: Diaper Toss Task

Ask them to "put this in the bin" with a clean diaper or cloth.

Day 6: Brushing Together

Model brushing your hair or teeth side-by-side. Invite them to mimic.

Day 7: Clean-Up Basket Time

After play, say, "Let's put this away!" and help them drop toys into a bin.

Parent Hack of the Week – The Morning Mini-Job

Give your toddler a task like "carry this cloth to the kitchen" or "hand me the sock." It's small, but they beam with pride—and it sets the tone for everyday contribution.

Week 4: Attention, Focus & Early Thinking

Day 1: Hide & Reveal Box

Hide a small toy under a cloth and say, "Where did it go?"

Day 2: Stack and Rebuild

Stack soft blocks and let them knock them down. Repeat together.

Day 3: Snack Sort Game

Mindful Moment

Offer two types of snacks (like banana pieces and puffs) and show sorting them into different bowls.

Why it matters

Encourages early classification, focus, and visual discrimination.

Try this

If they mix them again after sorting, that's still learning!

Day 4: Puzzle Exploration

Let them try fitting 1–2 chunky puzzle pieces with guidance.

Day 5: Push and Pull

Use a toy with a string or something they can drag and retrieve.

Day 6: Tap and Sound Discovery

Tap on glass, wood, and fabric. Say, "Listen!" and copy their response.

Day 7: Toy in a Cup

Drop a toy in a large cup and hand it to your toddler. Let them retrieve it.

Parent Hack of the Week – The Snack Drop Trick

Use a clean muffin tin and place one puff or fruit piece in each hole. Watching your toddler pick them out one by one turns snack time into a focus-building mini puzzle.

Reflect & Recharge: End of Month 14
Parent Story – The Little Leader

During clean-up, I asked, "Can you bring me the sock?" and Leo not only brought it, but grabbed another and dropped both in the laundry bin. He looked so proud—like he was leading the charge. It was one of those quiet, wow moments.

— *Amira, mom of a 14-month-old*

What if my toddler isn't doing these yet?

- Don't stress if they're not gesturing much yet—keep modelling in play and routines.

- Some toddlers imitate in silence for weeks before showing it outwardly.

- Small signs of trying (watching closely, copying later) still count.

> ### Mindful Reminder
>
> The more we slow down, the more we notice what our toddlers are really learning. It's not about big leaps—it's about thousands of tiny sparks, lit by your presence.

Month 15: Expressive Explorers

Focus: Vocabulary burst, pretend play, fine motor refinement, and emotional expression

Week 1: Words, Sounds & Everyday Language

Day 1: Name Game

Point to familiar people or objects and say, "That's Mama... that's your cup!"

Day 2: Copy My Sound

Make simple sounds like "ba-ba" or "moo." Pause and wait for baby to echo.

Day 3: Picture Naming Fun

Mindful Moment

Look through a board book and name 4–5 pictures slowly, with wide eyes and clear tone.

Why it matters

Builds recognition and sets a strong base for vocabulary development.

Try this

Pause and wait after each word. Give your toddler a chance to "say it" in their own way.

Day 4: Object Label Walk

While walking around the house, label what you see: "Light! Table! Spoon!"

Day 5: Gesture & Say

Use gestures while speaking: wave with "hi," pat your chest with "me," or point with "that."

Day 6: Singing Rhymes

Sing a simple rhyme with gestures ("Twinkle Twinkle," "The Wheels on the Bus").

Day 7: Talking Toy Time

Let your toddler "talk" to a stuffed toy. Respond as the toy in a playful voice.

Parent Hack of the Week – The Label Ladder

Pick 3 household items (e.g., cup, shoe, book) and name them all week during use. Repetition creates magic: one Day, your toddler might suddenly say it back.

Week 2: Pretend Play, Emotion & Expression

Day 1: Mirror Faces Game

Make happy, sad, surprised faces in the mirror and name them.

Day 2: Toy Feed

Hand a spoon or cup and say, "Feed the teddy!" Watch pretend play bloom.

Day 3: Brush & Care Play

Mindful Moment

Offer a brush and stuffed animal or doll. Model brushing its "fur" and hugging it.

Why it matters

Builds empathy, emotional labelling, and role imitation.

Try this

Say, "She's sad—can you help?" to spark kindness.

Day 4: Hide & Greet

Hide behind a blanket and say, "Where's mama?" then reappear: "Peekaboo!"

Day 5: Baby Dance Moves

Play music and move together. Encourage your toddler to clap or stomp.

Day 6: Emotional Book Time

Read a story and name characters' feelings: "She looks happy!" "Oh no, he's sad."

Day 7: Sound & Emotion Match

Say a feeling with a voice: "Happy!" (excited), "Tired" (yawn), "Mad!" (dramatic tone).

Parent Hack of the Week – The Emotion Echo

When your toddler shows a strong emotion, name it gently: "You're frustrated… it's okay." Giving words to feelings helps build emotional IQ—and diffuses tantrums before they erupt.

Week 3: Fine Motor Control & Independent Tasks

Day 1: Spoon Drop Play

Let your toddler pick up a spoon and drop it into a bowl or cup.

Day 2: Block Stack Practice

Give 2–3 stacking blocks and guide hands gently if needed.

Day 3: Little Pincer Practice

Mindful Moment

Place small snacks (peas, cereal bits) on a plate and let your toddler pick them up.

Why it matters

Strengthens pincer grasp—key for writing, dressing, and more.

Try this

Count or name each snack to boost language while building motor control.

Day 4: Velcro Fun

Let your toddler open/close Velcro on shoes, books, or cloth flaps.

Day 5: Flip-the-Page Game

Hand your toddler a board book and encourage page-turning.

Day 6: Tear & Drop

Tear paper strips and let your toddler crumple or drop them in a bin.

Day 7: Lid & Box Play

Give boxes with easy lids. Let them open and close freely.

Parent Hack of the Week – The Pincer Picnic

Snack time = fine motor practice. Use a muffin tray and put different bite-sized foods in each cup. Let your toddler pick, pinch, and eat—independence with every bite.

Week 4: Problem Solving, Curiosity & Social Games

Day 1: Object Swap Game

Offer one toy, then another. Watch your toddler choose or swap.

Day 2: "Where Did It Go?" Trick

Hide a toy under a napkin. Say, "Where is it?" Watch their delight when they uncover it.

Day 3: Cup & Block Play

Mindful Moment

Place a block under one of two cups. Shuffle and say, "Which one?"

Why it matters

Builds memory, prediction, and joy in discovery.

Try this

Let them watch first, then gradually make it more playful or tricky.

Day 4: Big vs. Small Toys

Offer toys of different sizes and describe: "Big ball... little cup!"

Day 5: Rolling Toy Test

Roll a car or ball and wait—do they follow or imitate?

Day 6: "Help Me" Requests

Ask them to hand you something: "Can you bring the spoon?"

Day 7: Clean-Up Challenge

Say, "Let's put all the blocks in the bin!" and make it a game.

Parent Hack of the Week – The Tiny Detective

Hide a small toy in plain sight, then ask, "Where's the duck?" Guide them just a bit. It builds attention, search-and-find skills, and pride when they "solve it."

Reflect & Recharge: End of Month 15
Parent Story – The First Real Word

We were playing with her toy duck, and I said, "Quack-quack!" like always. But this time, Mei looked straight at it and said, "Quaaa!" My heart skipped. It wasn't perfect—but it was hers. Her first real word.

— Xin Yue, mom of a 15-month-old

What if my toddler isn't speaking yet?

- Many toddlers focus first on motor skills or gestures—words follow.

- Keep modelling language and pairing words with action.

- If they understand instructions and show social engagement, you're on track.

> **Mindful Reminder**
>
> Words may be few, but expression is everywhere—through gestures, eye contact, play, and sound. Stay tuned to their cues. You're their favourite communication partner—and that's the foundation that matters most.

Month 16: Little Communicators

Focus: Word comprehension, imitation play, balance & mobility, and independent routines

Week 1: Listening, Comprehension & Response

Day 1: "Where's the…?" Game

Ask, "Where's your nose?" or "Where's the ball?" Pause for a response.

Day 2: Simple Two-Step Directions

Say, "Pick up the spoon and give it to me." Celebrate effort!

Day 3: Body Part Parade

Mindful Moment

Name and touch body parts: "These are your toes!" Wait for your toddler to touch them too.

Why it matters

Builds comprehension, body awareness, and introduces relational language.

Try this

Turn it into a bath time game or dressing routine.

Day 4: Toy Sound Match

Say the sound of a toy ("vroom" for car) and hand it over. Watch for recognition.

Day 5: Gesture + Phrase

Add gestures to daily phrases: "All done!" with open hands.

Day 6: Echo Reading

Read a line from a board book. Repeat key words and wait for your toddler to chime in.

Day 7: Call & Response Game

Say "Hi!" and wait. When they respond, cheer: "You said hi!"

Parent Hack of the Week – The Two-Step Magic

When your toddler starts understanding short commands, combine two: "Get your ball and sit here." It might take practice—but when they do it? Pure magic. You'll both feel it.

Week 2: Movement, Balance & Spatial Play

Day 1: Stair Climb & Sit

With close supervision, help toddler climb up 2–3 stairs and sit.

Day 2: Obstacle Path Crawl

Lay out pillows or boxes and encourage crawl/step-through.

Day 3: Tunnel Crawl Play

Mindful Moment

Create a tunnel with chairs and a blanket. Let your toddler crawl through while you cheer.

Why it matters

Supports gross motor development, spatial awareness, and bravery.

Try this

Sit at the other end calling their name. Peek inside to keep it playful.

Day 4: Standing Toy Toss

Encourage your toddler to toss soft toys into a basket while standing.

Day 5: Balance Pause

Ask toddler to "stand like a tree!" for 2 seconds. Try again with giggles.

Day 6: Up-Down Dance

Dance to a song that uses up/down or fast/slow. Move together.

Day 7: High-Five March

March around the room and give a high-five each time they pass you.

Parent Hack of the Week – The Pillow Runway

Line up soft cushions in a zig-zag. Watch your toddler step, fall, or crawl across—again and again. Bonus: It builds stability, and you get five solid minutes of movement magic.

Week 3: Imitation, Pretend & Routine Play

Day 1: Phone Talk

Hand them a toy phone. Model "Hello!" and pass it back and forth.

Day 2: Washcloth Wipe Time

Let your toddler help wipe the table, toys, or high chair tray.

Day 3: Self-Feeding Boost

Mindful Moment

Hand over the spoon and let your toddler scoop from their own bowl.

Why it matters

Encourages independence and coordination during everyday tasks.

Try this

Use thicker foods like mashed potatoes or yogurt to reduce spills and boost confidence.

Day 4: Pretend Cook Together

Give a pot and spoon. Stir, add pretend ingredients, taste together!

Day 5: Toy Sleep Ritual

Tuck a doll/stuffed animal into a cloth. Whisper, "Shhh… night-night."

Day 6: Shoe Time Helper

Let toddler help push their foot into shoes or socks. Say 'Find the sleepy shoe! Let's wake it up with your foot!

Day 7: Brush & Mirror Game

Give a brush and stand at a mirror. Say, "Your turn!"

Parent Hack of the Week – The Daily Helper Cheer

Turn routine tasks into play. "Helper, helper—here you come!" Invite your toddler to toss a diaper in the bin or bring their bib. In many Japanese families, toddlers serve small items on trays—try this with snacks to build independence. You're nurturing confidence through contribution.

Week 4: Curiosity, Creativity & Object Exploration

Day 1: Block Tower Try

Hand blocks one by one and let your toddler build a stack.

Day 2: Texture Sorting Time

Place smooth, rough, and soft objects in a bin. Let them explore and sort.

Day 3: Lid & Cup Match

Mindful Moment

Offer a few small containers and mismatched lids. Let your toddler explore which fit.

Why it matters

Builds problem-solving, hand-eye coordination, and early logic.

Try this

Let them "struggle" a bit—success feels sweeter after effort.

Day 4: Push & Pull Game

Let your toddler push toys across the room, then pull them back by string or hand.

Day 5: Crayon Scribble Time

Tape paper to the table. Offer chunky crayons to scribble freely.

Day 6: Ball Drop Challenge

Drop a ball into a tube or bucket. Say, "Ready… set… go!"

Day 7: Lid Tap Orchestra

Line up plastic lids. Tap with a spoon. Name sounds together.

Parent Hack of the Week – The Container Collection

Create a "play drawer" in the kitchen with different safe containers. It's not just mess—it's memory-building, imagination-boosting, focus-growing, joyful play.

Reflect & Recharge: End of Month 16
Parent Story – The Shoe Helper Surprise

We were rushing to leave when I felt a tap on my leg. Ella had one shoe in her hand and was trying to push her foot into the other. No words. Just determined, proud energy. She wanted to do it herself. I paused. Let her. It took longer—but watching her beam made the whole Day better.

— Nadia, mom of a 16-month-old

What if my toddler isn't doing this yet?

- Every toddler picks their pace—some climb before they talk, others talk before they run.

- Focus on progress: are they trying? Imitating? Exploring? That's growth.

- Celebrate effort. Even the wobble is a win.

> ## Mindful Reminder
>
> Independence doesn't arrive in leaps—it arrives in small moments of "I'll try." Let them. Then let them try again. These moments grow confidence, one wobbly spoon or mismatched shoe at a time.

Month 17: Curious Communicators

Focus: Expanding vocabulary, movement coordination, self-help skills, and social awareness

Week 1: Words, Sounds & Conversations

Day 1: Word of the Day

Pick a simple word (like "ball") and use it repeatedly during play.

Day 2: Book Talk

Point at a picture in a book and name it. Pause and wait for any response.

Day 3: Object Naming Hunt

Mindful Moment

During a walk around the house, name familiar objects: "Chair," "Spoon," "Door." Let your toddler try too.

Why it matters

Hearing repeated labels boosts comprehension and early vocabulary recall.

Try this

Touch the object each time. Toddlers often link meaning faster through multisensory input.

Day 4: Sound Game

Make animal or vehicle sounds and see if your toddler can match them.

Day 5: Name & Point Game

Say a family member's name and ask your toddler to point to them.

Day 6: Echo Song Time

Sing a familiar song and pause to let your toddler fill in the last word.

Day 7: Snack Talk

Name each item during snack: "Banana! Yum! More?"

Parent Hack of the Week – The Mealtime Chat Frame

Instead of just feeding your toddler, talk about everything happening: "Spoon goes in! Chew, chew! All done?" It turns mealtime into an interactive speech lab.

Week 2: Coordination, Climbing & Gross Motor Play

Day 1: Ball Roll & Catch

Roll a soft ball and try gentle rolling back and forth.

Day 2: Step Up Practice

Let your toddler step onto a low platform (curb, mat) with help.

Day 3: Box Fort Navigation

Mindful Moment

Use cardboard boxes or cushions to build a mini fort or maze. Let your toddler explore in and out of it.

Why it matters

Encourages problem-solving, spatial planning, and independence in a slightly more open-ended setting than the tunnel.

Try this

Add a favorite toy inside and ask your toddler to "go find it." You can sit inside too for peek-a-boo or pretend play

Day 4: Dance with Stops

Play music and pause it randomly. Say "Stop!" and freeze together.

Day 5: Blanket Pull Ride

Sit your toddler on a blanket and pull them gently across a soft floor.

Day 6: Chase & Giggle

Play a short game of chase around a safe space. Pause often for hugs.

Day 7: Throw & Fetch

Throw a plush toy and ask your toddler to bring it back.

Parent Hack of the Week – The Step Game

Keep a sturdy low step or mat in play areas. Toddlers love stepping up and down. Narrate each move: "One foot up! Down again!"

Week 3: Self-Help & Daily Routine Skills

Day 1: Sock Pull Practice

Let your toddler try pulling off their socks independently.

Day 2: Spoon Self-Feeding

Provide thick yogurt or mashed food for easy scooping success.

Day 3: Clean-Up Helper

Mindful Moment

After play, ask your toddler to put toys into a basket. Join in together.

Why it matters

Involving toddlers in routines teaches contribution, sequencing, and responsibility.

Try this

Use a short clean-up song to make it fun and predictable.

Day 4: Toothbrush Time

Offer a toddler-safe toothbrush and mirror for them to try brushing.

Day 5: Bib or Hat On/Off

Let them try to remove or place a soft hat or bib.

Day 6: Washcloth Wipe

Give a damp cloth and invite your toddler to wipe the table with you.

Day 7: Carry & Place Game

Let your toddler carry a soft item from one room to another and place it in a basket.

Parent Hack of the Week – The Tiny Task Trick

During routines, assign a mini task: "Can you carry this to the table?" It gives toddlers pride and makes them feel capable—because they are.

Week 4: Emotions, Social Play & Sensory Awareness

Day 1: Emotion Mirror Game

Make a happy, sad, surprised face in the mirror and label each one.

Day 2: Peekaboo with Names

Cover your face and say, "Where's Mama? Peekaboo!"

Day 3: Empathy in Action

Mindful Moment

Pretend a stuffed toy is sad or hurt. Say, "Oh no! Bunny is sad." Offer a hug together.

Why it matters

Practicing empathy helps toddlers begin to read emotions and build social responses. Even if they walk away mid-play, they're still absorbing emotional roles over time.

Try this

Show a comforting response and let your toddler join in.

Day 4: Sensory Bin Discovery

Offer a shallow bin with dry rice or soft fabric scraps. Let them explore.

Day 5: Bubble Pop Play

Blow bubbles and let your toddler chase and pop them.

Day 6: Hand Trace Fun

Place your toddler's hand on paper and trace around it.

Day 7: Blanket Snuggle Wind-Down

Cuddle under a soft blanket together and name favourite animals or people.

Parent Hack of the Week – The Bunny Bandage Game

Keep a few toy bandages for pretend play. When a stuffed animal is "hurt," help your toddler stick on a bandage. You're teaching care, names for feelings, and gentleness.

Reflect & Recharge: End of Month 17
Parent Story – The Clean-Up Breakthrough

"I used to clean up all the toys myself, but one Day, Mateo grabbed a block and dropped it into the basket. Then another. I clapped, and he beamed. Now, every evening, he runs to help. It's our little ritual of growing up."

— Carmen, mom of a 17-month-old

What if my toddler isn't saying many words yet?

- That's okay. Many toddlers understand far more than they can say.

- Keep labelling, repeating, and pausing—language is building behind the scenes.

- Talk to your paediatrician if there are no gestures or attempts to communicate.

> ## Mindful Reminder
>
> Your toddler is starting to notice everything—and everyone. They may not say it yet, but they understand more than you know. Every word, gesture, and game is helping their voice emerge.

Month 18: The Curious Connector

Focus: Vocabulary burst, pretend play, imitation, and connection through movement and speech

Week 1: Language Leap & Everyday Words

Day 1: Name Everything Walk

Narrate everything on a short walk: "tree," "car," "dog," with clear, excited tones.

Day 2: Word + Action Pair

Say "clap!" and clap. "Jump!" and hop. Help toddler follow with joy.

Day 3: Sound Echo Game

Mindful Moment

Say a playful sound like "ba!" and wait for your toddler to mimic. Take turns with silly tones.

Why it matters

Builds social turn-taking, sound recognition, and speech rhythm.

Try this

Add gestures—"ba!" with a hand clap, "la!" with a shoulder shrug—for a full-body echo game.

Day 4: Favourite Object Hunt

Ask "Where's your bear?" and wait for them to fetch or point.

Day 5: Everyday Label Time

While changing clothes, name each item: "Socks!" "Hat!" "Shirt!"

Day 6: Sing-Talk Moments

Narrate routines in a melody: "Time to eat, eat, eat!" – it increases word retention.

Day 7: Snack Talk Chat

Talk about snack texture: "Crunchy cracker," "Cold yogurt," "Sticky banana."

Parent Hack of the Week – The Bathroom Vocabulary Game

Change diaper time into a quick naming game: "Wipe... diaper... button... pants!" Use funny voices. Repetition + routine = word mastery on the go.

Week 2: Pretend Play & Imagination

Day 1: Toy Bedtime

Let your toddler cover a stuffed animal and say "Night-night."

Day 2: Kitchen Imitation

Offer a safe bowl and spoon. Let them "mix" like you do.

Day 3: Storytime Play-Along

Mindful Moment

Read a familiar story and let your toddler act out gestures—like pointing, clapping, or pretending to eat.

Why it matters

Builds memory, symbolic thinking, and emotional engagement.

Try this

Pick books with simple, predictable phrases or animal actions for easy re-enactment.

Day 4: Phone Talk Pretend

Give them an old phone or toy one. Model "Hello!" and let them copy.

Day 5: Dress-Up Time

Offer hats, scarves, or socks for silly pretend roles.

Day 6: Copy the Grown-Up

Hand your child a soft cloth while you clean or pretend to sweep.

Day 7: Toy Tea Time

Sit with a doll and cup set. Pretend to sip, pour, and serve. Inspired by UK teatime play—offer small pretend cups and let your toddler 'serve' like a host.

Parent Hack of the Week – The Pretend Pouch

Fill a pouch with pretend items: toy key, empty bottle, play spoon. Let your toddler choose and play "grown-up." You'll hear: "Uh-oh!" "Bye!" "All done!"—and witness imagination bloom.

Week 3: Movement, Rhythm & Body Awareness

Day 1: Follow the Leader

Walk slowly. Then hop, crawl, spin. Ask them to do the same!

Day 2: Obstacle Wiggle Path

Line up cushions and boxes. Let them climb, crawl, and balance.

Day 3: Body Word Game

Mindful Moment

Say "Touch your nose!" or "Where are your knees?" and help them find each body part.

Why it matters

Combines receptive language and physical awareness.

Try this

End with a gentle "hug yourself" or "big stretch" to wind down.

Cold Day Option: Play this game during bath time with warm water for comfort

Day 4: Dance & Pause

Play music. Dance together. Pause suddenly and freeze with a funny face.

Day 5: Mirror Moves

Stand together in front of a mirror and copy each other's movements.

Day 6: Ramp Walk & Roll

Set up a low, stable ramp with a board or cushion. Let them walk up or roll toys down.

Day 7: Ball Chase Time

Roll a ball gently and encourage them to chase and bring it back.

Parent Hack of the Week – The Laundry Basket Zoom

Sit your toddler in a basket and gently pull them across the floor. Add commentary: "Turning left!" "Bump ahead!"—a giggle-filled sensory and body control activity.

Week 4: Social Gestures, Sharing & Self-Awareness

Day 1: Give & Take Game

Offer a toy. Say "Your turn… my turn" as you trade back and forth.

Day 2: Look & Name Faces

Point to family photos. Name each person and wait for your toddler to try.

Day 3: "Me" & "You" Moments

Mindful Moment

Point to yourself: "Mama!" Point to them: "You!" Use a mirror to explore this together.

Why it matters

Builds early self-awareness and identity through simple comparisons.

Try this

Say "You are [name]!" in a joyful tone and wait for a smile or giggle.

Day 4: Sharing Snack Time

Offer two small bowls—hand one to your toddler and say "One for me, one for you!"

Day 5: Gesture Replay

Wave and say "Hi!" Encourage them to do the same with a doll or pet.

Day 6: Emotion Copy Game

Make happy, sad, and surprised faces. Let your toddler try copying.

Day 7: Thank You Time

Say "Thank you!" with a toy exchange. Nod and smile to model it clearly.

Parent Hack of the Week – The Mirror High-Five Trick

Stand at the mirror and say, "Let's high-five!" Then give one to your reflection and help your toddler do the same. It's fun, social, and builds emotional mirroring.

Reflect & Recharge: End of Month 18
Parent Story – The Mimic Surprise

I was brushing my hair when I noticed Mateo pick up his toy brush and copy me—same strokes, same concentration. He even said, "Hair!" It was the first time I saw him link action, word, and intention on his own. It felt like a peek into his thinking mind.

— Allan, dad of an 18-month-old

What if my toddler isn't saying many words yet?

- Word comprehension often comes before speech. Keep naming things and pausing.

- Focus on gestures, pointing, and sound mimicking—these are all forms of communication.

- If by 18 months there's no verbal word and little social responsiveness, consider a paediatrician check-in.

> **Mindful Reminder**
>
> At this age, your toddler learns most from what you *do*, not just what you say. Your playful tone, your modelling, your consistent presence—that's their greatest teacher. Keep showing up. They're learning how to connect—because of you.

Month 19: Little Problem-Solvers

Focus: Problem-solving, verbal expression, tool use, and pretend play with purpose

Week 1: Tools, Discovery & Early Logic

Day 1: Scoop & Pour Play

Give two bowls and a spoon. Let your toddler scoop dry cereal or small toys between them.

Day 2: Toy in a Box

Place a favourite toy in a closed box. Let them figure out how to open it.

Day 3: Lid & Match Game

Mindful Moment

Offer a few mismatched lids and containers. Let them try matching.

Why it matters

Builds problem-solving, memory, and fine motor coordination. That pause when they're unsure? That's their brain rewiring to try again.

Try this

Praise persistence, not perfection: "You tried another one! That's smart thinking!"

Day 4: Toy Rescue Tape

Lightly tape a toy to a table with painter's tape. Watch them peel it off.

Day 5: Push & Fit Challenge

Use shape sorters or boxes with slots. Encourage trying different angles.

Day 6: Drawer Riddle

Hide a familiar item in a drawer and ask, "Where's the spoon?" Let them hunt.

Day 7: Stack & Problem Play

Offer blocks or nesting cups. Let them figure out order or how high to go.

Parent Hack of the Week – The Spoon & Slot Fix

Cut a slot in a cardboard box and hand your toddler some spoons or cardboard pieces. Watching them figure out what fits becomes a puzzle-solving joyride—and a focused few minutes for you.

Week 2: Speech Spark & Expression

Day 1: Sound Stretch Game

Exaggerate words: "Biiiig baaaall!" Let them repeat the stretched version.

Day 2: My Voice Echo

Say their name softly, loudly, then in a whisper. See if they echo back.

Day 3: Name That Feeling

Mindful Moment

Narrate moments like "You're happy!" or "You look frustrated." Point to your own face too.

Why it matters

Builds emotional vocabulary and self-understanding through gentle labelling.

Try this

Use mirrors or books to show emotions and name them together.

Day 4: Ask & Answer Time

Ask simple questions: "Want water?" Pause. Celebrate any response—gesture or word.

Day 5: Phrase Echo

Say simple two-word phrases: "Big truck," "More banana," "All done." Wait for repeat attempts.

Day 6: Picture Point Talk

Flip through a photo book. Say names and point. Ask, "Where's Grandma?"

Day 7: Word + Touch

Say "head," "toes," "ears" and touch each together with them.

Parent Hack of the Week – The Snack Talk Trick

At snack time, offer two foods and name them: "Banana or cracker?" Pause. Let them choose. No pressure—just repetition and fun. Toddlers love the control—and it builds vocabulary fast.

Week 3: Creative Play & Imitation

Day 1: Brush Teddy's Hair

Hand a brush and a stuffed toy. Say, "Let's brush hair like we do!"

Day 2: Pot & Spoon Drummer

Let your toddler tap safely on pots, boxes, or the floor. Name the sounds: "BANG!" "TAP!"

Day 3: Real-Life Imitation Moment

Mindful Moment

Invite your toddler to help during real routines—like putting clothes in a hamper or pretending to stir while you cook.

Why it matters

Builds confidence, routine understanding, and social imitation.

Try this

Narrate steps as they copy. "You're helping! Stir stir stir!"

Day 4: Role Swap Game

Say "Your turn!" and offer a toy phone or pretend tool. Take turns pretending.

Day 5: Object Reuse Play

Use socks as puppets, blocks as phones, bowls as hats. Let them copy or invent.

Day 6: Doll Naptime

Offer a blanket and doll or stuffed animal. Let your toddler tuck them in.

Day 7: Toy Bath Time

Fill a small tub with water. Let them "bathe" a toy using a sponge or cup.

Parent Hack of the Week – The Laundry Fold Game

Hand them a small cloth or sock while you fold laundry. Say, "Your sock, my sock." They'll mimic, play, or fold it their way—and feel like a big helper in your world.

Week 4: Emotional Growth & Social Play

Day 1: My Turn, Your Turn

Offer a toy and say "Your turn." Take it gently back with "My turn."

Day 2: Hug Your Toy

Say, "Give Teddy a hug!" Pause and smile when they do.

Day 3: Help Me Moments

Mindful Moment

Ask for help with a simple task—"Can you bring Mama the spoon?" Let them feel valued.

Why it matters

Encourages empathy, confidence, and purpose in routines.

Try this

Use a warm tone. "Thank you! You helped Mama!"

Day 4: Say Hello Together

Model waving and saying "Hi!" to a friend, family member, or stuffed toy.

Day 5: Emotion Faces Mirror

Make a face—happy, sad, silly. Encourage them to copy. Say the feeling out loud.

Day 6: Give a Snack Game

Offer two pieces of snack and say, "One for you, one for me!" Encourage sharing.

Day 7: Cuddle Pause

Pause in the Day for a long, gentle cuddle. Say, "You're safe with me."

Parent Hack of the Week – The Sock Share Game

Offer a pair of socks. Say "One for me, one for you." Put one on each foot—then swap! Toddlers find it hilarious—and it builds early sharing and emotional connection.

Reflect & Recharge: End of Month 19
Parent Story – The Helping Giggle

I was sweeping the floor and muttered, "Oops, mess!" Next thing I knew, Aarav brought over his little toy broom and said, "Me!" he swept beside me, giggling the whole time. It wasn't about cleaning—it was about being *with* me. That was the real magic.

— Pranali, mom of a 19-month-old

What if my toddler isn't solving problems on their own yet?

- It's normal to observe first. They may watch you try before jumping in later.

- Keep puzzles simple and celebrate any trial—not just success.

- Delay is often strategy: some toddlers think before they act.

> **Mindful Reminder**
>
> This month, your toddler is learning how to think *through* action. That toy box they opened? The snack they chose? The sock they gave you? It all counts. You're raising a thinker. Stay steady. Stay present. One moment at a time.

Month 20: Tiny Thinkers in Motion

Focus: Memory, movement sequences, simple instructions, and early independence

Week 1: Following Instructions & Movement Routines

Day 1: Two-Step Requests

Ask your toddler to do two things: "Pick up the ball and give it to me."

Day 2: Body Part Boogie

Say, "Touch your nose… now your toes!" Add rhythm to make it fun.

Day 3: Dance Routine Try

Mindful Moment

Play a song with simple steps—clap, jump, turn. Try a few motions together.

Why it matters

Builds memory, motor planning, and follow-through.

Try this

Keep it short and silly. "Clap! Clap! Spin!"

Day 4: Snack Helper Game

Ask: "Can you bring your cup?" Then add, "Now sit at the table!"

Day 5: Shoe Spot Game

Ask: "Where are your shoes?" Celebrate when they go and find them.

Day 6: Pack the Bag

Name 2–3 items (toy, bottle, hat) to place in a bag. Watch as they remember.

Day 7: Freeze & Go

Say "Go!" and run with them. Then pause: "FREEZE!" Add giggles.

Parent Hack of the Week – The Tiny Assistant Trick

Start giving one small "task" a Day: carry socks to the basket, hold the toothpaste, close a drawer. Each tiny task makes them beam. You're building memory, movement, and pride—all in one.

Week 2: Language Bursts & Object Naming

Day 1: Object Line-Up

Line up 3–4 items. Name one and say, "Can you get the spoon?"

Day 2: Picture Naming

Open a photo book or picture book and ask "Where's the dog?" Let them point or say it.

Day 3: Everyday Talk Along

Mindful Moment

Narrate the Day using simple language: "We're washing hands… now drying… all done!"

Why it matters

Regular exposure to real-time words builds vocabulary faster than isolated flashcards.

Try this

Slow down your speech and smile—it's more engaging.

Day 4: Echo Time

Say "Ball," then wait. Say "Ball rolls!" Let them try saying or mimicking.

Day 5: Big vs Small

Hold two objects: "This is big… this is small." Let them choose or name.

Day 6: Color Match Chat

Sort 2–3 coloured items. Name the color each time: "Red cup. Red spoon."

Day 7: Favourite Word Parade

Say a word your toddler loves (like "truck" or "banana") every few hours. Watch their face light up and join in.

Parent Hack of the Week – The Label Everything Phase

Toddlers love repetition. Label objects a few times a Day: "Chair," "Mama's shoes," "Blue cup." Repeating what they're already curious about? That's language gold.

Week 3: Pretend Play & Emotional Insight

Day 1: Pretend Cooking

Offer a bowl and spoon. Say, "Stir the soup!" Join the meal too.

Day 2: Care for Teddy

Give a wipe or small cup to "help" a doll or stuffed toy.

Day 3: Emotion Practice Pause

Mindful Moment

Act out feelings: smile and say "happy," frown for "sad." Point to your face and theirs.

Why it matters

Helps toddlers connect physical expressions to emotional words.

Try this

Ask gently, "How are you feeling?" and answer for them with warmth.

Day 4: Knock-Knock Game

Pretend knock on a door. Say "Who's there?" and act surprised.

Day 5: Blanket Nap Play

Lay down a stuffed toy. Say "Shh… it's bedtime!" Watch toddler join in.

Day 6: Mirror Play & Talk

Sit in front of a mirror. Point and say, "This is YOU! That's your nose!"

Day 7: Pretend Phone Chat

Hand them a pretend phone: "Hello, Grandma? How are you?" Listen as they "talk."

Parent Hack of the Week – The Grocery Pretend Bag

Hand them a small bag and pretend they're shopping. "Can you get milk?" They'll pull out anything—but imagination, memory, and speech are all happening in that bag.

Week 4: Spatial Play, Balance & Coordination

Day 1: Ball Target Roll

Roll a ball toward a box. Say, "Let's try to get it in!"

Day 2: Crawl-Under Game

Drape a blanket between chairs and crawl under it together.

Day 3: Stack & Tumble Challenge

Mindful Moment

Offer stacking blocks and let your toddler build, then knock them down.

Why it matters

Teaches spatial reasoning, control, and cause-effect.

Try this

Celebrate even tiny stacks. Say, "One… two… whoa!"

Note: In some Scandinavian homes, building and knocking down is a key part of early forest school play—outdoors and free-form

Day 4: Jump Like a Frog

Pretend to be a frog. Crouch, then hop. Encourage them to try.

Day 5: Spoon Transfer Game

Scoop dry rice or cereal from one bowl to another with a spoon.

Day 6: Box Climb Crawl

Let them climb onto a low, safe box or foam mat. Clap for effort.

Day 7: Spin & Stop

Spin around holding hands. Say "Stop!" and freeze in a pose.

Parent Hack of the Week – The Climb & Shout Ladder

Put couch cushions in a small pile and say, "Climb up and ROAR!" Toddlers love climbing + roaring + falling onto softness = the ultimate coordination booster.

Reflect & Recharge: End of Month 20
Parent Story – The First Big Ask

I asked Malik to bring his shoes—just hoping. He turned, found them, and waddled over, beaming. I didn't even care that they were mismatched. He *understood* me. That moment made me believe in everything we've been building.

— Jamal, dad of a 20-month-old

What if my toddler isn't combining words or following 2-step directions?

- Start with repeating single actions often. "Bring the ball" is plenty.

- Repetition and routine are your best tools—turn it into a game, not a test.

- Stay playful. Even if they gesture instead of talk, that's communication, too.

Mindful Reminder

At this stage, your toddler is trying to *make sense* of everything. Words. Choices. People. Emotions. It's a lot—but you're the anchor in it all. Just keep showing up. One connected moment at a time.

Month 21: Curious Communicators

Focus: Language confidence, problem-solving through play, early routines, and emotional understanding

Week 1: Word Discovery & Early Phrases

Day 1: Object Hunt Talk

Say, "Can you find the ball?" Pause while they search.

Day 2: "More Please" Practice

Prompt them to say or sign "more" when wanting more snack or song.

Day 3: Talking Time Together

Mindful Moment

Narrate your routine slowly: "We're washing hands. Splash splash! Drying now."

Why it matters

Everyday narration helps link words with context—this builds comprehension fast.

Try this

Speak slowly, pause often, and invite them to say the last word: "Socks on your…?"

Day 4: Who Says What?

Make animal sounds with toys: "Cow says…?" Let them finish.

Day 5: Name Everything Walk

As you walk, name things: "Tree… car… bird… dog!" Point and pause.

Day 6: Mealtime Words

Say "bite," "more," or "all done" with clear gestures.

Day 7: Echo Your Toddler

Repeat a word or sound your toddler says—but expand it. "Ba!" becomes "Ball? Yes! You said ball!"

Parent Hack of the Week – The Last Word Trick

Pause during rhymes or stories: "Twinkle, twinkle, little…" Let them fill in the blank. Even one sound shows language is blooming.

Week 2: Sensory Curiosity & Early Problem-Solving

Day 1: Lid Matching Game

Give your toddler a few small containers with lids. Let them try matching.

Day 2: Spoon + Cup Puzzle

Place small items in a cup and offer a spoon. Let them "fish" it out.

Day 3: Texture Trail Fun

Mindful Moment

Lay down a line of textures: towel, bubble wrap, soft mat. Let your toddler walk or crawl across barefoot.

Why it matters

Mixed textures build sensory discrimination and body awareness.

Try this

Name each feel: "Rough… soft… bumpy…"

Day 4: Push + Pull Challenge

Give a container with toys inside. Let them pull toys out, then close the lid.

Day 5: Wet vs Dry Game

Touch a wet cloth and a dry one. Ask: "Which is wet? Which is dry?"

Day 6: Tap to Hear

Tap different objects (wood, metal, soft toy) and say what it sounds like.

Day 7: Puzzle Assist Time

Offer a simple puzzle. Guide hand-over-hand once, then let them try.

Parent Hack of the Week – The Texture Stash

Keep a small bin of textured scraps—felt, sponges, rubber, silk. Let them explore during quiet time. Each feel is a brain booster.

Week 3: Emotional Language & Toddler Identity

Day 1: Mirror Me Faces

Make happy, sad, surprised faces in the mirror. Ask, "How do I look?"

Day 2: Feelings in Books

Point to faces in a storybook: "She looks sad. What do you think?"

Day 3: Emotion Word Play

Mindful Moment

Name your own feelings aloud: "Mama's tired but happy."

Why it matters

Modelling helps toddlers begin labelling feelings and builds emotional IQ.

Try this

Match your tone with the word. Show what "frustrated" sounds and looks like.

Day 4: Hug or High-Five Choice

Ask: "Want a hug or a high-five?" Let them choose.

Day 5: "Yes" or "No" Questions

Ask simple questions: "Do you want the red cup?" Let them say or signal yes/no.

Day 6: Soothe Your Teddy

Offer a toy or teddy and say, "Is he sad? Want to help him feel better?"

Day 7: Song for Feelings

Sing "If You're Happy and You Know It…" Add new verses: "If you're sad, give a hug…"

Parent Hack of the Week – The Feelings Basket

Create a little collection of toys that match feelings—calm, silly, sleepy. Label each with emotion words as you play. Over time, your toddler will start to label their own moods too.

Week 4: Routines, Choice & Independence

Day 1: Snack Choice Offer

Let toddler choose between two snacks. Name them clearly: "Banana or apple?"

Day 2: Pyjama Pick Time

Offer two options for PJs. Say: "Which one today?" Celebrate the decision.

Day 3: Turn-Taking Toss

Mindful Moment

Use a soft ball. Say "My turn," then "Your turn." Keep it simple and slow.

Why it matters

Builds patience, listening, and social rhythm through shared play.

Try this

Use a silly voice when it's your turn—they'll giggle and stay engaged.

Day 4: Clean-Up Routine

Say, "Time to clean up!" Hand them one item to place in a basket.

Day 5: Book Flip Freedom

Let them turn pages at their own pace—even if they skip.

Day 6: Walk to the Door Game

Say, "Let's go to the door," and walk together. Add "Ready... steady... go!"

Day 7: "All Done" Gesture

Practice the baby sign or simple phrase after a meal, bath, or play.

Parent Hack of the Week – The Start-The-Choice Game

When transitions are tough, start a choice. "I'll pick your pants… you pick your socks!" You're giving control inside structure—and that's toddler magic.

Reflect & Recharge: End of Month 21
Parent Story – The Little Voice

I said, "Let's get your shoes," expecting the usual blank stare. Instead, Ethan said, "Shoe!" and ran to grab one—mismatched, but his. It was the first time I saw the *words in his mind* reach his mouth—and reach me.

— Sarah, mom of a 21-month-old

What if my toddler isn't using many words yet?

- Start with consistent routines and repeat key words daily.

- Gestures count! Many toddlers point, wave, or nod before speaking.

- Keep modelling—your child is listening even if they're not saying much yet.

> ### Mindful Reminder
>
> This month, your toddler may *try* words, choices, ideas, and boundaries. That's progress—not pushback. Keep your language warm, your patience high, and your expectations low. Growth is happening—even in silence.

Month 22: Bold Problem Solvers

Focus: Cognitive leaps, tool use, early imagination, and expressive language

Week 1: Everyday Problem-Solving & Confidence

Day 1: Container Challenge

Offer a container with a lid. Say, "Can you open it?" Let them try first.

Day 2: Puzzle Piece Discovery

Give a few puzzle pieces and a board. Cheer even small attempts.

Day 3: Drawer Game Exploration

Mindful Moment

Choose a low drawer filled with safe, varied objects. Let your toddler explore freely.

Let them struggle a bit. Curiosity + mild frustration = deeper learning

Why it matters

This builds curiosity, visual scanning, and motor planning.

Try this

Add a new item each week to spark memory and surprise.

Day 4: String Pull Surprise

Tie a toy to a short string. Show how to pull it toward them.

Day 5: Try-Try-Try Again Game

Hide a toy under one of two cups. Watch how they react and learn.

Day 6: Scoop & Dump Task

Offer a spoon and bowl with soft objects to scoop and dump.

Day 7: Sock Pairing Help

Hand them two matching socks and invite: "Can you find a friend?"

Parent Hack of the Week – The Hidden Cup Game

Use three small cups and hide a toy under one. Move slowly. Let your toddler guess. Over time, they'll watch more closely—and love the "ta-da!" win.

Week 2: Expressive Language & Imitation

Day 1: "Tell Me What You See" Walk

Point and name things. Ask, "What's that?" even if they just point or babble.

Day 2: Action Sound Play

Make a silly sound as you perform a task: "Zip!" (zipping bag), "Pop!" (open lid).

Day 3: Label & Wait

Mindful Moment

Hold up an item—cup, spoon, toy—and clearly name it: "This is a cup." Pause. Let them look or say something.

Why it matters

Waiting builds processing time, attention, and word recall.

Try this

Repeat only once. The silence is golden—it invites a response.

Day 4: Mirror Talk Time

Look in the mirror together and point to eyes, nose, ears.

Day 5: Pretend Call

Hold a toy phone and say, "Hi, Nana!" Hand it to them. Watch their reply.

Day 6: Gesture + Word Combo

Say "Drink?" while motioning. Let them mimic back.

Day 7: Mini Object Story

Hold two toys. "Dog runs... ball rolls..." Add sound effects. Short and fun.

Parent Hack of the Week – The "Pause & Peek" Trick

When reading a book or telling a rhyme, pause mid-sentence. Look curious. Many toddlers will chime in—even with a sound or gesture. That pause gives them power.

Week 3: Independent Routines & Body Awareness

Day 1: Help with Pants or Socks

Say, "Let's try pulling them up!" Guide, but don't rush.

Day 2: Self-Spoon Time

Offer a soft spoon. Let them try to eat alone. Mess is okay!

Day 3: Pyjama Play Practice

Mindful Moment

After bath, hand them their PJs. Let them help with sleeves or feet.

Why it matters

Builds autonomy and motor sequencing—two arms in, then legs!

Try this

Offer soft praise for any effort: "You got one arm in! Amazing!"

Day 4: Toothbrush Helper

Let them brush first. You can "finish the job" after.

Day 5: Clean-up Match Game

Ask: "Where does this go?" and hand them a block, spoon, or book.

Day 6: Choose Your Snack

Offer two snack options. Cheer their choice.

Day 7: Shoes by the Door Game

Say: "Let's find your shoes and bring them to me!" High fives all around.

Parent Hack of the Week – The Mirror Dressing Game

Prop a safe mirror at toddler height. Let them watch as they put on socks or zip up a jacket with help. Seeing effort = pride in action.

Week 4: Imaginative Play & Sensory Joy

Day 1: Wash the Toy

Give them a sponge and a plastic doll or truck. Say, "Let's give it a bath."

Day 2: Blanket Cave

Drape a sheet over a table. Say, "This is your cave!" Let them explore.

Day 3: Pretend Play Spark

Mindful Moment

Offer a cup and toy spoon. Model feeding a teddy, then hand it over.

Why it matters

Pretend play strengthens planning, empathy, and memory.

Try this

Keep it short—just 1–2 actions. Keep repeating all week.

Day 4: Water Drip Time

With supervision, let water drip from a small cup into another. Say "drip... drip..."

Day 5: Nature Basket Touch

Collect leaves, pebbles, or grass. Let them explore textures.

Day 6: Color Talk Sorting

Offer coloured blocks or toys and say, "Can you find all the blue ones?"

Day 7: Sensory Bag Squish

Fill a zip bag with gel and tiny toys. Tape shut. Let them poke and squish.

Parent Hack of the Week – The Blanket Tunnel Escape

Lay a large blanket over two chairs to create a tunnel. Let them crawl through, peek out, and crawl again. Each pass builds coordination—and giggles!

Reflect & Recharge: End of Month 22
Parent Story – The Big Answer

One evening, I asked Luca, "Where's your ball?" expecting him to point. He ran across the room, picked it up, and shouted, "Ball!" I wasn't ready for such a clear response. I laughed, clapped, and he beamed. That moment? Pure magic.

— Jess, mom of a 22-month-old

What if my toddler still doesn't speak much?

- Look for understanding—do they follow directions or point? That counts.

- Use short, repeatable phrases in your daily routines.

- Narrate less. Invite more. Turn talk into two-way play.

Mindful Reminder

Every question, every pause, every small "win" is a doorway to connection. You don't need to force words—you just need to keep inviting them in. One curious Day at a time.

Month 23: Big Feelings & New Ideas

Focus: Emotional expression, cause-effect learning, planning, and pretend play

Week 1: Emotional Intelligence & Expression

Day 1: Name That Feeling

When your toddler is upset or excited, say: "You're feeling mad… or happy… or surprised!"

Day 2: Emotion Faces in Mirror

Make silly faces—sad, happy, surprised—in the mirror. Let your toddler copy.

Day 3: Feelings Talk Moment

Mindful Moment

During calm time, name your own emotion: "I feel tired. I need a hug."

Why it matters

Teaches emotional awareness and the power of naming feelings.

Try this

Add gestures: a yawn for tired, arms crossed for grumpy.

Day 4: Favourite Toy Comfort

Encourage them to hug a soft toy when feeling sad or frustrated.

Day 5: "What's That Face?" Game

Show photos or books with faces. Ask, "What do you think he feels?"

Day 6: Happy Dance Break

Play upbeat music. Dance big! Say, "We're so happy today!"

Day 7: Comfort Object Search

Let your toddler find their blanket, stuffed toy, or lovey when upset.

Parent Hack of the Week – The Feelings Basket

Create a basket with toys or photos showing different faces (sad, silly, sleepy). Use it when your toddler's emotions spike. "Let's find the one that feels like you right now." It turns tantrums into connection.

Week 2: Planning, Cause & Effect

Day 1: Toy Toss Target

Set up a soft bin. Say, "Throw it in!" Let them aim and toss toys.

Day 2: Push & Roll Cars

Show how pushing softly rolls a car. Try again with a big push!

Day 3: "Try Again" Task

Mindful Moment

Give a slightly tricky toy (pop-up, button press). Watch them try, fail, and try again.

Why it matters

Supports persistence, frustration tolerance, and cause-effect understanding.

Try this

Offer verbal encouragement but no help unless needed: "Hmm, how can we do this?"

Day 4: Stack & Fall Game

Stack blocks and say, "Let's see how tall it gets!" Then… crash.

Day 5: Spoon Tap Sounds

Let them bang a spoon on different surfaces: "Loud? Quiet?"

Day 6: Hide & Find Two Toys

Hide two toys under cups. Say, "Let's find them!" Watch memory bloom.

Day 7: Pour & Catch Water Game

Give a cup and bowl for gentle water pouring in the tub or sink.

Parent Hack of the Week – The "Uh-oh, Try Again" Song

Make a tune: "Try again, try again, let's see what you can do…" Sing it when toys fall, towers tumble, or socks go on the wrong foot. It turns frustration into fun.

Week 3: Pretend Play & Social Scenarios

Day 1: Toy Bedtime

Lay a soft toy down. Say "Night night," cover with a cloth.

Day 2: Phone Chat Pretend

Hand them a toy phone and ask, "Who's calling?"

Day 3: Copy a Scene Moment

Mindful Moment

Model a mini-scene: stir a pot, feed a teddy, tuck them in. Let your toddler take over.

Why it matters

Boosts memory, empathy, and sequencing—key to early pretend play.

Try this

Use real routines they've seen you do, and keep it simple.

Day 4: Stuffed Animal Ride

Put a soft toy on a toy car or in a basket. Say, "Where's she going?"

Day 5: Puppet Talk Time

Use a sock puppet to say, "Hello!" and ask simple questions.

Day 6: Dress-Up Bit

Let them try wearing your hat, scarf, or sunglasses for fun.

Day 7: "Let's Go to the Store"

Pretend you're shopping. Hand them a bag and "buy" toys.

Parent Hack of the Week – The Pretend Pause

During bath or snack, pause and say, "Let's pretend we're at a restaurant!" Let them "order," serve, or stir. The real world becomes a playground—with you in it.

Week 4: Motor Skills, Routines & Self-Trust

Day 1: Brush Hair by Self

Hand them the baby brush and say, "You try!"

Day 2: Snack Bag Zip

Let them open a zipper bag (partly started by you).

Day 3: Dressing Choice Moment

Mindful Moment

Offer two shirts. Ask, "This one or that one?" Let them choose and help dress.

Why it matters

Builds decision-making, body awareness, and routine participation.

Try this

Stay calm if they switch. It's part of the process!

Day 4: Ball Toss Practice

Stand close and take turns tossing a small ball.

Day 5: Step Up & Down

With your hand, guide them up one step and back down.

Day 6: Clean-Up Help

Say, "Let's put all the blocks in here!" Offer praise as they help.

Day 7: Water Scoop

In the bath or sink, let them scoop water from one cup to another.

Parent Hack of the Week – The Sock Race

During dressing, say, "Let's race to get your socks on!" Count together. Make dressing a silly challenge instead of a power struggle.

Reflect & Recharge: End of Month 23
Parent Story – The Pretend Hug

I was talking on the phone when Praveer grabbed a teddy, held it to his ear, then hugged it hard. I asked, "Who are you talking to?" and he said, "Papa!" It was his first pretend play moment—and it felt like watching his heart grow.

— Neetika, mom of a 23-month-old

What if my toddler still throws tantrums or doesn't pretend play?

- Tantrums are age-appropriate. Offer comfort and name their emotion: "You're mad."

- Pretend play can start tiny—just one toy hug or spoon stir is enough.

- Stay playful and patient. They're watching and learning—even when silent.

Mindful Reminder

The world is full of big feelings—and your toddler is just learning how to hold them. Stay close, stay curious, and offer a playful way through. One moment at a time.

Month 24: Two and Thriving!

Focus: Celebrating mastery, self-expression, early choices, memory, and cooperative play

Week 1: Self-Confidence & New Skills

Day 1: Solo Snack Setup

Offer a bowl and spoon and let your toddler serve themselves something soft like yogurt.

Day 2: Step-by-Step Helper

Give a 2-step direction: "Pick up the book and bring it to the couch."

Day 3: Let Me Do It Moment

Mindful Moment

Invite your toddler to do a full mini-task—like putting toys in a bin—without helping.

Why it matters

Builds self-trust, memory, and a sense of competence.

Try this

Cheer their effort, not perfection: "You did that ALL by yourself!"

Day 4: Open/Close Practice

Offer twist-lid containers or a box with a flap to explore independently.

Day 5: Clothes Sort Game

Give them a few clean clothes and say, "Can you find the socks?"

Day 6: Tall Stack Challenge

Stack as many blocks as you can together—then knock it down in celebration.

Day 7: Jump and Count

Encourage 2-foot jumps and count them together.

Parent Hack of the Week – The "Me First!" Button

Let them push the elevator, turn the light switch, or zip their coat. When things feel out of control, little power moments help toddlers feel capable—and calm.

Week 2: Words, Memory & Understanding

Day 1: Match & Say

Point to photos or animals in a book. Ask, "What's this?" Let them answer.

Day 2: Daily Routine Recall

Ask, "What did we do after snack today?" Let them try to remember.

Day 3: Sound Labelling Moment

Mindful Moment

When your toddler hears a sound (car, bird, beep), pause and say, "What was that?"

Why it matters

Strengthens auditory memory, labelling, and curiosity.

Try this

Add excitement: "That was a big truck! Vroooom!"

Day 4: Echo Words Game

Say a word with silly emphasis—"ba-NA-na!" Let them echo it.

Day 5: Name the Action

Say: "You're jumping!" or "You're climbing!" Describe what they're doing.

Day 6: Toy Grouping Fun

Sort toys by color or type: "Let's find all the blue things!"

Day 7: Where Did It Go?

Hide a toy under a cloth and ask them to find it—boosts early memory.

Parent Hack of the Week – The "Remember Together" Trick

At bedtime, recall the Day together: "You played outside… then bubbles… then snack." Your toddler might fill in the blanks. It turns routines into stories—and stories into memory.

Week 3: Pretend Play & Role Exploration

Day 1: Doctor Check-Up

Let your toddler check a stuffed toy's heartbeat, ears, or toes.

Day 2: Toy Bath Time

Give dolls or animals a pretend wash in a small bin.

Day 3: Role Swap Moment

Mindful Moment

Let your toddler "be the parent." Offer a toy phone and say, "You call Nana!"

Why it matters

Supports empathy, imagination, and social roles.

Try this

Follow their lead—even if it gets silly.

Day 4: Cooking Show Pretend

Stir, mix, and serve invisible food. Narrate your steps with flair.

Day 5: Shopping Time

Set up a mini grocery area and let them "buy" and "pay."

Day 6: Toy Conversations

Make two animals "talk" to each other. Watch your toddler join in.

Day 7: Dress-Up Box Fun

Fill a box with hats, scarves, or costume bits and explore together.

Parent Hack of the Week – The "Big Kid Helper" Frame

Say, "You're the store helper today," or "Chef Liam is cooking!" Framing routines as pretend roles makes daily tasks more fun—and builds identity.

Week 4: Social Play, Celebration & Connection

Day 1: High-Five Game

Offer a high-five after tasks. Say, "Teamwork!"

Day 2: Snack Share

Give two pieces of snack and encourage offering one to you or a toy.

Day 3: Celebration Dance Moment

Mindful Moment

After your toddler completes a task or challenge, play music and do a silly dance together.

Why it matters

Reinforces effort, builds connection, and releases joy.

Try this

Use the same song each time—create a "We Did It" ritual.

Day 4: Circle Time Play

Sit in a small circle with family or toys. Pass an object and say each name.

Day 5: Group Book Time

Let your toddler pick the book. Invite everyone to sit together to read.

Day 6: Family Photo Fun

Look at printed family pictures and name everyone aloud.

Day 7: "Say Hi" Walk

Wave and greet people during a neighbourhood walk. Practice social cues.

Parent Hack of the Week – The "Good Job Bell"

Use a small bell, shaker, or clap to celebrate little wins: "You cleaned up? DING DING!" Ritual praise builds confidence and routine recognition.

Reflect & Recharge: End of Month 24
Parent Story – The "I Did It" Moment

Last week, Dhrishay zipped his jacket—slowly, stubbornly—without help. When he finished, he looked up and shouted, "I DID IT!" That proud little face... I'll never forget it. He's growing right in front of me.

— *Lochan, mom of a 2-year-old*

What if my toddler isn't doing all of this yet?

- Pretend play, words, and independence blossom on different timelines.

- Mastery often follows hundreds of quiet, hidden repetitions.

- Keep modelling, inviting, and celebrating small wins. They're learning every moment.

> **Mindful Reminder**
>
> Two is not just a number—it's a turning point. Your toddler is not just doing more, they're becoming more. Keep offering trust, connection, and joy. The best part? You're doing it together.

Year 2: Celebrating Another Year of Growth!

What an incredible journey this has been! Your little one has grown leaps and bounds over the past year, and so have you as a parent. From first steps to first words, each milestone has been a reflection of your love, patience, and dedication. **You are doing an amazing job!**

This year may have brought new challenges—toddler independence, big emotions, and endless curiosity—but through it all, you have guided your child with care and encouragement. **Every effort you make, no matter how small, is shaping their future in the most meaningful way.**

Now is a great time to **track and rate your child's progress** using the **Milestone Tracker** to see how they've developed across key areas.

As you step into Year 3, remember that each phase comes with new discoveries, new challenges, and new joys. **Trust yourself, embrace the journey, and continue to enjoy these precious moments.**

You've got this! Congratulations on completing Year 2—your love and dedication are laying the foundation for a bright and brilliant future for your child.

Understanding Your Child's Developmental Tracker

Every child develops at their own pace. These trackers are designed to provide a structured way to observe and support your child's growth, but they should not be seen as rigid timelines. It's completely normal for some children to excel in certain areas while taking more time in others.

How to Use the Tracker

Rate on a scale of 0-5 based on your child's current abilities in each category.

No need to rush or compare! Some children might be more advanced in speech but take longer with motor skills, and that's completely fine.

Use it as a guide, not a test. If your child isn't yet meeting certain milestones, observe their progress over time instead of worrying.

Celebrate small wins! Any progress, no matter how small, is valuable.

What If My Child is Behind in Some Areas?

Variability is normal – Development is not linear, and children often leap ahead in some skills while taking more time in others.

Support their growth through interactive play, reading, conversations, and hands-on activities that align with their interests.

Patience is key – Keep engaging them in activities without pressure or comparisons.

Seek guidance if necessary – If you have concerns, consulting a paediatrician or child development expert can provide reassurance and strategies for support.

Encouraging a Positive Learning Experience

This tracker is meant to **empower you as a parent** and help you understand your child's unique journey. Focus on their strengths, provide encouragement, and create a nurturing environment where learning feels fun and natural. Every child has their own timeline – trust the process, and enjoy watching them grow!

Remember: Progress over perfection! ❁

Domain	Emerging Milestones	Rating (0-5)
Communication & Language	Uses 10–50+ words by age 2; begins combining 2–3 word phrases	
	Points to familiar people, body parts, or pictures when named	
	Understands and follows simple instructions ("Give me the ball")	
	Enjoys songs, rhymes, and sound play	
	Begins labelling feelings or needs with simple words ("more," "all done," "happy")	
Social & Emotional Development	Engages in parallel play and begins showing interest in other children	
	Shows preferences for people, toys, or routines	
	Imitates adult actions and daily routines (sweeping, stirring)	
	Expresses basic emotions and begins learning to self-soothe with support	
	Uses gestures, facial expressions, or words to communicate needs	

Cognitive & Thinking Skills	Explores cause and effect through toys (push, drop, bang)	
	Finds hidden objects easily (object permanence fully developed)	
	Matches or sorts by one attribute (color, size, shape)	
	Starts solving simple problems through trial and error (e.g., shape sorter)	
	Begins recognizing familiar objects, animals, and people by name	
Fine & Gross Motor Skills	Walks independently, climbs furniture, pulls toys while walking	
	Begins running, kicking, and trying stairs with help	
	Scribbles with fist grip, turns pages of a board book	
	Stacks 2–6 blocks, drops objects into containers, begins using spoon or cup	
	Starts attempting self-dressing (taking off shoes, placing hat)	
Play, Creativity & Independence	Engages in pretend play (feeding doll, talking on toy phone)	
	Enjoys repeating actions and routines with variation	
	Explores textures, sounds, and movement through play	
	Follows familiar routines with cues (bath, bed, snack)	
	Begins making choices and asserting independence ("me do it")	

At the end of the year, let's pause to celebrate the energy, emotions, and discoveries that defined it.

Each wobble and word was part of your shared dance of growth.

Progress lives in play, patience, and presence.

This chapter ends, but your shared rhythm keeps evolving beautifully.

And as one chapter closes, another begins

As you step into Year 3, know this: your toddler is not just growing—they're becoming. And so are you. The next chapter brings even more wonder, more questions, and deeper connection. Let's keep growing together.

CHAPTER 4

Year 3: The Communicator Year

Advanced Speech, Social Play & Self-Awareness

Quote

"Listen earnestly to anything your children want to tell you... If you don't listen to the little stuff, they won't tell you the big stuff."

— Catherine M. Wallace

Mantra

I listen with patience. I speak with love. We grow through every word.

M.I.N.D. for Year 3

Moments That Matter

Pause and truly listen — your child is finding their voice.

Intentional Interaction

Talk, pretend, and read together — these build emotional and cognitive skills.

Nurture Through Love

Set gentle boundaries with empathy and presence.

Daily Growth

Every new question, emotion, or conflict is a brain-building opportunity.

Year 3: Growing Together

The leap from toddlerhood to early childhood is big—but beautiful. Year 3 is where imagination deepens, independence strengthens, and conversations begin to bloom. Your child is full of questions, ideas, and emotions—and your presence continues to be their safe anchor in a growing world.

You've already built strong routines, trust, and joyful moments. This year, those foundations will grow into even more independence, confidence, and connection.

What's New in Year 3

- Activities now shift gently to support decision-making, storytelling, emotional coaching, and peer interaction.

- Pretend play, real-world routines, and role modelling become key tools for brain-building.

- You'll notice deeper insights into emotional regulation, social behaviour, and creative independence.

- **The structure also evolves**: Instead of daily activities 7 Days a week, we now follow a **5-day rhythm**. Why? Because your toddler—and you—need room to explore, repeat, and rest.

Why the 5-Day Format Works Best Now:

- Toddlers are becoming more independent and need space to play freely.

- Parents benefit from flexibility and less pressure for daily structure.

- The focus shifts to quality, not quantity—making every activity count.

Think of it as *intentional rhythm* instead of *daily homework*. Use the extra 2 days each week for replaying favourites, spontaneous outings, or simply rest.

NEW: Monthly Bonus Spark

At the end of each month, enjoy a special **Bonus Spark**—a themed day of joyful connection. It might be a mini celebration, an imaginative adventure, or a playful ritual like "Gratitude Picnic" or "Little Chef Day."

Why it matters: These creative sparks build memory, variety, and magic into your routine—without extra pressure. It's a simple way to end each month with wonder and connection.

How to Use This Guide in Year 3

- Weekly rhythm includes:
- 5 short, brain-boosting activities, 1–2 expanded Mindful Moments, a fresh **Parent, Hack of the Week**, a warm **Reflect & Recharge** story
- New: **Monthly Bonus Spark**—a themed day of joyful connection and celebration
- Focus stays on playful learning, now with more independence and flexibility for both of you

Milestones to Watch in Year 3

Every toddler develops at their own pace, but here's what many begin showing between 24 and 36 months:

Emerging Skills (Early Year 3)

- Speaks 2–3 word phrases and names familiar people or objects
- Follows simple instructions and shows growing independence
- Engages in pretend play (feeding toys, role play)
- Walks, runs, and climbs with confidence

- Identifies basic body parts and everyday objects

- Begins to express emotions using words or gestures

- Participates in simple routines like clean-up or getting dressed

Expanding Skills (Late Year 3)

- Uses short sentences and asks simple questions

- Begins to play *with* peers (not just beside them)

- Shows early problem-solving with puzzles, tools, or choices

- Understands concepts like "big/little" or "more/less"

- Begins to take turns and follow 2-step instructions

- Labels and discusses feelings more clearly

- Shows signs of toilet readiness or interest

These are flexible ranges, not a checklist. Your child's development is a story—not a race.

Month 25: Big Feelings, Big Play

Theme: Emotional expression, peer connection, and real-world routines

Week 1: Feelings in Action

1. Emotion Faces Game

Make faces in the mirror and name them: "Happy! Sad! Silly!"

2. Story time Feelings Talk

Read a short book and point out how characters feel.

3. Comfort Toy Talk

Mindful Moment

Let your child comfort a stuffed toy. Ask, "Is Bunny sad?" and guide them to hug or soothe it.

Why it matters

Builds empathy and teaches how to respond to emotions.

Try this

Use it as a routine when your child feels overwhelmed.

4. Dance It Out

Play music and act out feelings with movement: "Excited jump! Tired stretch!"

5. Feelings Matching Game

Show happy/sad faces on cards or pictures and ask your child to match them.

Parent Hack of the Week – The Emotion Echo

When your toddler shows a big emotion, echo it in words: "You're upset—it's okay." Labelling calms chaos and builds emotional literacy.

Week 2: Independence in Motion

1. Shoe Sort Game

Ask your child to match pairs of shoes and line them up.

2. Carry and Place

Give them a task: "Take this spoon to the table."

3. Snack Time Setup

Mindful Moment

Invite your child to help set up snack time—placing cup, plate, or napkin.

Why it matters

Encourages responsibility and builds sequencing skills.

Try this

Use the same phrases each time: "Cup… then snack… then sit!"

4. Step and Jump Challenge

Set up cushions or steps for safe jumping fun.

5. Clean-Up Toss

Turn tidying up into a game: toss toys into the bin one by one.

Parent Hack of the Week – The "You're the Helper" Trick

Say, "I need your help!" even for simple tasks. Toddlers light up when they feel trusted—plus, it turns resistance into pride.

Week 3: Pretend, Play & Problem-Solve

1. Feed the Toy

Hand your toddler a spoon and toy and say, "Time to eat!"

2. Puzzle Time Together

Offer a 3–5 piece puzzle and solve it side-by-side.

3. Fix-It Fun

Mindful Moment

Hand your child a pretend tool (spoon, cardboard tube) and say, "Can you fix it?"

Why it matters

Encourages imagination, planning, and symbolic play.

Try this

Use real-life objects—"fix" the chair, the shoe, or a teddy's nose.

4. Sock Match Game

Hand them socks and ask, "Can you find the same?"

5. Pretend Phone Call

Give them a toy phone. "Call Grandma!" and chat.

Parent Hack of the Week – The Mini Repair Kit

Fill a small pouch with "tools" like a soft brush, spoon, toy screw. Your toddler will "fix" everything in sight. It builds confidence and invites endless open-ended play.

Week 4: Social Games & Peer Play

1. "Your Turn, My Turn" Toss

Use a soft ball to trade turns gently.

2. Name the Friend

Point to family or peers and name them joyfully.

3. Share & Switch

Mindful Moment

During play, hand your toddler a toy and say, "Want to trade?" Model how to share.

Why it matters

Builds early social awareness and turn-taking without pressure.

Try this

Keep trades light and playful—no forcing.

4. Photo Peek Book

Make a small album of familiar faces. Look through together.

5. Dance with a Buddy (You!)

Hold hands and spin to music. Simple joy.

Parent Hack of the Week – The Toy Picnic Trick

Lay out a blanket, place stuffed toys in a circle, and "serve" food. Toddlers love playing hostess—and sneak in tons of empathy and pretend planning along the way.

Monthly Bonus Spark – "Little Chef Day"

Let your toddler help prepare a simple snack: stir yogurt, tear lettuce, or spread butter with a toddler-safe tool.

Why it's magical: They feel grown-up, focused, and proud of contributing.

Optional twist: Wear aprons and "take orders" for snack orders.

Let the mess happen—this one's about memory-making.

Reflect & Recharge: End of Month 25
Parent Story – The First "I Helped"

I was rushing around making lunch, and Leila quietly pulled out napkins, unfolded them, and placed one at each seat. She looked up and said, "I help!" I paused. She wasn't just copying me—she *felt* like part of it. And I saw her pride glowing.

— *Maya, mom of a 25-month-old*

What if my toddler resists routines or refuses help?

- That's normal—it's part of autonomy. Keep offering gentle opportunities.

- Use play language: "Want to be the sock boss today?"

- If they say no, back off with warmth. The goal is invitation, not control.

Mindful Reminder

Independence isn't about doing things alone—it's about feeling capable *with you nearby*. Keep inviting. Keep trusting. They're becoming, one brave little step at a time.

Month 26: Confident & Capable

Theme: Independence, confidence, and flexible thinking

Week 1: Independent Moves

1. Step Climb Challenge

Let your toddler climb up and down a low step with your support nearby.

2. Spoon Scoop Snack

Offer a thick yogurt or mashed food for solo spoon feeding.

3. Snack Set Helper

Mindful Moment

Invite your toddler to place a cup and plate on the table before meals.

Why it matters

Sequencing tasks and setting the table builds autonomy and early planning skills.

Try this

Keep it consistent—make it "their job" before every snack.

4. Dress Me Race

Say, "Let's put on socks together!" and turn dressing into a friendly game.

5. Jump, Land, Clap

Try jump-and-land games with a clap to boost coordination.

Parent Hack of the Week – The Solo Snack Win

Let your toddler serve one dry snack (like puffs or crackers) from container to bowl. When they succeed, say: "You did that all by yourself." That sentence is a memory-maker—and motivation fuel.

Week 2: Language in Daily Life

1. Word Walk

Narrate a short walk: "Tree… bird… red car!"

2. What's Missing?

Hide one familiar item from a group and ask what's gone.

3. Echo Game

Mindful Moment

Say short, fun phrases with rising tone: "More snack?" or "All done?" Pause for them to echo.

Why it matters

Builds memory, rhythm, and two-way conversation cues.

Try this

Make it silly. Toddlers love repeating rhymes or dramatic tones.

4. Label in the Mirror

Point and say: "Eyes! Nose! Smile!"

5. Photo Storytime

Look through a photo book and name people, places, or feelings.

Parent Hack of the Week – The Elevator Talk Trick

Use elevator or car rides to talk about where you're going. "We're going up to get apples!" Repetition in routine spaces makes learning effortless.

Week 3: Pretend & Problem-Solving Play

1. Fix-It Toy Fun

Hand your child a safe tool and say, "Let's fix the chair!"

2. Sock Match Sort

Offer a few socks and ask: "Can you find a match?"

3. Toy Rescue Game

Mindful Moment

Tape a soft toy lightly to the table with painter's tape. Invite your child to "rescue" it.

Why it matters

Sparks problem-solving, persistence, and play planning.

Try this

Use playful urgency: "Can you help Puppy? He's stuck!"

4. Mini Market Roleplay

Pretend to buy/sell with play food or boxes.

5. Stack & Build Time

Use blocks or containers for tower fun.

Parent Hack of the Week – The Everyday Pretend Box

Keep a shoebox with pretend items—an old phone, empty bottle, paper "money." Toddlers replay real life here, turning observation into imagination. Confidence builds where fantasy and function meet.

Week 4: Social Routines & Cooperation

1. "Hi" Practice Game

Wave and say hello to toys, people, or pets.

2. Turn-Taking Toss

Roll or toss a soft ball back and forth with "Your turn!"

3. Goodbye Ritual

Mindful Moment

When leaving day-care or saying bye to a grandparent, create a ritual: "Wave, hug, blow kiss."

Why it matters

Helps toddlers prepare for transition and learn emotional closure.

Try this

Repeat it often. Rituals = predictability = calm.

4. Name Game Album

Flip through a photo album and say names together.

5. Movement Parade

March, clap, or dance around the room with music.

Parent Hack of the Week – The Snack time Song

Sing a simple song during snacks: "Crunch, crunch, apple munch!" Toddlers associate rhythm with calm moments—and it becomes your secret mealtime soother.

Monthly Bonus Spark – "Little Explorer Day"

Let your toddler "lead" a home scavenger hunt. Say, "Can you find something red? A spoon? A soft toy?"

Why it's magical: Builds vocabulary, confidence, and observation. Plus, it's pure joy when *they* are in charge.

Optional twist: Add a small backpack or magnifying glass for pretend explorer vibes.

Reflect & Recharge: End of Month 26
Parent Story – The Mirror Moment

After putting on her socks by herself, Ava stood in front of the mirror and said, "I look ready!" She grinned, did a spin, and ran off. I didn't help her dress—but I got to witness her pride. That's the win.

— Daniela, mom of a 26 month old

What if my toddler gets frustrated while trying to do things alone?

- Stay close but quiet—your presence helps more than correction.

- Avoid jumping in too fast. Let them ask or gesture for help.

- Use supportive language: "It's tricky, but you're trying—that's brave."

> ### Mindful Reminder
>
> Your toddler is discovering what it means to try, to struggle, and to succeed. That's real growth. Let them wobble, reach, and shine—your belief in them is the best guide they'll ever have.

Month 27: Confident Playmakers

Theme: Confidence, curiosity, and social language

Week 1: Movement with Purpose

1. Target Toss

Let your toddler aim and throw soft toys into a bin or basket.

2. Stair Step Try

Encourage safe step-up and down movement with support nearby.

3. Follow the Beat

Mindful Moment

Play a clapping rhythm and invite your toddler to copy the pattern.

Why it matters

Enhances auditory memory, body coordination, and attention.

Try this

Start simple, then let your toddler create the rhythm for you to follow.

4. Object-on-Back Walk

Balance a soft toy on their back while crawling or walking.

5. Speed Game

Call out "fast!" and run together, then "slow" and tiptoe.

Parent Hack of the Week – The Rhythm Walk

Add hand-claps, stomps, or songs while walking indoors or out. A regular walk turns into a coordination-building groove session.

Week 2: Language & Everyday Connections

1. Shopping Bag Sort

Pull items out of a grocery bag and name each one slowly.

2. "What's This?" Walk

Let your toddler point to things during a walk while you name them.

3. Snack Narration

Mindful Moment

Describe snack time in slow, rhythmic sentences: "First the cup... then the apple... now the bite."

Why it matters

Builds sequencing and receptive language.

Try this

Pause for toddler to fill in or echo key words.

4. Sound Echo Fun

Make fun sounds: "Beep!" "Pop!" "Whoosh!" and wait for repeats.

5. Word Match Photo Album

Look at family photos. Say the name, ask, "Where is Grandma?"

Parent Hack of the Week – The Breakfast Recap

During breakfast, talk about one memory from yesterday: "Remember when we saw the cat?" You'll be amazed what your toddler remembers— and what they add.

Week 3: Pretend Play & Creative Problem-Solving

1. Toy Tools Fixing Time

Let your toddler use pretend tools to "repair" items around the house.

2. Scoop & Sort Play

Offer two bowls and items to sort (blocks, spoons, pom-poms).

3. Toy Hotel

Mindful Moment

Set up a few stuffed toys on pillows and say, "They're sleeping at the hotel!" Invite your toddler to tuck them in, give them snacks, or brush their hair.

Why it matters

Supports empathy, narrative play, and self-care routines.

Try this

Change it up next time: let the toys go camping or fly on a plane.

4. Blanket Tent Build

Build a small fort or tent and play inside with books or toys.

5. Bubble Catch Game

Blow bubbles and let them chase and catch.

Parent Hack of the Week – The Busy Box Switch-Up

Fill a box with 5 random safe household items. Let your toddler explore. Next week? Swap 2 items out. Novelty + familiarity = hours of focused play.

Week 4: Social Growth & Everyday Roles

1. Hat Parade

Try on silly hats and name each one: "Sun hat!" "Daddy's hat!"

2. "Can You Help Me?" Task

Ask your toddler to carry a spoon, close a drawer, or wipe the table.

3. Sharing Snack Time

Mindful Moment

Offer a snack and ask, "One for me, one for you?" Practice taking turns while eating.

Why it matters

Encourages early generosity, fairness, and joint attention.

Try this

Use language like "You shared with Mama. That was kind."

4. Name the Friend

Point to family or toy friends: "That's Ellie! That's Sam!"

5. Tidy Up Dance

Put on music and clean together with flair.

Parent Hack of the Week – The Family Helper Frame

Say, "You're part of the team!" before giving a task. Toddlers beam when they belong.

Monthly Bonus Spark – "Little Librarian Day"

Set up a cosy book corner with 4–6 books. Let your toddler choose, stack, and "lend" them. Add a bag for book pickup or a stamp pad.

Why it's magical: Encourages care for books, builds choice-making, and invites early literacy pride.

Reflect & Recharge: End of Month 27
Parent Story – The Sharing Spark

We were eating crackers when Jonah broke his in two, handed me one, and said, "Here, Mama." It wasn't prompted. Just pure, tiny generosity. My heart melted.

— Emma, mom of a 27 month old

What if my toddler still resists sharing or helping?

- That's developmentally normal. Sharing is learned in stages.

- Keep modelling it in play: "I'll give you one, now you give one back."

- Don't force it—just repeat gently and celebrate small tries.

> ### Mindful Reminder
>
> Your toddler is watching everything. The way you model patience, kindness, and joy becomes their blueprint. Keep showing up, even when it feels unseen. They're soaking it all in.

Month 28: Big Feelings, Bigger Moves

Theme: Emotional awareness, motor mastery, and playful responsibility

Week 1: Emotion in Motion

1. Feel & Freeze

Act out feelings with movement: stomp when "mad," sway when "tired." Freeze after each.

2. Emotion Faces Hunt

Look through a magazine or book and find faces: "Happy! Sad! Surprised!"

3. Comfort in Routine

Mindful Moment

Create a mini goodbye routine for transitions: hug, high five, wave.

Why it matters

Predictable rituals soothe separation stress and help toddlers label emotions.

Try this

Let your toddler choose the ritual order each day.

4. Snack time Mood Talk

Ask: "Is this a happy snack? A silly snack?" Add voice tone and gesture.

5. Dramatic Toy Play

Act out a toy getting "lost," "hurt," or "happy," and let your toddler respond.

Parent Hack of the Week – The Emotion Shelf

Designate a shelf or box for comfort items: a soft toy, book, photo, or calming object. Label it: "When I feel big feelings." This gives toddlers a go-to place for self-regulation.

Week 2: Physical Confidence & Coordination

1. Ramp & Roll

Create a simple ramp using cardboard and race toy cars or balls.

2. Box Jump Challenge

Use a low, soft box to jump off safely, one foot or both.

3. Obstacle Explorer

Mindful Moment

Set up a mini obstacle course with cushions, boxes, or tape lines to walk across.

Why it matters

Builds spatial planning, gross motor control, and goal setting.

Try this

Let your toddler lead and redesign the course after a few rounds.

4. Animal Walk Parade

Crawl like a bear, hop like a frog, flap like a bird.

5. Push-Pull Path

Use a box or laundry basket to push and pull across different surfaces.

Parent Hack of the Week – The Cushion Maze

Lay out couch cushions in a zigzag or circle. Invite your toddler to climb, jump, or crawl over them. Change the shape daily for novelty + motor mastery.

Week 3: Pretend with Purpose

1. Pretend Cooking Time

Use real spoons or pots. Narrate: "Mix! Stir! Serve!"

2. Toy School Roleplay

Line up dolls or animals and pretend it's circle time.

3. Stuffed Animal Care Day

Mindful Moment

Let your toddler choose one toy to care for all day: feed, nap, clean, carry.

Why it matters

Strengthens empathy, role play, and emotional language.

Try this

Ask, "How is Bear feeling now? What does Bear need?"

4. Mirror Movement Game

Take turns copying each other's funny moves in front of a mirror.

5. Box Town Build

Use boxes to create a pretend house, shop, or zoo.

Parent Hack of the Week – The Real Job Pretend Frame

Say, "You're the chef today" or "You're my delivery helper!" Then act it out. Toddlers light up when pretend play connects to real tasks.

Week 4: Social Play & Everyday Skills

1. Photo Name Time

Flip through pictures and name people or events.

2. Help Me Fold

Give them a washcloth or soft item to fold with you.

3. Snack Helper Role

Mindful Moment

Ask your toddler to "set the table" for snack with cup, napkin, spoon.

Why it matters

Builds independence, order, and early planning.

Try this

Keep it consistent, let them lead the routine.

4. Storytime Pause & Predict

Stop during reading and ask: "What do you think happens next?"

5. Toy Pickup Parade

Make clean-up a musical, silly walk.

Parent Hack of the Week – The Tidy Tune

Invent a 10-second tidy-up song: "Clean-up time, clean-up time! We're putting toys away!" Sing it at the same time each day. The cue becomes the habit.

Monthly Bonus Spark – "Feelings Photo Booth"

Create a fun photo corner. Ask your toddler to pose: "Happy! Silly! Sad! Surprised!" Capture it if you want, or just enjoy the show.

Why it's magical: Strengthens emotional vocabulary, confidence, and self-awareness.

Reflect & Recharge: End of Month 28
Parent Story – The Tiny Teacher

While I was folding clothes, Happy sat beside his teddy and said, "Sit still! We're learning!" He clapped, nodded, then said, "Good job, Teddy." It was pretend, but it felt so real—like I was watching him grow into someone who notices, teaches, and cares.

— *Jasmine, mom of a 28 month old*

What if my toddler still doesn't express feelings clearly?

- That's okay—emotion language takes time.

- Keep modelling: "I'm feeling tired," "You look excited!"

- Use books and pretend play to introduce feeling words gently.

> **Mindful Reminder**
>
> Big feelings are part of growing up. The goal isn't to avoid them—it's to guide your toddler through them. Keep naming, noticing, and showing up. That's where emotional strength begins.

Month 29: Playful Growth & Real-World Routines

Theme: Self-confidence, memory, and practical independence

Week 1: Real-World Helpers

1. Water Plant Helper

Let your toddler use a small cup to water plants indoors or on the balcony.

2. Laundry Sort Game

Match socks or group clothes by color: "Find all the white ones!"

3. Snack Prep Time

Mindful Moment

Let your toddler help make snack: place crackers, peel bananas, or stir yogurt.

Why it matters

Teaches sequencing, builds confidence, and boosts motor coordination.

Try this

Narrate each step like a recipe: "Now stir... now scoop..."

4. Dusting with Socks

Put old socks on hands and let them "dust" low surfaces.

5. Key Finder Game

Hand over a safe, old key and say, "Can you find the door it fits?"

Parent Hack of the Week – The Clean-up Countdown

Instead of nagging, say, "Let's clean up in 5... 4... 3..." It turns transition into a game, and toddlers love the rush of a mini mission.

Week 2: Storytelling & Memory

1. Sequence Cards

Show 2–3 images of a routine (eat, wash, sleep) and talk through the order.

2. Stuffed Animal Recall

Hide 3 toys, ask, "Which one did we hide first?"

3. My Day in Pictures

Mindful Moment

Print 3 photos from recent days. Name the memory: "This was the park. This was snack time."

Why it matters

Builds memory and self-awareness through personal storytelling.

Try this

Let your toddler point and label photos in their own words.

4. Mirror Name Game

Look in the mirror and say names: "That's you, Lily! That's me, Mama!"

5. Book Retell Fun

After reading, ask your toddler what they remember. Even one word counts!

Parent Hack of the Week – The "What Happened Today?" Bath Chat

During bath, ask: "What did we do this morning?" Use their words or offer clues. This casual memory building becomes a calming, joyful ritual.

Week 3: Movement Meets Thinking

1. Step Jump Challenge

Use a pillow and say, "Jump over the mountain!"

2. Object Balance Race

Balance a small item on a spoon or hand while walking.

3. Indoor Maze Walk

Mindful Moment

Make a simple path with cushions or tape. Say, "Can you walk the maze?"

Why it matters

Boosts spatial planning, balance, and problem-solving.

Try this

Let them create their own path next time.

4. Slow vs. Fast Chase

Run fast, then slow. Name the speed as you go!

5. Toy Rescue Crawl

Put toys under chairs or behind pillows: "Go rescue Teddy!"

Parent Hack of the Week – The Obstacle Helper

Turn clean-up into a race: "Jump over the pillow... crawl to the book... now pick it up!" It's cleaning, disguised as an adventure.

Week 4: Early Choices & Expression

1. Cup or Spoon?

Offer two options at snack: "Do you want the red cup or blue one?"

2. Sock Drawer Helper

Ask: "Which socks today? You pick!"

3. Feelings Flash Cards

Mindful Moment

Show happy, sad, silly faces. Ask, "How are you feeling?"

Why it matters

Builds emotional vocabulary and self-expression.

Try this

Mirror the face they choose together.

4. Yes or No Game

Ask silly questions: "Do elephants wear shoes?" Giggle through the answers.

5. Dance & Freeze with Faces

Dance together, then freeze with a happy/sad/silly face.

Parent Hack of the Week – The "You Choose Today" Trick

Start the morning with one easy choice: shirt, snack, song. One small yes builds autonomy all day long.

Monthly Bonus Spark – "Toy Wash Station"

Fill a shallow tub with soapy water and let your toddler wash toy animals or trucks with a sponge or brush.

Why it's magical: Builds fine motor skills, pretend play, and responsibility all in one.

Optional twist: Dry toys with a towel, then "park" or line them up.

Reflect & Recharge: End of Month 29
Parent Story – The Day She Led the Way

Last weekend, I asked Sara if she wanted cereal or toast. She said, "Toast, please!" Then pulled out the jam, fetched her plate, and said, "I do it." I stood back. She buttered (messily), smiled, and said, "Yay, I did it!" It was a proud-messy-sweet kind of moment.

— Isabelle, mom of a 29-month-old

What if my toddler doesn't want to help or chooses "no" for everything?

- That's part of developing independence—they're practicing control.

- Keep offering easy choices, and stay consistent in tone.

- Use playful phrases: "Let's be the spoon boss today!"

> ### Mindful Reminder
>
> This month is full of little yeses and noes. It can feel like a tug-of-war—but it's really a dance. The goal isn't control; it's connection. Stay close, offer freedom within safe limits, and let your toddler feel like a growing, capable part of your world.

Month 30: Brave Minds, Busy Hands

Theme: Early choices, confidence in tasks, playful problem-solving

Week 1: Everyday Independence

1. Cup & Pour Game

Give your toddler a small jug and cup to pour water (supervised).

2. Pick & Wear

Let them choose between two outfits or shoes.

3. Snack Time Steps

Mindful Moment

Guide your child in prepping a simple snack: spreading jam or peeling a banana.

Why it matters

Builds sequencing and fine motor pride.

Try this

Narrate each step out loud: "First peel... then bite!"

4. Tidy-Up Toss

Turn clean-up into a tossing game with soft toys and a bin.

5. Find & Fetch

Ask, "Can you bring the red spoon?" Let them search and return.

Parent Hack of the Week – The Tiny Boss Trick

Let your toddler "lead" one mini-routine per day: light switch, opening the door, choosing snack. Being in charge builds calm confidence in daily transitions.

Week 2: Language, Sounds & Simple Questions

1. Point & Label Walk

Go outside and name things: "Dog. Tree. Truck."

2. Yes/No Talk Time

Ask fun questions: "Do bananas fly?" Pause for response.

3. Sound Show

Mindful Moment

Say silly sounds: "Moo! Beep! Boom!" Let them copy or invent new ones.

Why it matters

Enhances phonemic awareness and turn-taking.

Try this

Add movement: stomp for "boom," wave for "woosh."

4. Name the Action

Describe what they're doing in short bursts: "You jumped! You stirred!"

5. Toy Talk Practice

Hold a toy and say, "What does bear say?" Let them speak or act it out.

Parent Hack of the Week – The Mirror Echo

Stand at the mirror and make silly sounds or sentences together. Toddlers love the double feedback—your voice and their reflection.

Week 3: Tools, Touch & Problem Solving

1. Lid Match Game

Set out containers and mismatched lids. Let them figure it out.

2. Push & Pop Toy Time

Use pop-up toys or press-and-release buttons for cause-effect fun.

3. Block Bridge Challenge

Mindful Moment

Stack blocks like a bridge. Ask, "Can this toy cross?" Encourage testing and fixes.

Why it matters

Boosts spatial reasoning and persistence.

Try this

Celebrate every attempt—not just the success.

4. Toy Rescue Tape

Lightly tape a toy to the table and let them "rescue" it.

5. Shape Puzzle Sort

Offer a 3- to 5-piece puzzle. Let them lead the solve.

Parent Hack of the Week – The Drawer Switch Game

Fill one drawer with new safe items (kitchen tools, soft brushes). Toddlers love a change of scenery, and it resets playtime curiosity in seconds.

Week 4: Pretend Play & Early Social Stories

1. Toy Bedtime Roleplay

Tuck in a stuffed animal: "Shh... time to sleep."

2. "Can I Help You?" Play

Pretend to cook or clean, then ask your toddler to help.

3. Dress the Teddy

Mindful Moment

Offer doll clothes or scarves and invite your child to dress a toy.

Why it matters

Builds care, planning, and fine motor focus.

Try this

Let them choose the "outfit" and name it.

4. Pretend Picnic

Lay out a cloth and share snack time with toys.

5. Emotion Voice Game

Say "Hi!" in different tones: excited, sleepy, sad. Let them copy.

Parent Hack of the Week – The Tiny Waiter Game

Hand them a notepad and say, "Can I order milk and crackers?" Let them pretend to serve. Builds listening and pretend sequencing.

Monthly Bonus Spark – "Build-A-Box Day"

Grab a cardboard box and turn it into a car, house, or bus. Use crayons, stickers, and imagination.

Why it's magical: Invites teamwork, creative design, and dramatic storytelling.

Reflect & Recharge: End of Month 30
Parent Story – The Big Step Alone

I watched Avi climb onto the couch solo and sit down with his snack—no help, no prompting. Just calm determination. He looked up and grinned. That moment wasn't about climbing. It was about ownership.

— Himani, mom of a 30-month-old

What if my toddler doesn't want to be "independent" yet?

- Some toddlers cling harder before new bursts of growth. That's okay.
- Keep offering small steps: "Want to try this part yourself?"
- Model independence with joy. They're watching you even when they don't join.

Mindful Reminder

Confidence comes quietly. It's not just loud victories—it's also the quiet moments when your toddler tries, stumbles, and gets back up with your gentle presence nearby. That's growth in motion.

Month 31: Playful Minds, Growing Confidence

Theme: Social play, flexible thinking, and imagination in action

Week 1: Building Flexibility & Focus

1. Stack and Switch

Offer different shapes (blocks, cups) and encourage your toddler to stack them in new ways.

2. Treasure Sort Game

Mix small objects (spoons, blocks, socks). Ask: "Can we sort by size? By color?"

3. Story Stretch

Mindful Moment

Read a short story, then change one part: "What if the bunny flew instead of ran?"

Why it matters

Fosters imagination and flexible thinking.

Try this

Pause and let them offer their own silly twist.

4. Freeze & Find

Pause music and ask them to find a specific toy fast: "Find the duck!"

5. Switch It Up Snack

Serve snack in a cup instead of a plate. Watch how they adapt.

Parent Hack of the Week – The What-If Walk

Take a short walk and ask silly questions: "What if dogs could drive? What if trees danced?" Watch your toddler think, giggle, and invent along with you.

Week 2: Pretend Play & Emotional Language

1. Feelings for Teddy

Say, "Bear is sad. What should we do?" Let your toddler comfort or help.

2. Story Dress-Up

After reading, grab a hat or scarf and act like a character from the story.

3. Mirror Faces Play

Mindful Moment

Look into the mirror together. Make faces: happy, mad, silly. Label each.

Why it matters

Boosts emotional awareness and empathy.

Try this

Ask, "Can you show me a proud face?"

4. Pretend Play Clean-Up

Use a spray bottle (water) and cloth to pretend clean with their toys.

5. Mood Music Game

Play different music (slow, fast, dramatic). Ask, "How does this sound feel?"

Parent Hack of the Week – The Emotion Toolbox

Create a "toolbox" with calming tools: a soft toy, a small book, or a sensory bottle. When big feelings come, ask, "Want to get your toolbox?"

Week 3: Independence & Motor Mastery

1. Put Away Pairs

Ask your toddler to match socks, shoes, or cups and put them away.

2. **Obstacle Crawl Path**

Set up cushions and boxes for crawling and climbing.

3. Spoon & Scoop Challenge

Mindful Moment

Use dry rice or cereal and two cups. Let them scoop and transfer slowly.

Why it matters

Builds wrist control, focus, and fine motor skills.

Try this

Count scoops aloud for extra rhythm and attention.

4. Push the Laundry

Let them push an empty laundry basket from one room to another.

5. Unlock & Open Time

Offer safe locks, lids, or drawers to explore.

Parent Hack of the Week – The Quiet Helper Game

Whisper a "mission": "Can you quietly carry this to the table?" Making it secret makes it irresistible—and boosts concentration.

Week 4: Language & Social Turn-Taking

1. Yes/No Puppet Game

Use a puppet to ask silly questions: "Do cats wear socks?"

2. Name That Action

Narrate what you and your child are doing in real-time.

3. Listening Walk

Mindful Moment

Go outside and listen together. Whisper: "What can you hear? A bird? A car?"

Why it matters

Encourages auditory focus and mindfulness.

Try this

Pause often. Let your toddler lead the listening.

4. Talk & Toss

Toss a soft ball back and forth, saying one word each turn.

5. Favourite Toy Interview

Ask, "What does Bunny like? What does Bunny eat?" Let your child answer as the toy.

Parent Hack of the Week – The Dinner Talk Trick

Place 2 toys or objects on the table and ask them to "talk." You might hear wild stories, but what you're really hearing? Language blooming.

Monthly Bonus Spark – "Backpack Explorer Day"

Give your toddler a small bag or backpack. Let them fill it with 3 items, then go on a pretend hike around the house or yard.

Why it's magical: It invites autonomy, imagination, and narrative play in one simple moment.

Reflect & Recharge: End of Month 31
Parent Story – The Confidence Climb

Martha had always waited for help on the stairs. But this week, she looked back, grinned, and said, "I do it." And she did. Step by step, steady and proud.

— Jack, dad of a 31-month-old

What if my toddler gets frustrated when trying something new?

- Pause before jumping in. Sometimes they need a few beats to problem-solve.

- Use phrases like, "You're working hard on that!"
- If needed, offer just the first step. Let them finish it.

> **Mindful Reminder**
>
> It's not just what your toddler is doing—it's what they believe they *can* do. Your encouragement becomes their inner voice. Keep it calm, warm, and steady. They're becoming brave thinkers, one tiny decision at a time.

Month 32: Confident Play, Creative Days

Theme: Imagination, early planning, group interaction, and problem-solving

Week 1: Pretend Play & Real-World Imitation

1. Little Chef Pretend

Offer pots, spoons, and bowls. Say, "What are you cooking today?"

2. Toy School Time

Line up toys and pretend it's circle time. Sing a rhyme or count aloud.

3. Baby Doll Care

Mindful Moment

Let your toddler feed, change, or rock a doll. Join them as co-parents.

Why it matters

Strengthens empathy and sequencing through real-life play.

Try this

Narrate in soft tones: "You're so gentle. Baby likes that."

4. Dress-Up Exploration

Provide scarves, hats, or shoes. Let them become someone new.

5. Pretend Clean-Up Time

Offer a spray bottle and cloth. Ask: "Can you help clean the table?"

Parent Hack of the Week – The Role-Play Reset

When routines stall (getting dressed, eating), shift into pretend mode: "Can the superhero brush teeth? Can the kitty wear socks?" It turns power struggles into playful moments.

Week 2: Language, Memory & Expression

1. Action Story Time

Read a book and ask your toddler to act out parts.

2. Two-Word Talk Game

Model pairs: "Blue ball," "Big spoon." Let them try their own.

3. Sound & Feelings Echo

Mindful Moment

Say emotional words with matching tone: "Happy!" (bright), "Tired..." (slow).

Why it matters

Connects feelings, sounds, and expression.

Try this

Ask, "Can you say it too?"

4. Animal Sounds Parade

Act like different animals with movement and sounds.

5. Daily Recap Game

Ask, "What did we do this morning?" Help them recall.

Parent Hack of the Week – The Memory Talk Trick

At bedtime, recap the day: "You built a tower, we saw a dog, you ate yogurt..." It builds memory, language, and connection before sleep.

Week 3: Planning, Focus & Problem Solving

1. Toy Rescue Hunt

Hide a toy under a cloth or box. Say, "Where did it go?"

2. Build & Balance Game

Use blocks to build towers, ramps, or fences.

3. Fix-It Station

Mindful Moment

Set out toy tools and broken toys/items. Ask, "Can you fix this?"

Why it matters

Encourages planning, fine motor control, and task pride.

Try this

Sit beside them and narrate their work.

4. Snack Sort Game

Offer 2-3 snack types. Ask: "Put all the crackers here. All the grapes here."

5. Draw & Guess Game

Scribble or draw shapes and ask, "What do you see?"

Parent Hack of the Week – The Slow Fix Challenge

Hand your toddler a spoon, sock, or container and say, "Hmm... this needs help." Wait. They love stepping in as problem-solvers—especially when you playfully pause first.

Week 4: Social Sharing & Group Play

1. Toy Swap Game

Hand a toy, wait, then offer: "Want to switch?"

2. Name the Friend

Show family or friend photos. Ask, "Who is this?"

3. Shared Blanket Play

Mindful Moment

Sit on a blanket together with toys. Say, "Let's play here!"

Why it matters

Introduces boundaries, space-sharing, and shared focus.

Try this

Model offering a toy: "Want a turn?"

4. Pass the Ball

Sit in a circle with family or toys. Take turns rolling the ball.

5. Help with a Job

Invite them to help give a toy to someone else: "Can you give this to Papa?"

Parent Hack of the Week – The Snack Share Trick

Use a small plate and place two pieces of snack. Say, "One for you, one for me." Keep swapping. You're teaching turn-taking with every nibble.

Monthly Bonus Spark – "Story Box Day"

Fill a box with 3 random items (a sock, a spoon, a toy). Say, "Let's tell a story!" Take turns inventing a tale using all three.

Why it's magical: Builds imagination, sequencing, and early narrative skills.

Reflect & Recharge: End of Month 32
Parent Story – The Pretend Picnic

Adwita packed crackers and her teddy into a tiny backpack. She laid out a towel and called me over: "Come picnic!" She poured pretend tea and offered air-cookies. I sat. We shared invisible bites and real laughter.

— Anita, mom of a 32-month-old

What if my toddler skips pretend play or isn't interested in dressing up?

- Some children prefer physical or puzzle play. That's okay.

- Model short, silly pretend play without pressure.

- Join their play first, then gently add a pretend layer.

Mindful Reminder

Pretend play isn't about acting—it's about trying ideas on for size. Even a spoon turned into a spaceship means your toddler is exploring what could be, not just what is. That's powerful growth.

Month 33: Brave Bonds & Big Ideas

Theme: Confidence, communication, and early perspective-taking

Week 1: Trying New Things

1. Yes Table Time

Set up a low table with new play items (tape, containers, measuring spoons). Say, "You can try all of these!"

2. Upside Down Book Fun

Hand them a book upside down. Let them figure it out. Say, "Hmm, does that look right?"

3. The First Try Smile

Mindful Moment

Give a new tool (crayon, spoon, sock) and step back. Watch, wait, then smile when they try.

Why it matters

Builds confidence and risk-taking in a safe environment.

Try this

Use the phrase, "Trying is winning!"

4. Sock Slide Game

Let them walk or scoot in socks on a smooth surface.

5. Snack Scoop Challenge

Give dry cereal and a spoon. Let them serve themselves.

Parent Hack of the Week – The Brave Bin

Create a bin labelled "Try It!" and rotate 1-2 items weekly: a tricky puzzle, new spoon, big hat, etc. Make trying things the goal, not finishing them.

Week 2: Everyday Problem-Solving

1. Toy Rescue Rope

Tie a toy to a scarf. Let them pull it up from a chair.

2. Snack Puzzle Plate

Serve a snack where they have to unwrap, unscrew, or open containers.

3. The Helper Pause

Mindful Moment

When they struggle, pause. Ask, "Want help, or want to try again?"

Why it matters

Builds patience, autonomy, and decision-making.

Try this

Use this moment when socks, lids, or shoes frustrate them.

4. Upside-Down Sort

Give 3 toys and 3 containers upside down. Let them flip and match.

5. Chair Fort Fix

Set up a blanket fort that falls easily. Let them rebuild it together.

Parent Hack of the Week – The Shoe Switch Trick

Let them put shoes on the wrong feet. When they notice, say, "You figured that out!" The real win isn't perfection—it's self-correction.

Week 3: Conversations & Feelings

1. Name That Voice

Use silly voices: robot, whisper, giant. Ask, "Whose voice is this?"

2. Toy Talks First

Make a toy "talk" to your toddler: "Hi! Want to play?"

3. Mood Mirror Game

Mindful Moment

Make a face and say, "This is my thinking face. Can you show me your feeling face?"

Why it matters

Builds emotional awareness and introduces perspective.

Try this

Add a mirror. Let them look and name the face.

4. Back-and-Forth Book Chat

Ask one question per page: "What's the dog doing?"

5. Peek-a-Who Talk

Hide a puppet and change its voice. "Who's that?"

Parent Hack of the Week – The Two-Toy Chat

Use two stuffed animals to model short, funny conversations: "Hi! I have juice!" "Yum, me too!" Your toddler will start adding lines.

Week 4: Physical Play & Social Flexibility

1. Follow-the-Leader Walk

Take turns leading and copying simple moves.

2. Stop and Go Dash

Play a running game where they stop when you say, "Freeze!"

3. Partner Pretend

Mindful Moment

Give them a block or toy and say, "Let's play this together." Follow their lead.

Why it matters

Fosters social flexibility and creative collaboration.

Try this

Avoid directing. Just mirror and extend what they do.

4. Toy Trade-Up Game

Offer a toy and ask, "Want to trade? What else can we play with?"

5. Tunnel & Talk

Crawl through a tunnel and meet in the middle. Say, "Hi there, explorer!"

Parent Hack of the Week – The Dance Turn Switch

Start a dance, then pause and say, "Your turn to make a move!" Toddlers love leading when grownups copy.

Monthly Bonus Spark – "Little Backpack Adventure"

Pack 3 small items in a backpack: toy, snack, and surprise (like a scarf). Go on a pretend "trip" across the house or yard.

Why it's magical: It blends independence, narrative play, and exploration in one joyful spark.

Reflect & Recharge: End of Month 33
Parent Story – The Brave Fix

Last week, my daugther dropped her spoon and said, "Uh-oh." Before I could move, she picked it up and said, "I fix it!" It was small, but it felt like a giant leap in confidence.

— Amit, dad of a 33-month-old

What if my toddler gets stuck and always asks for help?

- Ask, "Do you want to try first, or want me to help?"

- Model your own problem-solving out loud: "Hmm, I wonder how to open this. Let me try."

- Celebrate effort more than outcome.

Mindful Reminder

Trying is one of the biggest skills a toddler can learn. When you pause and believe in their effort, they start believing too. Confidence begins with small, steady "I did it" moments.

Month 34: Little Leaders, Big Ideas

Theme: Confidence, choice-making, and early reasoning

Week 1: Decisions & Independence

1. Snack Choice Game

Offer two snack options. Ask: "Which one do you want?" Let them decide.

2. Pick the Outfit

Hold up two shirts. "This or that?" Let your toddler choose and help dress.

3. Helper in Charge

Mindful Moment

Say, "You're in charge of wiping the table today!" Hand them a cloth and let them lead.

Why it matters

Builds initiative, responsibility, and confidence.

Try this

Repeat small tasks weekly—watch pride and routine grow.

4. Toy Sorting Time

Mix toys, then sort by size, color, or type together.

5. Water Cup Transfer

Offer two cups and a pitcher of water. Let your toddler pour (with help).

Parent Hack of the Week – The Decision Cheer

Start saying "Good choice!" after they make any decision—even small ones. It shifts your focus to effort, not outcome, and builds decision-making confidence.

Week 2: Curiosity, Memory & Everyday Logic

1. "What's Missing?" Game

Place 3 toys, hide one. Ask, "What's gone?"

2. Color Hunt Walk

Go on a walk and say, "Find something green!"

3. Puzzle Talk

Mindful Moment

As they work on a puzzle, narrate: "You're looking… you turned it… you tried again!"

Why it matters

Encourages persistence, spatial reasoning, and focus.

Try this

Let them take the lead—support with words, not hands.

4. Laundry Sort Together

Match socks, fold towels, or sort by person.

5. "Tell Me What's Next" Routine

At bedtime, ask what comes next: "After we brush teeth, then what?"

Parent Hack of the Week – The Noticing Game

At mealtime or outside, say, "I noticed you did ___." Naming specific actions helps toddlers build attention and recall—and shows that you're really watching.

Week 3: Creative Exploration & Symbolic Thinking

1. Scribble & Tell

After a scribble drawing, ask, "What did you make?"

2. Box Play World

Give a box and some figures. Say, "Let's make a house or a ship!"

3. Reuse Pretend

Mindful Moment

Take a common item like a scarf or spoon and say, "Let's pretend it's something else!"

Why it matters

Boosts flexible thinking and symbolic play.

Try this

Use one item for many things: scarf = cape, picnic blanket, tunnel cover.

4. Dance Like an Animal

Say, "Can you move like a frog? A bird? A slow turtle?"

5. Build Together

Use blocks to build a tower, then a wall. "What else could we make?"

Parent Hack of the Week – The Pretend Prop Basket

Fill a small bin with "open-ended" items: an old phone, headband, spoon, scarf. These props spark big pretend worlds without needing expensive toys.

Week 4: Feelings, Empathy & Social Routines

1. Toy Hospital

Pretend a stuffed toy is sick. Ask: "What should we do?"

2. "How Do You Feel?" Cards

Show drawings of emotions. Ask: "Which face are you today?"

3. Snack for a Friend

Mindful Moment

Offer two snacks and say, "One for you, one for me. Want to give one to Bunny too?"

Why it matters

Nurtures empathy, sharing, and social awareness.

Try this

Let your child be the snack giver—it fosters pride in caring.

4. Goodbye Practice Game

Say goodbye to toys as you tidy up: "Bye car! See you later!"

5. Caring Hands Time

Encourage a back rub, gentle hug, or toy tuck-in as part of wind-down.

Parent Hack of the Week – The Emotion Mirror

Sit together in front of a mirror. Ask, "Can you show me your tired face? Your silly face?" It's part game, part emotion lab—and they love it.

Monthly Bonus Spark – "Little Leader Day"

Let your toddler plan one simple thing—maybe what snack to eat, what toy to take on a walk, or where to sit for a story.

Why it's magical: They feel powerful in their world—and practice real decision-making in a safe space.

Reflect & Recharge: End of Month 34
Parent Story – The Snack Decision Win

It was snack time. Usually, I just handed Leandro whatever was easy. But today, I asked, "Banana or cheese?" He paused, pointed, and said,

"Cheese!" The pride on his face was so real. Just a tiny choice—but it made him feel big.

— Ana, mom of 34 month old twins

What if my toddler always says "No!" or wants the opposite?

- It's developmentally normal. Toddlers are testing power.

- Offer playful choices: "Do you want to hop to the kitchen or crawl?"

- Let them lead when possible—it balances out the no's.

> ### Mindful Reminder
>
> This month is about voice—your toddler's, and yours. Keep using your calm, consistent voice even when they test boundaries. They're learning how to choose, decide, and lead—with you as their model.

Month 35: Everyday Experts

Theme: Practical thinking, independence, and self-expression

Week 1: Problem-Solving in Action

1. Snack Puzzle

Give your toddler two small containers. Put snacks inside. Ask them how to open them.

2. Toy Rescue Game

Tape a toy gently under a table or chair. "Can you rescue it?"

3. Step-by-Step Talk

Mindful Moment

Choose a simple task (like washing hands). Say each step slowly: "Turn on water... get soap... rub..."

Why it matters

Builds sequencing, memory, and follow-through.

Try this

Pause between steps and let your child lead.

4. Treasure Under the Cup

Hide a small item under one of three cups. Mix and guess.

5. Stack, Knock, Repeat

Stack blocks and say, "Let's knock them down!" Then repeat.

Parent Hack of the Week – The Gentle Clue Trick

When your toddler struggles, don't jump in. Say, "Hmm… what do you think?" A pause plus a clue grows confidence faster than help ever could.

Week 2: Communication & Everyday Expression

1. Two-Word Builder

Say a phrase like "big ball" or "more snack." Let them try to repeat or respond.

2. Name the Step

Narrate your task: "I'm putting socks in the basket. Now I'm folding."

3. Picture Talk Walk

Mindful Moment

Flip through a photo book or printed pictures. Point and ask: "Who's this?" "Where are we here?"

Why it matters

Boosts recall, language, and personal connection.

Try this

Add your toddler's name often—"That's you at the beach!"

4. Echo Song

Sing a familiar song, pause, and let them fill in the next word.

5. Gesture + Sound Play

Wave with "hi," pat your chest for "me," or act out feelings.

Parent Hack of the Week – The Morning Recap Ritual

Each morning, review yesterday: "We played at the park. You saw a cat. Then bath time!" It anchors memory and makes language part of real life.

Week 3: Independence & Everyday Tasks

1. Shoe Match Time

Put out 3 pairs of shoes. Ask: "Can you find two that match?"

2. Wipe the Table Task

Hand them a cloth and ask them to clean their spot.

3. Simple Snack Station

Mindful Moment

Let your toddler peel a banana, pour cereal, or scoop fruit with a spoon.

Why it matters

Supports self-care skills and fine motor confidence.

Try this

Let them mess up—it's part of learning.

4. Jacket on Game

Practice putting on a jacket or sweater. Cheer even half-success.

5. Tidy-Up Toss

Toss toys into a basket like a game. "Can you get three in?"

Parent Hack of the Week – The Pre-Task Countdown

Before starting any routine, try "Ready... steady... go!" It builds anticipation—and makes transitions feel like a game.

Week 4: Play, Imagination & Confidence

1. Pretend Tool Time

Give a spoon or cardboard tube. "Can you fix the chair?"

2. Toy Tea Party

Pour pretend tea, serve guests, take turns sipping.

3. Role Reversal Play

Mindful Moment

Say, "You be the parent!" Let your child tell *you* what to do.

Why it matters

Builds confidence, social skills, and emotional insight.

Try this

Go along with their silly ideas—they love the power shift.

4. Dance Like a Creature

"Be a butterfly! Now a lion!" Change movements with music.

5. Story Flip Game

Read a favourite book and ask, "What happens next if the cat flies?"

Parent Hack of the Week – The Pretend Pause Trick

Right before bath or bedtime, pause and say, "What if we were penguins getting ready for bed?" Even one silly moment resets tension and sparks joy.

Monthly Bonus Spark – "Yes Day Mini-Moments"

Let your toddler pick three small things today: what to eat, what toy to bring outside, or which book to read. Say "Yes!" with extra excitement. **Why it's magical:** Saying yes to little things builds trust and gives them a safe sense of control.

Reflect & Recharge: End of Month 35
Parent Story – The Step-by-Step Surprise

I asked Charlie to help with laundry, just for fun. I handed him a sock and said, "Put this in." He grabbed it, looked at the basket, and said, "More sock?" Then he went back for more. I didn't expect him to take it so seriously—but he did. It felt like a tiny, wonderful shift.

— *Cydney, mom of a 35-month-old*

What if my toddler avoids daily tasks or routines?

- Break it into one tiny step. Let them lead that step only.

- Add play or imagination: "Can you carry the spoon like a robot?"

- Cheer effort, not outcome: "You *tried* that by yourself!"

> **Mindful Reminder**
>
> Confidence comes from practice—especially in the small things. Let them fumble. Let them lead. You're showing them they can do hard things... with you right there, steady and kind.

Month 36: Mini Milestones, Mighty Moments

Theme: Milestone mastery, social play, and expressive independence

Week 1: Building Everyday Mastery

1. Sock Slide Game

Invite your child to slide across the floor in socks. Great for balance and giggles.

2. Name the Step Routine

Break daily tasks into steps: "First socks, then shoes."

3. Try It First

Mindful Moment

Before stepping in, ask, "Want to try by yourself first?"

Why it matters

Encourages confidence and self-direction without pressure.

Try this

Use a gentle tone—this works especially well during dressing or snack setup.

4. Cup Transfer Challenge

Let your child pour water from one cup to another.

5. Color-by-Word Hunt

Say, "Find something red!" Let them explore and return with an item.

Parent Hack of the Week – The Pause & Wait Strategy

Before offering help, pause for a full five seconds. That small window often sparks amazing independence.

Week 2: Expression Through Movement & Talk

1. Animal Movement Parade

Walk like a bear, hop like a frog, stretch like a cat.

2. Opposite Play

Say "fast/slow" or "loud/quiet" and model both.

3. Feelings in Motion

Mindful Moment

Ask your child to "show me happy feet" or "angry arms." Act it out together.

Why it matters

Links emotion to body expression and builds self-awareness.

Try this

Turn it into a game when feelings run high.

4. Silly Rhyming Words

"Dog, frog, log, snog!" Invite them to make up nonsense too.

5. Dance & Freeze with Feelings

When the music stops, freeze and show a face: happy, sad, surprised.

Parent Hack of the Week – The Movement Melt Trick

When tension runs high, say, "Let's move like jelly!" Movement diffuses frustration faster than logic.

Week 3: Peer Play & Social Awareness

1. Toy Share Circle

Sit with two toys. Say, "One for you, one for me!" Practice switching.

2. Hello Song Time

Sing hello to everyone in the room (stuffed animals included).

3. Playdate Prep Talk

Mindful Moment

Before meeting others, say, "Let's take turns and use kind words."

Why it matters

Prepares your toddler for smoother peer interactions.

Try this

Keep it light and short—model the words with their toys.

4. Snack Trade Game

"I give you a cracker, you give me a grape!" Practice trading.

5. Photobook Friend Talk

Look at a picture of a friend or cousin. "What do you like to play with them?"

Parent Hack of the Week – The Two-Toy Trick

When play turns possessive, offer a second toy nearby. "You both have one!" It keeps peace without forcing sharing.

Week 4: Real-Life Role Play & Imagination

1. Chef for the Day

Pretend to cook with real tools: mixing spoon, empty pot.

2. Doctor Kit Fun

Use a toy or real spoon as a "thermometer" for check-ups.

3. Fix-It Helper

Mindful Moment

Invite your child to "fix" something around the house with pretend tools.

Why it matters

Encourages problem-solving, care, and real-world imitation.

Try this

Let them fix things beside you while you do chores.

4. Pet Care Pretend

Brush a stuffed animal or take it for a pretend walk.

5. Cashier Checkout Game

Use real or pretend coins. Say, "Buy something and give me money!"

Parent Hack of the Week – The Pretend Invitation Trick

Instead of asking your toddler to "get dressed," say, "Can you be a firefighter getting ready?" They'll suit up in seconds.

Monthly Bonus Spark – "Little Tour Guide Day"

Let your toddler "lead" a tour of the house. "This is my room. Here's the kitchen!" Ask questions along the way. **Why it works:** Rehearsing what they know boosts confidence and narrative skills.

Reflect & Recharge: End of Month 36
Parent Story – The Jacket Victory

I used to wrestle Isla into her coat every morning. One day, I asked, "Want to do it yourself first?" She tugged it on, slowly, and then beamed. I realized she wasn't refusing—she just wanted to try. That shift made mornings smoother for both of us.

— Rachel, mom of a 36-month-old

What if my child still needs help with basic tasks?

- That's totally normal. Independence comes in bursts.

- Try letting them do one part: just the zipper pull, or only one shoe.

- Keep offering chances—even if they say no sometimes.

> ### Mindful Reminder
>
> As your child turns 3, remember: they're not just doing more, they're understanding more. Trust their pace. Celebrate the effort. And know your presence is still their greatest comfort.

Year 3: Another Year of Incredible Growth!

Congratulations! You and your little one have completed another year of discovery, learning, and joyful moments. Your child is growing into an independent, curious, and expressive individual, and it's all thanks to your love, patience, and dedication. **You are doing an incredible job!**

This past year has likely been filled with boundless energy, big emotions, and an eagerness to explore everything around them. There may have been challenges along the way, but through it all, **your guidance, support, and encouragement have made a world of difference.**

Take a moment to **track and rate your child's progress** using the **Milestone Tracker** to see how they have developed across key areas. As you step into Year 4, new adventures and exciting challenges await. Keep trusting yourself, stay patient, and most importantly, **enjoy these precious moments**—they are shaping your child's future in ways you can't even imagine.

You've got this! Congratulations on completing Year 3! Your love and dedication are building a strong, confident, and happy child.

Understanding Your Child's Developmental Tracker

Every child develops at their own pace. These trackers are designed to provide a structured way to observe and support your child's growth, but they should not be seen as rigid timelines. It's completely normal for some children to excel in certain areas while taking more time in others.

How to Use the Tracker

- **Rate on a scale of 0-5** based on your child's current abilities in each category.
- **No need to rush or compare!** Some children might be more advanced in speech but take longer with motor skills, and that's completely fine.

- **Use it as a guide**, not a test. If your child isn't yet meeting certain milestones, observe their progress over time instead of worrying.

- **Celebrate small wins!** Any progress, no matter how small, is valuable.

What If My Child is Behind in Some Areas?

- **Variability is normal** – Development is not linear, and children often leap ahead in some skills while taking more time in others.

- **Support their growth** through interactive play, reading, conversations, and hands-on activities that align with their interests.

- **Patience is key** – Keep engaging them in activities without pressure or comparisons.

- **Seek guidance if necessary** – If you have concerns, consulting a paediatrician or child development expert can provide reassurance and strategies for support.

Encouraging a Positive Learning Experience

This tracker is meant to **empower you as a parent** and help you understand your child's unique journey. Focus on their strengths, provide encouragement, and create a nurturing environment where learning feels fun and natural. Every child has their own timeline trust the process, and enjoy watching them grow!

Remember: Progress over perfection!

Domain	Emerging Milestones	Rating (0-5)
Communication & Language	Begins speaking in 2–4 word phrases to express wants and ideas	
	Understands and responds to simple questions ("Where's your shoe?")	
	Points to named objects, animals, or people in books or photos	
	Uses naming, labelling, and pointing to share attention ("Look! Dog!")	
	Starts repeating rhymes, familiar lines from songs or books	
	Begins identifying common words or letters from books or signs through repeated exposure	
Social & Emotional Development	Shows affection for familiar people (hugs, smiling, seeking contact)	
	Begins showing awareness of others' emotions (comforts, copies)	
	Experiences big feelings and seeks comfort or solutions	
	Plays near other children (parallel play) and watches others interact	
	Starts using words or gestures to express preferences ("No want that!")	

Cognitive & Thinking Skills	Recognizes and names common objects, body parts, and everyday actions	
	Matches objects by function or category (spoons in cups, shoes together)	
	Explores cause and effect (pouring, flipping, pushing buttons)	
	Completes simple shape sorters or knob puzzles	
	Remembers locations of favourite toys or routines ("Snack comes after nap")	
	Begins noticing patterns or quantities through play (e.g., "More blocks!" or "One, two!")	
Fine & Gross Motor Skills	Runs without falling, climbs furniture safely, kicks a ball	
	Begins jumping with both feet and walking up/down stairs with help	
	Scribbles with crayons using whole hand or emerging grip	
	Turns pages in board books, begins stacking small blocks	
	Feeds self with spoon and begins using a cup independently	
Play, Creativity & Independence	Engages in pretend play with objects (feeds doll, drives car)	
	Enjoys singing, clapping, dancing to familiar songs	
	Starts simple dressing tasks (putting on hat, pulling up pants)	
	Helps with daily routines (tidying, bringing items, washing hands)	
	Chooses between 2–3 options with growing confidence ("Red cup or blue?")	

As you reflect on this year of growing independence and big feelings, take pride in your shared resilience.

Every challenge shaped new understanding; every joy deepened your connection.

Growth isn't always loud — sometimes it's in the quiet "I love yous."

This chapter ends, but your bond grows bolder with each step forward.

And now, Year 4 begins — the age of curiosity and courage.

Big questions, brave attempts, and blooming confidence take centre stage.

You're not just guiding a child; you're walking beside a thinker, a doer, a little dreamer becoming more *themself* each day.

CHAPTER 5

Year 4: The Independent Thinker

Creativity, Emotional Reasoning & Logical Skills

Quote

"Children are not things to be moulded, but people to be unfolded."

— *Jess Lair*

Mantra

I empower without control. I guide without fear. I love without limits.

M.I.N.D. for Year 4

Moments That Matter

Let them make choices and take the lead — independence begins now.

Intentional Interaction

Encourage open-ended questions and hands-on play.

Nurture Through Love

Support self-expression while teaching kindness and patience.

Daily Growth

Help them build logic and emotional regulation through consistent guidance.

Year 4: Independence in Action

"Your child isn't just growing—they're becoming their own person."

Year 4 is where early childhood truly begins. Your toddler is now a confident explorer—asking questions, making choices, and trying things all on their own. They're not just participating in the world anymore—they're starting to shape it. And you? You're guiding them toward confidence, compassion, and real-world readiness.

This year is all about building life-ready skills through everyday moments. From emotional expression and decision-making to teamwork and problem-solving, your child is stepping into a bigger world—and learning how to thrive in it.

What's Evolving in Year 4

- **Life Skill of the Month:** A practical life-readiness theme—like cooperation, self-care, or communication—anchors the month and helps you zoom out to the big picture.

- **The 5-Day Rhythm Continues:** Five focused activities per week offer the right mix of inspiration and flexibility—enough to stay playful and fresh without feeling overwhelming.

- **Weekly Rhythm:** 5 focused activities, 1 Mindful Moment, and a Parent Hack to try right away.

- **Reflect & Recharge:** A What If... check-in and a relatable Parent Story to remind you—you're not alone.

Milestones to Watch in Year 4

Your child's development is unfolding at its own pace, but many 3–4 year olds begin to:

- Speak in clear 4–6 word sentences and tell simple stories

- Ask "why" questions and express ideas and preferences

- Engage in pretend play and cooperative games with peers

- Follow 2–3 step instructions and anticipate routines

- Identify colours, shapes, and basic quantities

- Show early problem-solving and planning skills

- Begin regulating emotions with guidance

- Demonstrate improved coordination in both fine and gross motor tasks

These aren't boxes to tick—they're glimpses into the many ways your child will bloom.

How to Use This Guide

- **Weekly Rhythm:** 5 focused activities, 1 Mindful Moment, and a Parent Hack to try right away.

- **Life Skill of the Month:** A guiding theme that brings focus and real-world relevance.

- **Reflect & Recharge:** A What If... check-in and a relatable Parent Story to remind you—you're not alone.

Let's begin Year 4 with curiosity, confidence, and connection—one joyful life skill at a time.

Month 37: Look Closer, Think Deeper

Week 1: Eyes Wide Open

1. Backyard Noticing Walk

Go outside and ask, "What do you see that wasn't here yesterday?"

2. Snack Detective Game

Hand them a familiar snack and ask, "What colours do you see? What shapes?"

3. Listen & Look Pause

Mindful Moment

Sit quietly for 30 seconds and ask, "What sounds do you hear? What do you see?"

Why it matters

Teaches present-moment awareness and strengthens focus.

Try this

Turn it into a bedtime wind-down routine.

4. Shadow Hunt

Go on a shadow search. "Can you find your shadow? Mine?"

5. Sky Watch Session

Lay down and look at the sky together. "What shapes do you see in the clouds?"

Parent Hack of the Week – The 'Noticing Hat' Trick

Grab a play hat or pretend crown. Say, "This is our noticing hat!" Put it on and take turns pointing out tiny details around you. It becomes a fun, mindful ritual anywhere—home, park, or errands.

Week 2: Observation in Everyday Play

1. Toy Sort Challenge

Pick 3-5 small toys. "Can we sort by color? Size? Shape?"

2. Laundry Patterns

Sort clothes and point out patterns: stripes, dots, solids.

3. Sink or Float Time

Mindful Moment

During bath or water play, guess what will float or sink.

Why it matters

Encourages prediction, observation, and early reasoning.

Try this

Use everyday items—plastic spoon, sponge, coin.

4. Color of the Day Hunt

Pick a color and find things around the house or outside that match.

5. Mirror Game

Make a face and ask them to match it. "What do you see on my face?"

Parent Hack of the Week – The Silent Minute Game

At any point in the day, say "Silent Minute!" and pause all noise or movement. After 60 seconds, ask: "What did you hear? What did you see?" Great for calming and curiosity!

Week 3: Observation Through Stories & Feelings

1. Book Detective Time

During Storytime, stop and ask, "What do you notice in this picture?"

2. Feeling Faces Match

Look at a picture book or flashcards. Match the emotion face to your child's expression.

3. What's Different Game

Mindful Moment

Show 3 toys. Turn around and remove 1. "What's missing?"

Why it matters

Boosts memory, comparison, and attention.

Try this

Start simple and add more items over time.

4. Emotion Mirror

You show a "mad face," your child copies. Then switch.

5. Draw & Describe

Scribble together and talk about what you drew: "A mountain! A rainbow?"

Parent Hack of the Week – The 'Spot the Detail' Trick

At the grocery store or on a walk, say, "I spy something round… green… that rolls!" Toddlers love guessing—and it builds visual vocabulary and concentration.

Week 4: Movement & Nature Noticing

1. Nature Texture Walk

Touch tree bark, smooth stones, soft grass. Describe each texture aloud.

2. Sound Chase Game

Say, "Where is that sound coming from?" when you hear birds, traffic, wind.

3. Bubble Focus

Mindful Moment

Blow bubbles slowly. Watch them float, pop, or land.

Why it matters

Teaches visual tracking and calming observation.

Try this

Count each bubble out loud as it pops.

4. Animal Spotting Game

Look for dogs, cats, birds on a walk. "What's that one doing?"

5. Balance Walk Challenge

Lay a string or tape line on the ground. Ask, "Can you walk across like a tightrope walker?"

Parent Hack of the Week – The 'One New Thing' Rule

Each day, ask: "What's one new thing you noticed today?" It could be a crack in the sidewalk or a bird's feather. This tiny habit rewires your toddler's brain for curiosity.

Life Skill of the Month: Observation

This month's focus is helping your child become a *curious noticer.* Practice spotting, describing, and wondering out loud together:

- "I wonder what's behind that tree?"
- "Let's see how many blue things we can find at lunch."
- "Look! That ant is carrying something—what do you think it is?"

Everyday observation builds focus, vocabulary, and emotional insight. All it takes is a moment of shared wonder.

Reflect & Recharge
Parent Story – The 'See It First' Game

Lately, my daughter loves spotting things before I do. "I saw it first!" she yells with a grin—whether it's a butterfly or a banana. It started as a game but now, it's our shared ritual. She's paying more attention to the world, and I get to see it through her eyes.

— Vidya, mom of a 3-year-old

What if my child seems distracted or uninterested in "noticing" activities?

- That's okay—observation develops over time.

- Try in quieter moments (bedtime, snack) when distractions are low.

- Celebrate even tiny observations. "You saw that tiny ant! Good eye."

> ### Mindful Reminder
>
> Learning to observe teaches kids to be present, engaged, and curious. Don't worry about "doing it right." Just notice together—and enjoy the view.

Month 38: Try, Tweak, Triumph

Week 1: Trial & Error Play

1. Puzzle Piece Fit Test

Offer a 6–8 piece puzzle. Let them try different placements, even if "wrong."

2. Scoop, Pour, Repeat

Give dry beans or cereal with bowls, spoons, and scoops. Watch the experimenting.

3. Upside Down Challenge

Mindful Moment

Offer a toy or cup upside down and wait.

Why it matters

Encourages problem-solving and cognitive flexibility.

Try this

Use playful prompts: "Hmm… what's going on here?"

4. Tower Rebuild Time

Build a tower. Let them knock it down and rebuild it a new way.

5. Obstacle Reroute Game

Set up cushions. When they bump into one, say, "Can you find a new way around?"

Parent Hack of the Week – The "Try Again Basket"

Keep a small bin with slightly challenging toys or tasks (e.g., puzzle with missing piece, shape sorter). Label it the "Try Again Basket." Let your child pick from it anytime—they'll start practicing persistence without pressure.

Week 2: Imagination in Action

1. Pretend Repair Shop

Give a toy and ask, "What's broken? How can we fix it?"

2. Story Scene Builder

Read a short book, then re-create the scene with toys.

3. What Could It Be?

Mindful Moment

Offer a box, stick, or sock and ask, "What could this be?"

Why it matters

Boosts creativity and symbolic thinking.

Try this

Let them surprise you with wild ideas!

4. Reverse Role Play

"You be the parent, I'll be the child." Let them instruct you.

5. Imagination Station Setup

Rotate household items for open-ended pretend (e.g., cardboard box + ladle = spaceship?)

Parent Hack of the Week – The "What Happens Next?" Trick

During any pretend play, pause and ask, "Then what happens?" It sparks storytelling, extends attention, and gives them control of the narrative.

Week 3: Social Growth & Confidence

1. My Job Today Game

Give a mini task: "You're the snack setter today."

2. Feelings Weather Check

Ask, "What's your mood today? Sunny? Stormy?"

3. Kind Hands Reminder

Mindful Moment

Before playdates or family time, touch your hand to theirs and say, "Let's remember to use kind hands today."

Why it matters

Builds self-regulation and physical awareness.

Try this

Repeat regularly—it becomes a loving ritual.

4. Pass the Emotion Ball

Toss a soft ball and say an emotion as you pass.

5. "Can I Help?" Practice

Encourage your child to offer help to you or a peer: "Want me to carry that?"

Parent Hack of the Week – The "Social Pause" Trick

When your child interrupts or gets frustrated in play, whisper, "Let's pause and see." This 2-second break often resets emotions and teaches waiting skills.

Week 4: Movement + Exploration

1. Crawl Maze Challenge

Use chairs and blankets to make a tunnel or maze. Let them figure it out.

2. Big Step, Little Step Game

Alternate stepping high, low, wide, tiny.

3. Sound & Move Match

Mindful Moment

Play sounds (drumbeat, clap, soft bell) and match them to movement.

Why it matters

Integrates auditory processing and gross motor coordination.

Try this

Let them make the sound for you to move to next.

4. Nature Collection Walk

Find 3 leaves, stones, or twigs. Ask: "How are they the same? Different?"

5. Animal Movement Freeze

"Be a kangaroo! Now freeze like a turtle!"

Parent Hack of the Week – The "2-Move Reset" Trick

When your child feels stuck or grumpy, suggest: "Do two moves!" Jump then tiptoe. This small burst of movement often shifts mood and energy instantly.

Life Skill of the Month: Resilience

This month is about trying—even when things don't go right the first time. Practice saying:

- "Hmm, that didn't work. Want to try again?"

- "Let's try it a different way!"

- "It's okay to take a break and come back."

You're teaching your child that mistakes are part of learning—and that effort matters more than perfection. Every wobble is a win.

Reflect & Recharge
Parent Story – The Upside-Down Spoon Win

Elias was trying to eat yogurt with his spoon flipped backward. I almost corrected him—but stopped. He stared at it, flipped it around, and said, "That way better!" It took an extra minute, but he figured it out—and I learned to wait.

— Claire, mom of a 38-month-old

What if my child gives up easily or gets frustrated fast?

- Stay nearby, but don't rush to fix things.

- Offer encouragement like, "That's tricky, but you're thinking about it."

- Celebrate the trying, not the finishing. "You kept going!"

Mindful Reminder

Resilience is built in the in-between moments—when your child tries, fails, and *chooses* to try again. You are their mirror. Show patience, and they'll learn persistence.

Month 39: My Turn, My Try

Week 1: Everyday Independence

1. Morning Job Picker

Offer 2 tasks: "Do you want to get your socks or pour water?" Let them choose.

2. Wipe, Fold, Put Away

Show how to wipe a surface, fold a towel, or place items where they belong.

3. Start the Routine Together

Mindful Moment

Begin a task together, then step back: "You start, I'll watch."

Why it matters

Builds confidence while knowing you're still near.

Try this

Use for tasks like putting on shoes, setting the table.

4. Snack Setup Station

Create a shelf or tray where your child can access snack items independently.

5. Mirror Practice Game

Let them brush hair, try dressing, or make faces while you observe and cheer.

Parent Hack of the Week – The "Half Start"

Trick Begin the task, then say: "Can you finish it?" (e.g., pulling up pants halfway). It gives them a boost of success and builds initiative.

Week 2: Emotional Check-Ins

1. Color Feelings Chart

Make a simple mood board: Blue = sad, Yellow = happy, Red = mad. Ask them to point daily.

2. Feelings Face Drawing

Let them scribble a face. Ask, "Is this a happy or a tired face?"

3. Emotion Mirror Pause

Mindful Moment

Look in a mirror and ask: "Can you show me how your face feels today?"

Why it matters

Builds awareness of facial cues and emotions.

Try this

Repeat during calm moments, not just big emotions.

4. Story Feelings Spotting

Read a book and pause: "How do you think they feel now?"

5. Happy/Sad Dance Game

Play music and move in happy, sad, silly styles.

Parent Hack of the Week – The "Mood Label Boost"

Whenever your child expresses something (whine, pout, grin), try naming it gently: "You look a little frustrated. Is that right?" Even if they don't respond, you're giving language to feelings.

Week 3: Flexible Thinking & Problem Solving

1. Switcheroo Sorting

Sort by one category (color), then switch (size or use). "Let's try another way."

2. Backwards Book Reading

Read a story backward. Ask: "What came before this?"

3. Fix-It Together

Mindful Moment

Break a tower or line of blocks. Ask, "What can we do now?"

Why it matters

Builds resilience and creativity.

Try this

Let your child lead the fix.

4. Snack Puzzle Tray

Cut snacks into fun shapes. Let them put pieces back together.

5. Toy Remix Play

Use blocks with animals, or kitchen items with cars. Invite new combinations.

Parent Hack of the Week – The "Try Another Way"

Phrase Make this your go-to script when something doesn't work. It avoids judgment and teaches persistence.

Week 4: Movement & Social Skills

1. Follow Me Steps

Take turns leading a short movement game: big steps, tiptoes, twirls.

2. Dance Freeze Name Call

Dance, freeze, then call out a name. The person dances next.

3. Trade & Talk

Mindful Moment

During play, model this: "Here, I'll trade this car for that block."

Why it matters

Encourages respectful peer exchange.

Try this

Practice at home before playdates.

4. Toy Parade

Line up toys and let each have a "turn" to walk or ride across the room.

5. Kind Words Call-Out

Catch your child using kind words or tone. Say, "That was kind! Thank you.

" Parent Hack of the Week – The "Kindness Echo"

When your child says or does something thoughtful, repeat it aloud. "You gave your toy to Max! That was kind." It reinforces prosocial behaviour.

Life Skill of the Month: Taking Initiative

Invite your child to take charge of small things: choosing a sock, starting a clean-up song, offering help. Try:

- "What job would you like to do today?"

- "Want to be the snack captain?"

- "Let me know when you're ready to start!" This builds internal motivation and self-starting skills for years to come.

Reflect & Recharge Parent Story – The Jacket Moment

Today I held out my Kiyah's coat and she said, "No, I do it." I watched as she struggled with the zipper, fumbled, then finally got it. Her eyes sparkled. "I did it!" she said. That look? Worth everything.

— Abhilasha, mom of a 39-month-old

What if my child refuses to do things they can do?

- Don't force. Offer gentle reminders: "I believe in you. I'll wait."

- Use routine to reduce power battles. "It's coat time. You can start or I can help."

- Celebrate tiny efforts: "You pulled one sleeve! That counts."

> **Mindful Reminder**
>
> Independence doesn't mean doing everything alone. It means *wanting to try.* Your support is still the soil where their confidence grows.

Month 40: Bold Hearts, Bright Ideas

Week 1: Building Focus Through Fun

1. Start-Stop Sound Game

Clap a rhythm, stop suddenly. Let your child guess what comes next or copy you.

2. Tray Time Sorting

Offer a tray with 3 categories: colours, sizes, or shapes. Let them sort objects playfully.

3. One Step at a Time

Mindful Moment

Ask, "What comes next?" during everyday routines like snack prep or dressing.

Why it matters

Teaches sequencing, memory, and focus.

Try this

Keep the steps light and visual: "First plate, then banana, then napkin."

4. Letter Hunt at Home

Pick 2 letters (like A and M). Find items that start with those sounds.

5. Mirror Dance Freeze

Dance together, freeze in silly shapes, and copy each other.

Parent Hack of the Week – The 'Task Countdown' Trick

Say, "We'll do 3 things: shoes, snack, story!" It builds memory and helps your child follow a sequence—without pressure.

Week 2: Feelings in Real Life

1. Color of the Day Check-In

Ask, "What color is your feeling today?" Link it to their mood.

2. Emotion Stamps Drawing

Draw or stamp faces (happy, mad, etc.). Let your child choose and explain.

3. Story of a Feeling

Mindful Moment

After a tantrum or giggle fit, tell a short story: "Once there was a little person who felt ___."

Why it matters

Builds emotional vocabulary and narrative thinking.

Try this

Keep it warm and playful—don't force it.

4. Feeling Scavenger Hunt

"Can you find something that makes you feel silly? Cozy? Brave?"

5. Name the Feel in Books

While reading, pause: "How do they feel now?"

Parent Hack of the Week – The 'Mood Basket'

Create a small bin with items for calming down (soft toy, stress ball, book). Let your child choose what helps when feelings get big.

Week 3: Real-World Thinking & Problem Solving

1. Pattern Snack Stacking

Alternate snacks (cracker, fruit, cracker). Ask, "What's next?"

2. Puzzle Mix Challenge

Mix pieces from two puzzles. Sort and solve together.

3. Fix and Figure It Out

Mindful Moment

Place a toy "stuck" on a ledge or behind a chair. Ask, "How can we get it?"

Why it matters

Encourages planning and spatial problem-solving.

Try this

Celebrate every idea—even silly ones.

4. Story Builder Cards

Use images or toys to make up a 3-part story (who, where, what).

5. Shape Walk Outside

Find circles, squares, triangles in signs or buildings.

Parent Hack of the Week – The 'Let's Try It Another Way' Phrase

Use when your child gets stuck. It replaces frustration with curiosity—and teaches flexible thinking.

Week 4: Social Awareness in Action

1. Kind Action Jar

Add a pompom each time your child is kind. Celebrate full jars!

2. Role Reversal Play

"You be the grown-up. Tell me what to do!"

3. Sharing a Story

Mindful Moment

Let your child tell a story to a toy or another family member.

Why it matters

Builds confidence, expression, and audience awareness.

Try this

Encourage silly stories, too—laughter builds connection.

4. Snack Sharing Game

Offer two snacks and say, "Which one do you want to share with me?"

5. Pass the Compliment

Say something kind about your child, then ask, "Want to give one back?"

Parent Hack of the Week – The 'Social Snapshot'

Point out kind behaviour in others: "Did you see how that friend helped?" It builds social awareness through observation.

Life Skill of the Month: Focus in Everyday Moments

Help your child strengthen their attention span through natural routines:

- Invite them to help set up snack with 3 steps.
- Let them finish simple songs or rhymes.
- Say, "Let's watch and see what happens next!" during Storytime.
- Use open-ended questions: "What do you think we should do now?" Focus grows from little chances to slow down, notice, and stay curious—together.

Reflect & Recharge Parent Story – The Puzzle Moment

I watched Theo struggle to finish a shape puzzle. He looked ready to give up—but then he whispered, "Try again." And he did. Slowly, proudly.

"I did it!" he yelled, and hugged me so hard I almost cried. He's learning how to stick with things—and so am I.

— Elena, mom of a 40-month-old

What if my child loses interest quickly?

- Start small—one-minute focus counts.

- Follow their lead. Attention grows with interest.

- Give praise for effort, not outcome: "You kept trying—that's amazing!"

> ### Mindful Reminder
>
> Attention is built through curiosity, not pressure. Every time you slow down together—whether stacking blocks or spotting shapes—you're growing your child's focus in the most powerful way: with love and presence.

Month 41: Little Leaders, Big Questions

Theme: Curiosity, confidence, and early reasoning

Week 1: Confident Communication

1. What Happens Next?

Read a story and pause before each page. Ask, "What do you think will happen?"

2. Yes/No Sort Game

Hold up silly items: "Is this a banana? Is it blue?" Encourage verbal reasoning.

3. Repeat After Me Talk

Mindful Moment

Say short phrases: "Time for snack!" and let your child echo.

Why it matters

Builds verbal memory and confidence.

Try this

Use fun tone changes—whisper, sing, giggle.

4. Story Stone Toss

Use picture cards or stones. Pick three, invent a story together.

5. Book Talk Roles

Let your child "read" the pictures while you add drama. They'll feel like a real storyteller.

Parent Hack of the Week – The Predictable Pause

Pause during a familiar sentence. Let your child finish it. It builds confidence through joyful guessing.

Week 2: Movement & Thinking Together

1. Animal Sound Stretch

Move like animals: hop like a frog, flap like a bird—add sound effects!

2. Shape Hop Game

Tape paper shapes on the floor. "Jump to the triangle! Now the square!"

3. Feather or Rock

Mindful Moment

Lie down and breathe together: "Soft like a feather. Heavy like a rock."

Why it matters

Encourages body awareness and calm-down routines.

Try this

Use it before bed or after big energy bursts.

4. Follow-the-Foot Game

Walk tracing a zigzag line or stepping only on certain colours.

5. Mirror Motion Game

Copy each other's movements slowly. Who's leading? Who's following?

Parent Hack of the Week – The Body Clue Trick

Ask: "Is your body telling you it's tired? Hungry?" Toddlers learn emotional cues from physical signals.

Week 3: Everyday Logic & Choice-Making

1. Snack Sort Challenge

Give a variety of snacks to sort by color, shape, or type.

2. What Comes Next?

During routines, pause: "We brushed teeth—what's next?"

3. Reason Out Loud

Mindful Moment

Narrate your actions: "I'm putting the milk back first—it gets warm fast."

Why it matters

Models planning, logic, and everyday reasoning.

Try this

Invite them to do the same: "What would you do first?"

4. Fix the Order Game

Use picture cards of a routine (e.g., brush, pyjamas, sleep). Ask your child to reorder them.

5. Yes/No Riddle Game

Think of an object. Let them ask yes/no questions to guess.

Parent Hack of the Week – "Hmm… That Makes Sense" Phrase

Even when your child is off, say this to show you value their thinking. It boosts persistence and creativity.

Week 4: Social Expression & Pretend Play

1. Pretend Play Family Roles

Act out jobs like cook, doctor, or pet groomer.

2. Toy Switch Talk

"Teddy gives the truck to Bunny. What does Bunny say?" Practice back-and-forth talk.

3. My Turn, Your Turn Roleplay

Mindful Moment

Model turn-taking with puppets or toys. Switch roles and let them direct.

Why it matters

Builds conversational rhythm and social empathy.

Try this

Use it to soften sibling conflicts or reinforce fairness.

4. Emotion Hat Game

Put on a "happy hat" or "grumpy scarf" and act it out.

5. Pretend Phone Call

Let them call a toy or loved one. "Hello! How are you?"

Parent Hack of the Week – The Everyday Actor Trick

Use props (sunglasses, apron, bag) to play roles. Real-world objects bring pretend play to life.

Life Skill of the Month: Following Curiosity

Your toddler is full of questions—this month, follow them!

- Keep a "Wonder Notebook" for questions they ask. Revisit together.

- Explore answers through books, play, or simple searches: "Let's find out!"

- Narrate your own curiosity: "Hmm, I wonder why that bird is so loud."

- Create a "Wonder Jar" where they drop drawings or ideas they're curious about.

Curiosity builds focus, confidence, and flexible thinking. Show them that wondering *is* learning.

Reflect & Recharge
Parent Story – The Wonder Jar Moment

One morning, Samar dropped a tiny drawing of a cloud into our wonder jar. I asked why, and he said, "I want to know why clouds don't fall." I paused—I didn't know either. So we looked it up. Later he pointed at the sky: "They're floating because they're light." That moment? It was more than learning. It was a spark.

— *Urshila, mom of a 41-month-old*

What if my child asks too many questions?

- That's curiosity at work! It's a good thing.

- Say "Let's find out together"—you don't have to know it all.

- If questions repeat, it means they're processing. Be patient.

> ## Mindful Reminder
>
> You don't need to be the answer machine. Just be their fellow explorer. Every time you say, "Hmm, good question," you're teaching that questions aren't annoying—they're the beginning of learning.

Month 42: Problem-Solvers in Progress

Theme: Flexible thinking, planning, and learning through mistakes

Week 1: Try, Tweak, Repeat

1. Tower Fall Rebuild

Let your child build a tower and watch it fall—then brainstorm ways to build it stronger.

2. Scoop & Spill Play

Use rice or pasta for sensory fun. Ask, "What happens if we go slow? Fast?"

3. "Let's Try Again" Talk

Mindful Moment

After something breaks or spills, say, "Hmm… how can we fix this?"

Why it matters

Encourages resilience and creative repair thinking.

Try this

Add humour to mistakes: "Oops! That cup went swimming."

4. Tiny Tool Tester

Offer spoons, lids, tongs. Ask, "What can we pick up with this?"

5. What's Missing? Game

Lay out 3 toys, then hide one while your child closes their eyes. Ask, "What's gone?"

Parent Hack of the Week – The Oops Strategy

Start saying, "Oops! What's next?" when things don't go right. This keeps the tone light while your child learns persistence and playful problem-solving.

Week 2: Choices, Plans & Cause-Effect

1. Snack Station Setup

Ask your child to choose and arrange their own plate: "Fruit or crackers first?"

2. Traffic Light Movement

Say "green" to go, "yellow" to slow, "red" to stop. Add silly twists!

3. If... Then Play

Mindful Moment

Use cause-effect talk in pretend scenarios: "If Bear gets wet, what happens?"

Why it matters

Strengthens logic and narrative understanding.

Try this

Switch it up—let your child ask the "if" question.

4. Build-a-Routine Game

Ask, "What should we do after bath? Then what?" Create bedtime steps together.

5. Two-Step Listening Game

Say, "Touch your toes, then clap!" or "Get a book, then sit down."

Parent Hack of the Week – The Visual Choices Trick

Use real objects or photos when offering choices. It empowers toddlers to feel in control and sharpens visual memory.

Week 3: Thinking with the Body

1. Obstacle Plan Path

Let your child help plan a crawl-jump-run course using pillows or tape.

2. Treasure Balance Challenge

Balance small items on a spoon while walking. "Let's make it to the basket!"

3. Body Detective Game

Mindful Moment

Say, "Your body looks wiggly—is it tired? Hungry? Bored?"

Why it matters

Builds interoception and self-awareness.

Try this

Let them ask you what your body might be feeling.

4. Freeze, Think, Act

Practice stopping mid-play to ask, "What should we do next?"

5. Slow-Mo Dance Party

Move to music in super slow motion. Add pauses to "think with your feet."

Parent Hack of the Week – The "Plan It with Your Body" Game

Let your child lead a movement plan: "First hop. Then spin. Then crawl!" They'll giggle—and grow spatial sequencing skills.

Week 4: Pretend, Predict & Problem-Solve

1. Story Riddle Time

Make up clues: "I'm big. I fly. I take people far away…" (Airplane!)

2. Toy Tool Problem Day

Give a "broken" toy and tools. Ask, "How do we fix it?"

3. "Let's Be Scientists"

Mindful Moment

Try experiments like dropping different objects in water. "What do you think will happen?"

Why it matters

Introduces prediction, testing, and observation.

Try this

Use dramatic flair—"Time for the experiment zone!"

4. Retell a Story from Pictures

Show a book without reading and ask your child to tell you what's happening.

5. Switch & Solve Clean-up

Pick up toys by category, shape, or sound. "Let's clean up all the things that roll!"

Parent Hack of the Week – The Scientist Role Play

Call your child "Professor ___" and ask for their ideas on solving little puzzles. It builds identity around thinking, not just getting answers right.

Life Skill of the Month: Problem-Solving & Memory in Motion

This month, help your child flex their "figuring-it-out" muscles while boosting memory and attention:

- Ask open-ended questions: "Hmm, what could we try?"

- Practice two-step instructions: "Get your shoes, then open the door."

- Play "What's Missing?" or "What comes next?" during routines.

- Celebrate effort more than outcome: "You had such a smart idea!"

- Turn routines into little missions—"We have a sock emergency! Who can help?" Problem-solving isn't about perfection. It's about curiosity, trying again, and remembering what worked.

Reflect & Recharge Parent Story – The Wobbly Tower Win

We were building blocks and the tower kept falling. I was ready to say, "Let's do something else," but Katie said, "Wait. We need the big one on the bottom!" She got it. That shift—from meltdown to mastery—was all hers.

— Leah, mom of a 42-month-old

What if my child gives up too fast?

- Join them—don't rescue, just stand beside them.

- Use a mantra: "We try, we learn."

- Celebrate micro-successes: "You figured out the first part!"

> ### Mindful Reminder
>
> Mistakes aren't failures—they're fuel for growth. Every "Oops!" moment is a gift. With your steady calm beside them, your child is learning something far more valuable than answers: how to think.

Month 43: Thinkers in Motion

Theme: Logical thinking, spatial awareness, and everyday math

Week 1: Patterns, Predictions & Problem-Solving

1. Pattern Hunt

Find patterns around the house: stripes on clothes, tiles, or routines.

2. Block Build & Match

Build a simple block tower and ask your child to copy it.

3. "What Comes Next?" Talk

Mindful Moment

Use socks, blocks, or snacks to make a color or size pattern. Ask, "What comes next?"

Why it matters

Strengthens early logic and prediction skills.

Try this

Let your child create their own pattern and quiz you!

4. Puzzle Flip Game

Turn puzzle pieces upside down and solve using only shapes.

5. Snack Sort

Give 2-3 snack items. Ask them to sort by color, size, or type.

Parent Hack of the Week – The "One More Step" Game

When playing or building, pause and ask, "What could we add next?" This opens the door to flexible, creative thinking.

Week 2: Exploring Size, Shape & Space

1. Big/Small Hunt

Find objects around the house that are bigger/smaller than their hand.

2. Shape Sorting Baskets

Use containers to group round, square, or triangle items.

3. Shape Walk

Mindful Moment

Tape shapes on the floor and walk to each: "Can you hop to the circle?"

Why it matters

Builds body coordination and visual-spatial awareness.

Try this

Let your child take the lead in calling out shapes.

4. Measuring Play

Use string, spoons, or blocks to "measure" toys.

5. Tallest Tower Challenge

Build with boxes or blocks. "Can we make it taller than you?"

Parent Hack of the Week – The Shape Finder Trick

Point out shapes while walking or shopping: "That sign is a triangle!" Kids love real-world connections.

Week 3: Thinking Through Movement

1. Obstacle Course Patterns

Design a simple path: jump, crawl, step over.

2. Ball Target Toss

Set up targets and let them aim. Vary distance.

3. Body Sequence Game

Mindful Moment

Say: "Touch head, then knees, then toes!" Add more steps slowly.

Why it matters

Builds working memory and body-mind connection.

Try this

Let your child invent a sequence for you to follow.

4. Roll & Count

Roll a ball 3 times and count aloud.

5. Move to the Beat

Clap, stomp, or tap in rhythm to music.

Parent Hack of the Week – The "Copy My Move" Ritual

Make it part of morning or wind-down: you do a move, your toddler copies. Builds attention, imitation, and bonding.

Week 4: Everyday Math & Choices

1. Snack Math

Offer 5 crackers. Ask, "How many after we eat 2?" Use fingers!

2. Toy Count & Clean

Count toys while tidying: "We put away 1...2...3 dinosaurs!"

3. "Big Math Words"

Mindful Moment

During play, casually use terms like "more," "less," "equal," and "in between."

Why it matters

Builds early math vocabulary through natural interaction.

Try this

Ask your child to teach their toy what each word means.

4. Choice Time Chart

Make a chart with 2-3 choices and let them point and pick.

5. Count & Clap Game

Say a number (1-5), then clap that many times together.

Parent Hack of the Week – The Tiny Tally Game

Start making tally marks on paper for anything: jumping jacks, snacks eaten, socks folded. Kids love marking "real" numbers.

Life Skill of the Month: Early Math Thinking

This month, your child is building a math mindset without flashcards:

- Let them group, compare, and sort objects freely.

- Talk casually about amounts: "You have more blocks than me!"

- Ask playful math questions: "If we add one more car, how many?"

- Celebrate process, not perfection. When math feels like play, confidence grows naturally.

Reflect & Recharge Parent Story – The Cracker Count Surprise

Vivaan was stacking crackers and I asked, "How many do you have?" He counted, "One, two, three, four!" Then he gave me one and said, "Now I have three." I nearly cried. He wasn't just counting—he was thinking.

—Tanya, mom of a 43-month-old

What if my child isn't interested in numbers?

- Look for math moments in play, not worksheets.
- Use their interests: cars, snacks, animals—anything can be counted or sorted.
- Keep it low-pressure. Curiosity always comes before skill.

> **Mindful Reminder**
>
> Early math is about noticing, comparing, and predicting. It lives in play, snacks, and routines. You don't need to teach math—you just need to make space for it to emerge.

Month 44: Builders of Belonging

Theme: Social identity, empathy, and emotional self-expression

Week 1: My Place in the World

1. Name & Place Game

Say your child's full name, then yours. Talk about where you live, and show on a map or photo.

2. Family Handprints

Trace everyone's hands on paper and decorate them. Hang them in a visible place.

3. "Who Do We Love?" Circle

Mindful Moment

Sit in a circle with dolls, stuffed animals, or family photos. Say aloud who you love and what you love about them.

Why it matters

Builds belonging and emotional language.

Try this

Let your child name people and add their own reasons.

4. Same & Different Sorting

Use pictures or toys to group by size, color, or other features. Talk about what makes them unique.

5. Neighbourhood Walk & Talk

Notice homes, shops, or nature. Say, "This is part of our world."

Parent Hack of the Week – The "That's Us!" Wall

Create a simple visual wall with family photos, drawings, or special places. Say, "That's our story!"

Week 2: Feelings & Friendship

1. Emotion Faces Chart

Draw or print basic faces (happy, sad, excited). Ask, "How do you feel today?"

2. Kindness Roleplay

Use dolls to act out helping, hugging, sharing.

3. Feelings Mirror

Mindful Moment

Stand together at the mirror. Make different expressions and label them.

Why it matters

Helps children identify and name feelings in themselves and others.

Try this

Ask, "What does your face say today?"

4. Friend Match Up

Look at a photo book. Point to friends and family: "Who do you like playing with?"

5. Hug Meter Game

Ask, "Do you want a tiny hug or a big one?" Follow their lead.

Parent Hack of the Week – The Emotion Echo

When your child shares a feeling, repeat it: "You felt left out. That can be hard." This builds emotional trust.

Week 3: Teamwork & Turn-Taking

1. Pass the Toy Game

Sit with toys and pass one around while saying each name.

2. Clean-Up Race

Team up to tidy with a timer. "Let's do it together!"

3. The Turn Timer

Mindful Moment

Use a small sand timer during shared play. Say, "Your turn until the sand runs out."

Why it matters

Builds patience, fairness, and a sense of time.

Try this

Let your child flip the timer to feel in charge.

4. Story Builder Circle

Start a story, then pause. Let your child add the next part. Keep going together.

5. Puzzle Pair Work

Complete a puzzle or shape-sorter side-by-side. Talk about helping each other.

Parent Hack of the Week – The "You Go, I Go" Ritual

In daily routines (like putting on shoes or brushing teeth), take turns and say it aloud: "You go, I go!" It adds rhythm and cooperation.

Week 4: Self-Expression & Identity

1. All About Me Drawing

Invite your child to draw themselves. Ask, "What do you love about you?"

2. Dress-Up Parade

Try on fun clothes or costumes. Let your child describe who they are.

3. I Am Statements

Mindful Moment

Say together: "I am strong. I am kind. I am learning."

Why it matters

Reinforces positive self-image and confidence.

Try this

Ask them to make their own "I am" phrase.

4. My Favourites Game

Ask about favourite color, toy, snack. Celebrate their preferences.

5. Name Dance

Spell out their name in movement: jump for J, tiptoe for T!

Parent Hack of the Week – The "I See You" Phrase

When your child does something independently or creatively, say, "I see you figuring it out. I love that!" It validates effort over perfection.

Life Skill of the Month: Belonging & Identity

Your child is discovering who they are and where they fit. This month, you can nurture that by:

- Sharing family stories, photos, and traditions
- Naming emotions out loud and making room for them
- Encouraging group play with gentle turns and teamwork
- Celebrating your child's ideas, interests, and style Belonging builds confidence. It starts with being seen, heard, and loved for who they are.

Reflect & Recharge
Parent Story – The Self-Portrait Surprise

Zara drew a big circle, then added curls and two tiny hands. She said, "It's me! I like me!" I nearly cried. It wasn't the drawing—it was the joy in her voice. She saw herself, and she liked what she saw.

— Aria, mom of a 44-month-old

What if my child doesn't want to share or participate in group play?

- Respect their pace—some kids warm up slowly

- Practice teamwork at home in low-pressure ways

- Narrate feelings: "You want to play alone now. That's okay."

- Offer parallel play and let connection unfold naturally

Mindful Reminder

Belonging starts with being known. Every name remembered, every feeling echoed, every story shared says: "You matter." Keep showing up. That's what makes them feel at home in the world.

Month 45: Little Planners, Growing Minds

Theme: Sequencing, planning, and real-world thinking

Week 1: Planning in Everyday Play

1. Snack Plan Game

Ask, "What do you want first: apples or crackers?" Let your child plan the snack order.

2. Toy Setup Time

Invite your child to choose 3 toys to set up before play begins.

3. "What Comes First?" Talk

Mindful Moment

Ask: "We brush, then what? Pyjamas!"

Why it matters

Builds sequencing and early routine memory.

Try this

Let your child finish the next step.

4. Morning Checklist Drawing

Draw simple pictures of morning steps. Let your child check them off.

5. Build-a-Scene

Offer blocks or figurines. Ask, "What do we need first to build a zoo?"

Parent Hack of the Week – The "Plan and Play" Trick

Start play by saying, "What's your idea? What should we do first?" It builds focus and ownership.

Week 2: Thinking in Steps

1. Laundry Sort Challenge

Ask, "Can we sort shirts, pants, and socks? What do we do first?"

2. Treasure Hunt Map

Draw a simple map. Follow it together to find a hidden toy.

3. Sound Step Story

Mindful Moment

Use sound words (clap, tap, stomp) and let your child arrange them into a sequence.

Why it matters

Combines rhythm, working memory, and planning.

Try this

Repeat and switch roles.

4. Routine Puzzle Time

Cut photos of daily routines. Ask, "Which comes first?"

5. Walk & Talk Plan

Go on a walk. Say, "Let's go here, then here, then home."

Parent Hack of the Week – The "What Next?" Prompt

Whenever there's a pause, ask, "What happens next?" It strengthens sequencing in real time.

Week 3: Motor Planning & Focus

1. Step-Hop Path Game

Make a path with pillows or mats. Create a pattern: step, hop, step...

2. Pour & Transfer Station

Let your child pour water or grains from one container to another. Ask them to plan their moves.

3. Slow-Mo Sequence

Mindful Moment

Say, "Let's brush in slow motion: up... down... rinse..."

Why it matters

Builds body-mind connection and thoughtful movement.

Try this

Use it during dressing or clean-up.

4. Jump-Then-Freeze Game

Jump, stop, pose. Then repeat.

5. Shape Build Plan

Give shapes or blocks and say, "Let's build a triangle tower! What first?"

Parent Hack of the Week – The "Show Me Your Plan" Phrase

Instead of jumping in, say, "Show me how you want to do it." Gives space to think, try, and adjust.

Week 4: Story Thinking & Pretend Plans

1. Picture Plan Stories

Use picture cards to create a sequence. Ask, "What's the story?"

2. Pretend Store Setup

Act out: "First we open shop. Then we sell!"

3. Story Sandwich Game

Mindful Moment

Say: "First the bunny slept... then... what?" Let them fill the middle.

Why it matters

Encourages imagination and flexible storytelling.

Try this

Use toys or snack items to act it out.

4. Costume Sequence Time

Dress in parts: "First the hat... then the cape!"

5. Dollhouse Plans

Ask, "Where should the baby sleep? What happens after that?"

Parent Hack of the Week – The "First, Then, Last" Talk

Use these three words in any story, routine, or play. They create a natural structure your child can grow with.

Life Skill of the Month: Sequencing & Planning

Your child is ready to build their thinking muscles by:

- Predicting steps in stories and routines
- Organizing tasks from start to finish
- Making choices and building play around them
- Beginning to understand time and order

Planning teaches patience, confidence, and focus. And it starts with tiny steps.

Reflect & Recharge
Parent Story – The Breakfast Builder

I asked Arjun what we should eat. He said, "Eggs first. Then toast. Then jam!" He even got out the plate. I realized it wasn't about food. It was about watching him organize his world—one thoughtful, tiny plan at a time.

— Kavita, mom of a 45-month-old

What if my child just rushes without planning?

- Use fun language: "Let's pretend we're slow-motion robots!"
- Give visual cues: "We do this first, then that."
- Celebrate each step completed, not just the end.

Mindful Reminder

Planning doesn't always look neat. But every time your child pauses, chooses, or adjusts—they're growing. Stay curious. Stay close. The steps will start to connect.

Month 46: Think, Talk, Try Again

Theme: Early reasoning, emotional flexibility, and self-regulation through playful thinking

Week 1: Thoughtful Choices & Emotional Language

1. Yes/No Debate Game

Ask silly questions: "Should dogs wear shoes?" Let your child argue yes or no—and why.

2. How Did That Feel? Walk

Recall a recent event (playdate, park, mealtime) and talk about how it felt. Ask, "What did your face look like then?"

3. Breathing Rainbow

Mindful Moment

Draw a rainbow with seven arches. Trace each with your finger while taking a slow breath.

Why it matters

Calms the body while focusing attention.

Try this

Use it during transitions or after overstimulation.

4. Feelings Puzzle Match

Draw faces with different emotions. Cut and mix halves. Let your child match and name them.

5. Which One Do You Choose?

Offer choices (book vs. walk, puzzle vs. drawing). After they choose, ask, "Why that one?"

Parent Hack of the Week – The "What Made You Pick That?" Question

After a choice or action, gently ask why. Toddlers love being seen as thinkers—it boosts both confidence and early logic.

Week 2: Planning, Patience & Follow-Through

1. 3-Step Dance Plan

Say, "Let's plan a dance: Jump, spin, clap!" Then perform it together.

2. Toy Rescue Plan

Tape a toy to a chair. Ask, "What should we do first?" Follow their plan—even if it's silly.

3. The Quiet Timer Game

Mindful Moment

Set a 1-minute timer and say, "Let's see how still we can be until the bell rings."

Why it matters

Teaches body control in a calm, fun way.

Try this

Use it as a reset button when energy runs high.

4. Puzzle Pick Challenge

Let your child choose a puzzle. Ask, "How will we finish it?" Let them take the lead.

5. Slow Snack Sort

Let them separate and count pieces: "Put three grapes here, two crackers there."

Parent Hack of the Week – The "Plan First, Play Later" Trick

Before jumping into something new, pause and say, "Let's make a plan." Even one step helps toddlers feel in charge of their actions.

Week 3: Real-World Routines & Confidence Builders

1. Getting Dressed Race

Set out two outfits. Let them choose, then time how long they take to dress (with help if needed).

2. Tidy Time Role Play

Pretend you're robots, chefs, or "clean-up superheroes" during chore routines.

3. The Reset Button Ritual

Mindful Moment

Say, "Let's hit the reset button!" Touch your forehead gently and take a deep breath together.

Why it matters

Turns meltdown moments into playful recovery.

Try this

Add a silly sound or gesture when things feel stuck.

4. Routine Sequencing Cards

Draw or print three steps of a task (brushing teeth, setting the table). Ask your child to put them in order.

5. Play-Work Station

Give a sponge, cloth, or brush and invite your child to "help" in real tasks like wiping or sorting.

Parent Hack of the Week – The "You're the Coach" Strategy

Let your child guide you through a task they know well. Say, "Tell me what to do next!" This builds autonomy and sequencing skills.

Week 4: Flexible Thinking & Conversation Confidence

1. Opposites Sort Game

Mix toy pairs: hot/cold, big/small, wet/dry. Ask, "Can you sort these opposites?"

2. Story Switch-Up

Read a familiar story and change one detail. Ask, "What if the bear was purple?"

3. Emotion Charades

Mindful Moment

Act out a feeling with no words. Let your child guess, then switch.

Why it matters

Teaches body cues and empathy.

Try this

Use unexpected emotions like "embarrassed" or "proud."

4. Curious Questions Corner

Create a space for "Why" questions. Write them on paper together. Try answering a few each day.

5. Toy Talk Theatre

Use toys to hold a conversation: "Hello, Bunny. What did you do today?"

Parent Hack of the Week – The "What Else Could It Be?" Game

Hold up a spoon, block, or shoe and ask, "What else could this be?" Imaginative answers show flexible thinking—and toddlers love it.

Life Skill of the Month: Reasoning with Flexibility

This month, you're building your child's ability to *think through* situations—not just react:

- Model thinking out loud: "I spilled it, so first I need a towel…"
- Use pretend or real plans before action: "Let's make a 3-step plan!"
- Encourage "silly logic": "What if cats could cook?" to strengthen creative reasoning
- Let your child guide a routine or activity, asking questions along the way

The goal isn't perfection—it's confidence in thinking and trying again.

Reflect & Recharge
Parent Story – The Big Why

Leo kept asking, "Why do birds fly?" and "Why can't cars jump?" At first I answered. Then one day I said, "Why do *you* think?" He blinked, thought hard, and said, "Because they got feathers and wings!" It was joy, pride, and wonder all at once.

— Nina, mom of a 46-month-old

What if my child resists planning or always wants to change the game?

- That's flexible thinking in motion—it's a great sign!
- Let them take the lead sometimes, but keep gentle boundaries
- Use routines as anchors, not limits: "Let's plan snack time *your* way!"

> **Mindful Reminder**
>
> A thinking child is a powerful learner. Let them make plans, change their minds, and think out loud. It's not chaos—it's growth. You're not raising a follower. You're raising a thinker.

Month 47: Builders of Big Ideas

Theme: Creative thinking, visual memory, and playful exploration of real-world roles

Week 1: See, Remember, Recreate

1. Shape City Build

Show a picture of a city or building. Give blocks or recycled materials and say, "Let's make our own!"

2. Memory Tray Game

Place 5 familiar items on a tray. Cover them, take one away, and ask, "What's missing?"

3. Picture It Pause

Mindful Moment

Close your eyes together. Say, "Let's picture your bedroom. What color is your bed? Where's your teddy?"

Why it matters

Builds visual memory and internal reflection.

Try this

Use during wind-down time to gently shift to calm.

4. Match & Mix Puzzle

Mix two puzzles. Let your child find what goes where. Say, "Hmm, that looks right—how can we check?"

5. Mirror Drawing Challenge

Fold paper. You draw one side of a shape or picture. Let your child complete the other half.

Parent Hack of the Week – The "Picture in Your Head" Prompt

When your child loses something or forgets a step, ask, "Can you make a picture of it in your head?" Watch their inner world light up.

Week 2: Everyday Math & Logic

1. Snack Pattern Game

Lay out snacks in a pattern: cracker, raisin, cracker... Ask, "What comes next?"

2. Biggest to Smallest Hunt

Line up toys by size. Ask, "Which is biggest? Smallest?" Mix them and repeat.

3. Step-By-Step Thinking

Mindful Moment

During any task (setting the table, brushing teeth), talk aloud: "First this... now that..."

Why it matters

Boosts sequencing and executive functioning.

Try this

Let your child take over the narration next time.

4. Dot & Count Painting

Use cotton swabs or stamps. Count dots aloud as you paint.

5. Guess & Check Estimation Game

Ask, "How many blocks will fit in this box?" Test it and count together.

Parent Hack of the Week – The "Oops! Let's Count Again" Trick

Make small counting errors on purpose. Let your child catch and correct you—it builds confidence and sharpens number sense.

Week 3: Pretend Roles & Empathy Building

1. Roleplay a Job

Pretend to be a chef, teacher, or doctor. Let your child lead the routine and set the rules.

2. Feelings for Others Game

Look at storybook characters or toys. Ask, "How do they feel? Why?"

3. The "Helper Heart" Pause

Mindful Moment

Before play, ask: "What's one way we can be helpful today?" Keep it small—like sharing a toy or making someone smile.

Why it matters

Centers kindness as part of everyday thinking.

Try this

Celebrate the helper moment later in the day.

4. Friendship Problem-Solving Roleplay

Act out scenarios: "What if your friend wants the same toy?" Talk through solutions together.

5. Dress-Up Conversation Parade

Wear silly hats or costumes. Greet each other and start pretend conversations.

Parent Hack of the Week – The "What Would They Do?" Prompt

When emotions rise, ask: "What would Firefighter Max (or another pretend character) do right now?" It shifts the frame from reactive to reflective.

Week 4: Sound, Rhythm & Expression

1. Rhyme Hunt

Say a word like "cat." Ask, "What rhymes with cat?" Use toys, books, or nonsense words.

2. Make Your Own Song

Pick a routine (washing hands, getting dressed) and make up a silly song about it together.

3. Sound Breaths

Mindful Moment

Breathe in slowly, and exhale making a soft sound like "shhh," "mmm," or "ahh."

Why it matters

Teaches breath control and emotional regulation through sensory feedback.

Try this

Use when transitioning or calming down.

4. Echo Rhythms Game

Clap or tap a simple rhythm. Let your child echo it. Then switch roles.

5. Emotion Song Time

Sing a familiar tune using feeling words: "If you're happy and you know it," "I'm feeling sleepy today…"

Parent Hack of the Week – The "Sing It Instead" Trick

When your child resists instructions, sing them instead: "Let's pick up toys, let's pick up toys!"—it softens resistance and keeps the mood light.

Life Skill of the Month: Creative Recall

This month is about remembering in motion—helping your child take what they saw, heard, or felt… and bring it back with their own twist.

- Recreate scenes from memory using blocks, drawings, or pretend play
- Play recall games: "What did we see at the park?" "What came after breakfast?"
- Let your child invent endings to familiar stories
- Encourage them to tell their version of the day, in any order

Creative recall powers everything from memory and storytelling to flexible thinking. It's not just about what they remember—but how they bring it to life.

Reflect & Recharge
Parent Story – The Half-Finished Drawing

Milo stared at my half-heart drawing and said, "I'll do the other side." He made it a rainbow heart and added his name. I didn't expect that—it was better than perfect. He didn't just copy. He completed.

— Elise, mom of a 47-month-old

What if my child forgets things often?

- That's normal! Recall skills are just blooming now.

- Practice with small routines: "What's the next step?"

- Give visual cues or let them take photos to remember

- Celebrate the effort to remember—not just accuracy

Mindful Reminder

Observation is the root of wonder. When your child stops to *notice,* they start to understand. Every pause, picture, and playful recall builds not just memory—but meaning.

Month 48: Creative Thinkers & Tiny Problem-Solvers

Theme: Imagination, persistence, and early innovation

Week 1: Tinker & Test

1. Build & Balance Time

Use blocks or recycled boxes to make towers and bridges. "Will it fall or hold?"

2. What If Tool Box

Offer safe items like measuring spoons, clothespins, or a funnel. Ask, "What can we make with these?"

3. Tinker Talk

Mindful Moment

Say aloud, "Let's try this... Hmm, what now?"

Why it matters

Models flexible thinking and experimentation.

Try this

Narrate your own trial-and-error as you play alongside.

4. Loose Parts Creation

Give random materials (buttons, bottle caps, paper scraps) and say, "What can you invent?"

5. Drop & Bounce Test

Drop different objects and guess which bounce. Ask why.

Parent Hack of the Week – The Inventor's Table

Set aside a small tray or corner for "invention parts." Label it and watch what your child begins to build.

Week 2: Imagination in Motion

1. Story Step Adventure

Turn movement into a tale: "We're stepping over lava! Now crawling through a tunnel!"

2. Pretend Passport Play

Make simple paper passports and "travel" to places. "What do we see in the jungle?"

3. Body Improv Game

Mindful Moment

Say an object: "Washing machine!" Let your child move like it. Then switch roles.

Why it matters

Encourages creativity, body awareness, and role flexibility.

Try this

Laugh together—goofy movement lowers pressure.

4. Sound Story Challenge

Tell a story using only sounds or actions. Let your child guess what's happening.

5. Animal Shadow Parade

Use flashlights and stuffed animals to make shadows. Create a parade of creatures on the wall.

Parent Hack of the Week – The "What Else Could It Be?" Game

Any object—sock, spoon, box—ask, "What else could it be?" Keep the ideas flowing and the giggles coming.

Week 3: Language, Logic & Expression

1. Mystery Sound Match

Make sounds (clap, tap, jingle) and guess the source.

2. Question of the Day

Ask fun ones: "Would you rather fly or swim?" Talk through answers.

3. "Tell Me More" Time

Mindful Moment

When your child shares something, ask, "Can you tell me more?"

Why it matters

Builds descriptive thinking and self-expression.

Try this

Use during car rides or calm snack times.

4. Pattern Play

Make simple sequences (sock-shoe-sock) and ask what comes next.

5. Backwards Story Game

Start with the ending: "The monster went to bed. What happened before that?"

Parent Hack of the Week – The Banana Phone Trick

Grab a banana (or toy phone) and make it ring. "Hello? Is it your idea calling?" Pretend play boosts speech and listening.

Week 4: Working Together & Taking Turns

1. Side-by-Side Station

Set up a task to do together (sorting laundry, matching lids). Talk about roles.

2. Idea Builder Game

Start drawing a house. Let your child add to it, then switch again.

3. Pause & Pass

Mindful Moment

During play, hold up a hand and say, "Let's pause and see who's ready."

Why it matters

Builds social rhythm and patience.

Try this

Practice before games or shared snacks.

4. Compliment Circle Time

Take turns saying nice things: "You're kind. You're fun to play with."

5. Co-Build Challenge

Work together on a big puzzle, train track, or sculpture.

Parent Hack of the Week – The "Let's Plan It Together" Phrase

Before a new activity, say: "Want to plan this with me?" Including your child builds cooperation and motivation.

Life Skill of the Month: Creative Collaboration

This month is all about working *with* others—sharing space, sharing ideas, and building together:

- Start team tasks like puzzles or snack prep
- Take turns telling stories or adding ideas
- Invite your child to plan a mini project with you
- Praise flexible thinking: "That was such a creative way to help!"

When kids create *together*, they learn to listen, adapt, and lead.

Reflect & Recharge
Parent Story – The Double Builder Breakthrough

Asha and her cousin were building with blocks when things got tense. One wanted a tall tower, the other a tunnel. I nearly stepped in—but then Asha said, "Let's build both!" They turned the design sideways, made a tunnel under the tower, and clapped. I realized she didn't just solve a problem—she created something better.

— Mira, mom of a 48-month-old

What if my child insists on their idea only?

- Celebrate the idea, then add: "Let's try yours AND mine."
- Offer turn-taking: "First your way, then mine."
- Model flexible phrases: "I hadn't thought of that!"

Mindful Reminder

Imagination doesn't live in isolation—it flourishes in connection. Every shared plan, silly twist, or compromise is shaping a child who can invent *and* include. That's where true creativity begins.

Year 4: Celebrating Another Year of Incredible Growth!

Congratulations! You and your child have completed yet another remarkable year of learning, exploration, and growth. Your little one is becoming more independent, expressive, and curious about the world—and it's all because of your love, patience, and unwavering support. **You are doing an amazing job!**

Year 4 has likely been filled with endless questions, growing confidence, and an eagerness to learn and try new things. There may have been challenges—big emotions, newfound independence, and boundless energy—but through it all, **your guidance and encouragement have helped shape your child into a bright and capable little individual.**

Now is the perfect time to **track and rate your child's progress** using the **Milestone Tracker**, celebrating their achievements and identifying areas for further growth.

As you step into Year 5, new opportunities for learning, creativity, and social growth await. Keep believing in yourself, trust your instincts, and most importantly, **enjoy these precious moments.** Your love and dedication continue to build a strong foundation for your child's future.

You've got this! Congratulations on completing Year 4! Your efforts are shaping a bright, confident, and happy child, and the best is yet to come.

Your Child's Developmental Tracker

Every child develops at their own pace. These trackers are designed to provide a structured way to observe and support your child's growth, but they should not be seen as rigid timelines. It's completely normal for some children to excel in certain areas while taking more time in others.

How to Use the Tracker

- **Rate on a scale of 0-5** based on your child's current abilities in each category.

- **No need to rush or compare!** Some children might be more advanced in speech but take longer with motor skills, and that's completely fine.

- **Use it as a guide**, not a test. If your child isn't yet meeting certain milestones, observe their progress over time instead of worrying.

- **Celebrate small wins!** Any progress, no matter how small, is valuable.

What If My Child is Behind in Some Areas?

- **Variability is normal** – Development is not linear, and children often leap ahead in some skills while taking more time in others.

- **Support their growth** through interactive play, reading, conversations, and hands-on activities that align with their interests.

- **Patience is key** – Keep engaging them in activities without pressure or comparisons.

- **Seek guidance if necessary** – If you have concerns, consulting a paediatrician or child development expert can provide reassurance and strategies for support.

Encouraging a Positive Learning Experience

This tracker is meant to **empower you as a parent** and help you understand your child's unique journey. Focus on their strengths, provide encouragement, and create a nurturing environment where learning feels fun and natural. Every child has their own timeline – trust the process, and enjoy watching them grow!

Remember: Progress over perfection!

Milestones Tracker:

Domain	Emerging Milestones	Rating (0-5)
Communication & Language	Speaks in full 4–6 word sentences, shares ideas, asks questions	
	Uses descriptive words and expands vocabulary through stories and play	
	Follows 2–3 step directions independently	
	Begins using positional language (under, next to, behind) and emotion words (proud, frustrated)	
	Tells simple stories with a beginning and end	
	Recognizes familiar letters, sounds, or words in books, signs, or names	
Social & Emotional Development	Forms friendships and plays cooperatively (turn-taking, group play)	
	Understands basic rules and routines; transitions with more ease	
	Names and expresses emotions with more detail ("I'm nervous, not sad.")	
	Uses problem-solving in peer conflicts ("Let's take turns.")	
	Demonstrates growing empathy and awareness of others' feelings	

Cognitive & Thinking Skills	Solves more complex puzzles, builds with intention (e.g., towers, patterns)	
	Sorts, matches, and classifies by multiple features (size, function, shape)	
	Begins sequencing (first/then/last) and early logic ("If it's wet, it rained.")	
	Remembers steps in routines and stories, retells events with detail	
	Explores early math naturally—counting, comparing, measuring in play	
Fine & Gross Motor Skills	Hops on one foot, climbs, balances on a beam or line	
	Throws and catches medium-sized balls with growing accuracy	
	Holds pencil or crayon with finger grip, begins forming shapes or letters	
	Uses scissors to cut along lines or around shapes	
	Independently dresses, buttons, zips, and feeds self with utensils	
Play, Creativity & Independence	Plays out real-life roles (doctor, cook, teacher) with rich pretend play	
	Invents stories, songs, or characters during unstructured play	
	Helps with daily chores and routines (setting table, tidying up)	
	Shows pride in helping or completing tasks independently	
	Begins expressing preferences in activities and asking for responsibilities	

This year brought big ideas, brave choices, and a deepening sense of self.

Pause to see how much your child — and you — have grown inside and out.

Every moment mattered, even the messy ones.

This chapter ends, but the heart of your parenting story beats stronger than ever.

Now, as Year 5 begins, a new kind of magic unfolds — where independence takes root and imagination soars.

Let's step into this next chapter with wonder, wisdom, and a whole lot of heart.

Year 5: The Ready-for-the-World Year

Early Independence, Self-Regulation & School Readiness

Quote

"Let the child be the scriptwriter, the director and the actor in his own play."

— *Magda Gerber*

Mantra

I give them roots and wings. This is the year we both become ready.

M.I.N.D. for Year 5

Moments That Matter

Stay close even as they step into new spaces — your presence still matters.

Intentional Interaction

Foster independence with encouragement and open-ended challenges.

Nurture Through Love

Support their growing need for autonomy with loving boundaries.

Daily Growth

Each day prepares their body, brain, and heart for the world ahead.

Welcome to Year 5: Ready for the World

Theme: Confidence, Curiosity & Real-Life Readiness

"Your child isn't just growing—they're stepping into who they are."

This year marks a powerful shift—from playful exploration to purposeful engagement. Your child is now a full-fledged little thinker with big feelings, brave ideas, and a deepening sense of self. They're starting to ask why, imagine what if, and navigate friendships, routines, and emotions with growing independence.

And you? You're not fading into the background—you're becoming the trusted guide, steady cheerleader, and wise coach they need by their side.

What's New in Year 5

- The *Life Skill + Real-Life Readiness* section is now unified—giving you a clear lens into what your child is building each month and how it matters for real-world growth.

- Plus, enjoy **a new *Game of the Month***—a playful, purposeful way to boost learning through connection.

- **Same Flexible Rhythm**: 4 themed weeks, 5 core activities per week, 1–2 Mindful Moments, a sticky Parent Hack, a relatable Parent Story, and a science-backed Mindful Reminder.

- **No Pressure Learning**: No drills, no worksheets, no rush—because real learning is already happening. Through play, stories, problem-solving, and connection, your child is building lasting understanding in the most powerful ways.

What to Expect This Year

By age 5, many children begin to:

- Express complex thoughts and ask layered questions

- Tell full stories, understand time, and follow multi-step routines

- Show leadership in group play and greater emotional maturity

- Solve problems creatively and explore big ideas with confidence

- Build deeper friendships and stronger self-identity

- Strengthen motor coordination, independence, and decision-making

These aren't checkboxes—they're emerging strengths on your child's one-of-a-kind path.

How to Use This Guide

- **Pick what fits.** You don't have to do everything—choose what works for your family's rhythm and your child's interests.

- **Start with the Life Skill.** Each month's theme gives you a focus—watch how it connects to real-world growth in the combined *Life Skill + Readiness* section.

- **Try the Game of the Month.** It's an easy, joyful way to reinforce learning through laughter and connection.

- **Reflect & Recharge.** The final section each month is your grounding space—because mindful parenting starts with feeling seen.

- **Above all:** Keep showing up with curiosity and compassion. That's where all the magic happens.

This Year Is About...

- Encouraging independence *without losing connection*

- Growing emotional language, social flexibility, and empathy

- Building focus, self-regulation, and real-world responsibility

- Letting curiosity lead—and trusting that deep learning will follow

You're not just getting ready for school—you're nurturing readiness for *life*.

Let's begin Year 5—where curiosity meets capability, and confidence takes flight.

Month 49: Confident Communicators

Theme: *Building expressive language, listening skills, and conversational flow*

Week 1: Everyday Expression

1. Feelings in Full Sentences

Model and prompt full-sentence feeling statements: "I feel happy because we played outside."

2. Talk About the Day

At breakfast or bedtime, ask: "What happened first? What did you like most?"

3. Conversation Stones

Mindful Moment

Use small stones or pictures. Each person picks one and shares a thought or story.

Why it matters

Promotes turn-taking, memory recall, and thoughtful expression.

Try this

Use real-life objects like a leaf, key, or toy car to spark conversation.

4. Describing Game

Pick an object and describe it together without naming it. Let the other guess.

5. Voice Volume Practice

Use a soft toy or whisper zone to practice "indoor voice" vs. "outdoor voice."

Parent Hack of the Week – The "Say More" Prompt

When your child says something short, pause and say, "Say more about that." It invites richer conversation without correction.

Week 2: Storytelling & Sequencing

1. Draw Then Tell

Let your child draw a picture. Ask, "What's happening here? What comes next?"

2. Story Chain

Take turns adding one line to a story: "Once upon a time..." (Parent says one line, child continues.)

3. Picture Pause

Mindful Moment

Look at a family photo or picture book. Ask: "What do you remember about this? How did you feel?"

Why it matters

Connects language, memory, and emotional reflection.

Try this

Use a favourite toy or birthday photo for deeper recall.

4. Sequence Cards Game

Mix up 3-4 cards that show a simple routine (brushing teeth, making a sandwich). Ask your child to put them in order.

5. What Happened Before?

During daily play or storytelling, ask: "What happened before this part?"

Parent Hack of the Week – The "Story Sandwich" Trick

Say, "Tell me what happened first, then what, and finally what?" This simple formula helps kids begin building narrative structure.

Week 3: Questions, Answers & Curiosity

1. Wonder Wall

Create a space for your child's questions. Write them down and revisit: "Why do bees buzz?"

2. Yes/No Riddle Game

Think of an object. Let your child ask yes/no questions until they guess it.

3. Slow Listening Pause

Mindful Moment

Say, "Let's listen without interrupting. Let's try to hear everything before we speak."

Why it matters

Supports patience, active listening, and emotional regulation.

Try this

Take turns with silly topics to keep it light.

4. Ask the Toy Game

Have a stuffed animal "ask" your child about their day. Let your child answer and create questions too.

5. Question of the Day

At breakfast, ask something fun: "Would you rather fly or swim like a fish?"

Parent Hack of the Week – The "Curiosity Clock"

Pick one moment a day to pause and say, "Let's get curious." Whether it's a tree, sound, or action—showing curiosity teaches it.

Week 4: Conversations in the Real World

1. Grocery List Talk

Involve your child in naming or describing grocery items. Ask, "What else do we need?"

2. Pretend Phone Calls

Roleplay calling Grandma, a favourite toy, or even a firefighter. Practice greetings and storytelling.

3. Mirror Words

Mindful Moment

Stand face-to-face and repeat simple phrases with matching expression.

Why it matters

Builds speech clarity, emotional expression, and rhythm.

Try this

Switch roles. Let your child lead the words.

4. Thank You Practice

Use pretend or real moments to model and practice "thank you," "please," and polite conversation.

5. Role-Play Problem Solving

Act out real-life moments: "What do we say if someone bumps into us?"

Parent Hack of the Week – The "You Start, I'll Follow" Trick

Let your child begin the conversation or activity. It empowers them and builds confidence in social interaction.

Life Skill + Real-Life Readiness: Expressive Communication

This month, your child is learning to share more than just needs—they're beginning to express memories, ideas, questions, and emotions. Whether it's a classroom, a family dinner, or a playdate, confident communication sets the stage for:

- Making and keeping friends
- Understanding and expressing needs
- Navigating instructions and group settings

Support this growth by:

- Modelling descriptive and emotion-rich language
- Encouraging longer answers without pressure
- Pausing to really listen—then responding with connection

Even small exchanges build lifelong communication skills.

Game of the Month: Picture Charades

Cut out or draw simple pictures (a cat, a sun, a toothbrush). Take turns acting them out while the other guesses. Add silly twists—try it with sound only or silently.

Why it works: Encourages expressive language, turn-taking, and fun through communication.

Reflect & Recharge
Parent Story – From Questions to Confidence

"My daughter used to just point or say one word. Last week, she told me a full story about what happened at the park—who was there, what she did, and how she felt. I realized she's not just talking—she's connecting."

— *Jenny, mom of 49 month old*

What if my child doesn't want to talk much?

- Keep modelling warm, patient conversations

- Use toys or pretend to take the pressure off

- Celebrate effort: "That was a great sentence! I loved hearing your idea."

> ### Mindful Reminder
>
> Connection comes before conversation. The more safe, seen, and heard your child feels, the more freely their words will flow. You don't have to pull the words out—you just have to open the door.

Month 50: Everyday Explorers

Theme: *Real-world thinking, observation, and initiative*

Week 1: Observing the World Around Us

1. Color Clue Hunt

Ask your child to find three red things, then three green, and so on. Vary the room or go outside.

2. Texture Detective

Let them touch and describe items: smooth spoon, bumpy rock, soft cloth.

3. Listen & Label

Mindful Moment

Sit quietly for a minute. After, ask, "What sounds did you hear?" Help label: birds, footsteps, wind.

Why it matters

Builds attention and auditory memory.

Try this

Add a challenge—"Did you hear anything that surprised you?"

4. Same & Different Snack Sort

Use 2-3 snacks (crackers, raisins, fruit). Compare: "Which is crunchier? Bigger? Sweeter?"

5. Shadow Walk

Go outside and find your shadow. Watch how it moves and grows. Try tracing it with chalk.

Parent Hack of the Week – The "I Spy Differently" Trick

Say, "I spy something round... or something that smells sweet!" This shifts focus from object names to qualities and characteristics.

Week 2: Practical Life & Independence

1. Snack Maker Challenge

Offer 2-3 options and let your child create their own plate. Ask, "What do you want to eat first?"

2. Mini Sorting Station

Set out clean socks, lids, or utensils. Ask your child to sort by size, type, or color.

3. The Pause Before Help

Mindful Moment

Say: "Do you want help or want to try first?"

Why it matters

Builds self-trust and autonomy.

Try this

Wait 10 seconds before stepping in.

4. Laundry Assistant Game

Ask your child to find all the shirts, or all socks, from a basket.

5. Watering Routine

Let your child water a plant each day. Say, "You're in charge of helping it grow!"

Parent Hack of the Week – The "You Lead" Script

Use phrases like, "What do *you* think comes next?" or "Show me how you would do it." It empowers your child to take initiative.

Week 3: Building Thinking Routines

1. What Happens Next? Game

During a task or routine, pause and ask, "What should we do now? Then what?"

2. Pattern Play

Make simple color or shape patterns with toys or snacks. Ask your child to copy, then create their own.

3. One Thing at a Time

Mindful Moment

Choose a task (brushing teeth, putting on shoes). Say: "Let's focus only on this one thing until it's done."

Why it matters

Strengthens focus and reduces overwhelm.

Try this

Add a calm rhythm: "Step one... step two... all done."

4. Story Steps Drawing

Ask your child to draw what happened first, next, and last in a favourite story or real-life event.

5. Compare & Decide

Hold up two outfits, toys, or snacks. Ask: "What's different? Which one do you pick and why?"

Parent Hack of the Week – The Thinking Out Loud Trick

Narrate your reasoning aloud: "I'm putting my keys here so I remember them later." It models thoughtful decision-making.

Week 4: Nature, Movement & Curiosity

1. Animal Moves Game

Move like different animals: slither like a snake, jump like a frog, stretch like a cat.

2. Outside Object Collection

Gather 5 things from nature (leaf, stick, pebble). Sort, describe, and create a story with them.

3. Wind Watch

Mindful Moment

Go outside and notice: "Can you see the wind moving anything?"

Why it matters

Builds observation and environmental awareness.

Try this

Add a scarf or pinwheel to visualize it.

4. Up/Down Walk

On a walk or stairs, say: "Let's count each step up... now down!" Add movement vocabulary.

5. Treasure Hunt with Clues

Hide a toy. Give simple verbal clues: "It's under something soft... near your shoes!"

3. Let Me Try First Pause

Mindful Moment

Ask, "Want to try first and then I'll help if needed?"

Why it matters

Builds initiative while showing support.

Try this

Step back physically to give them space to act.

4. Toy Organizer Time

Ask: "How should we put the toys back today? By color? By type?"

5. Water Plant Duty

Let your child be in charge of watering a small plant.

Parent Hack of the Week – The "Job Card Jar"

Create cards with simple tasks (set table, tidy shoes, water plants). Let your child pick one as their daily job—and celebrate follow-through.

Week 2: Following Through & Feeling Capable

1. Morning Ready Checklist

Draw or print simple steps: get dressed, brush teeth, pack bag. Let your child check them off.

2. Clean-up Song Sprint

Play a favourite song and tidy up together before it ends.

3. "I Did It" Reflection

Mindful Moment

Ask, "What did you do all by yourself today?" Then pause to truly acknowledge it.

Why it matters

Builds pride and internal motivation.

Try this

Say, "That was a big help. Thank you."

4. Shoe Spot Leader

Create a shoe area and ask your child to guide everyone in using it.

5. Lid Match Task

Give your child a drawer of containers and lids. Let them sort and match independently.

Parent Hack of the Week – The "Start with You" Approach

Say, "I'll do one, then you do one." Whether it's folding towels or putting away groceries, starting together helps them stay engaged.

Week 3: Everyday Problem Solving

1. Snack Picker Plan

Offer 3 snacks. Let them choose one and explain their decision.

2. Fix-It Toy Time

Use toys with loose wheels or puzzles with missing pieces. Ask, "What can we do about this?"

3. The Pause-and-Plan Prompt

Mindful Moment

Before rushing in, say: "Let's pause. What could we try first?"

Why it matters

Strengthens planning and self-direction.

Try this

Use a hand gesture like a slow-down wave to signal the pause.

4. Problem Roleplay

Act out mini dilemmas: "We both want the red cup! What now?"

5. Daily Choices Chart

Let them pick from a visual chart for clothes, snacks, or bedtime books.

Parent Hack of the Week – The "What's Your Idea?" Phrase

Instead of solving the issue, say, "Hmm, what's your idea?" Toddlers love being asked and often surprise you with clever thinking.

Week 4: Personal Pride & Self-Leadership

1. Mirror Motivation Time

Let them look in the mirror and say something they did well: "I zipped my coat!"

2. Show & Teach Moment

Ask your child to show a younger sibling or stuffed toy how to do a task.

3. Proud Pause

Mindful Moment

Pause after a task and say, "Look what you did! Let's just notice that for a second."

Why it matters

Helps your child soak in their achievement and feel truly seen.

Try this

Take a deep breath together while looking at the finished job.

4. Responsibility Sticker Chart

Add a sticker after each completed job. Celebrate weekly with a dance or high five.

5. "I Can Help!" Roleplay

Act out real-world moments where they offer help: opening doors, handing things, comforting someone.

Parent Hack of the Week – The "Pride Jar" Trick

At the end of the day, each person adds a pebble or button for something they felt proud of. Watch the jar grow over time.

Life Skill + Real-Life Readiness: Responsibility in Daily Life

This month is all about building a child who *wants* to help—not just *can*. When your child takes ownership of small tasks, they:

- Feel confident, valued, and capable
- Learn to follow through even when something isn't fun
- Build early executive function: planning, doing, reflecting

Responsibility is best built through trust, structure, and lots of joyful praise. Your belief in them becomes the voice in their own head.

Game of the Month: Task Race Relay

Make a list of 3 simple tasks: put away a toy, match socks, bring a spoon. Time how long it takes! Let your child make the next list.

Why it works: Makes chores fun, builds memory, and introduces time-awareness.

Reflect & Recharge
Parent Story – The Snack Hero Moment

"We were running late and I dropped everything while packing lunch. Without a word, Kiyaan picked up the spoon and said, 'I'll help.' That moment told me he wasn't just watching me all these months—he was becoming part of it."

— Ruchi, Mom of 51 month old

What if my child refuses to help or gets distracted halfway?

- Offer choices: "Which job do you want to start with?"

- Break it down: One small task feels doable

- Use play: Pretend you're robots or cleaning superheroes

Mindful Reminder

Children thrive when trusted. Letting them help isn't about perfection—it's about believing in their ability. Even small responsibilities plant the seeds of self-worth and contribution.

Let the little helper inside them shine.

Month 52: Bold Voices, Calm Choices

Theme: Communication, decision-making, and emotional regulation

Week 1: Everyday Choices & Confidence

1. Snack Choice Talk

Offer two snack options. Ask, "Which one do you want today and why?"

2. Yes/No Roleplay

Take turns saying yes or no to silly suggestions. "Should we eat socks for lunch?"

3. Stop and Breathe Before Choosing

Mindful Moment

Say, "Let's take one breath before we decide."

Why it matters

Encourages pause before impulse.

Try this

Add a gentle hand signal as your decision-pause cue.

4. Pick the Plan Game

Ask, "Should we tidy first or do the puzzle first? You choose."

5. Which Story First?

Let them pick the order of bedtime books.

Parent Hack of the Week – The "What's Your Pick?" Trick

Use this daily: "What's your pick?" It turns decisions into confident, thoughtful moments—even with small things.

Week 2: Clear Words, Strong Feelings

1. Big Feeling Cards

Show feeling faces. Ask, "What do you feel today?"

2. Feeling Sound Match

Make a sound (growl, sigh, laugh) and match it to a feeling.

3. My Calm Place Visualization

Mindful Moment

Guide your child to close their eyes and imagine a cosy, safe place.

Why it matters

Helps regulate emotions using imagination.

Try this

Ask afterward, "What did you see in your calm place?"

4. Talk It Out Roleplay

Pretend a toy is upset. Say, "How can they say what they need?"

5. Feeling Switch Game

Act out changing from one emotion to another (happy to sleepy, silly to calm).

Parent Hack of the Week – The "Try the Words First" Cue

When your child is upset, say: "Try your words first." Then wait. This encourages emotional clarity over reaction.

Week 3: Listening & Understanding

1. Whisper Directions Game

Whisper a task ("Tap your toes, then clap!"). Let them listen closely.

2. Tell Me More Time

When they share something, say, "Tell me more!" and really listen.

3. Echo the Feeling

Mindful Moment

Reflect what you hear: "You sound frustrated. That makes sense."

Why it matters

Builds emotional intelligence and feeling-seen moments.

Try this

Mirror their facial expression for empathy.

4. Book Pause Questions

While reading, pause to ask, "Why do you think they did that?"

5. Back-and-Forth Build

Take turns telling one line of a story. See where it goes!

Parent Hack of the Week – The "Look + Listen" Trick

Say: "I'm looking at you and listening." Model focused attention—it teaches them to do the same.

Week 4: Calming Tools & Brave Talk

1. Calm-Down Basket

Let your child help create a small bin with calming tools: soft toy, squishy ball, calm-down jar.

2. Brave Voice Practice

Practice asking for what they need: "Can I have a turn?" "I don't like that."

3. Breath Buddy Pause

Mindful Moment

Use a soft toy on their tummy to watch it rise and fall as they breathe.

Why it matters

Builds regulation through body awareness.

Try this

Use before transitions or tough moments.

4. "Not Yet" Talk

Reframe frustration by saying: "Not yet... but you're getting there."

5. Create Your Own Calm Song

Make up a short song together for use during meltdowns or hard transitions.

Parent Hack of the Week – The Calm Choice Phrase

Say: "Do you want a breath, a hug, or quiet time?" This gives power *and* calm in moments of intensity.

Life Skill of the Month: Communicating with Confidence

Your child is learning to:

- Make thoughtful choices and explain them
- Express emotions clearly and safely

- Listen with care and speak with intention
- Use strategies to calm down instead of acting out

These are lifelong skills that shape how they show up at school, at home, and in friendships. Your modelling, patience, and space to practice are the secret sauce.

Game of the Month: Emotion Freeze Dance

Play music and pause it randomly. Shout an emotion: "Happy!" or "Tired!" Your child must freeze and act it out.

Why it works: Boosts emotion recognition, movement, and fun regulation.

Reflect & Recharge Parent Story – The Calm Words Moment

"Tisha had a big meltdown when I took the markers away. But this time, she said, 'I'm mad because I wasn't done.' It stopped me in my tracks. We breathed, and she got to finish her picture calmly. She didn't need to shout—she needed words."

— *Navita, Mom of 52 month old.*

What if my child always defaults to whining or yelling?

- Model it: "You can say, 'I'm mad because...'"
- Wait it out gently—don't jump to fix, let them try words
- Praise any effort: "You used your words—that was awesome."

Mindful Reminder

Words are tools—but learning to use them takes time. Each small moment where you wait, model, and listen is shaping a communicator who feels heard, respected, and capable. Let their bold voice grow gently.

Month 53: Strong Bodies, Flexible Minds

Theme: *Physical coordination, perseverance, and trying new things*

Week 1: Movement with Purpose

1. Jump Count Game

Jump and count aloud. Add actions: "2 jumps, then a spin!"

2. Obstacle Path Play

Set up cushions, tape lines, or toys for jumping, crawling, or balancing.

3. Slow Walk, Big Feel

Mindful Moment

Walk slowly heel-to-toe, feeling each step.

Why it matters

Builds body awareness and calm focus.

Try this

Play soft music in the background.

4. Balance Challenge Time

Try standing on one foot, then switching.

5. Copy My Move Game

You move (hop, tiptoe, stomp), they copy—then trade roles.

Parent Hack of the Week – The "Body Boss" Trick

Say, "Your body is the boss today!" Let them lead movement games, building confidence and motor planning.

Week 2: Perseverance & Problem Solving in Play

1. Block Rebuild Game

Knock down a tower and ask: "Want to try building a new way?"

2. Puzzle Switch-Up

Mix two puzzles together. Let your child figure it out.

3. Try Again Talk

Mindful Moment

Say: "Trying again is brave. Let's see what happens next time."

Why it matters

Builds resilience and reduces fear of failure.

Try this

Say, "Mistakes are how we grow."

4. Scoop & Pour Station

Let them transfer rice, lentils, or water using spoons, funnels, or bottles.

5. Try a New Tool

Use tongs, tweezers, or chopsticks to move small items.

Parent Hack of the Week – The "Almost!" Phrase

When something is tricky, say, "You almost did it! Want to try again or take a break?" It validates effort over outcome.

Week 3: Exploring Space & Coordination

1. Animal Moves Obstacle Course

Hop like a frog, crawl like a bear, tiptoe like a cat.

2. Toss & Catch Challenge

Try soft balls or socks. Start close, then move farther apart.

3. Body Check-In Pause

Mindful Moment

Ask: "How does your body feel? Tired? Wiggly? Strong?"

Why it matters

Builds physical awareness and emotional connection.

Try this

Model your own check-in too.

4. Shadow Tag

Try to step on each other's shadows outside.

5. Shape Hop Floor Game

Tape different shapes on the floor. Call them out and hop to each.

Parent Hack of the Week – The "How Did That Feel?" Reflection

After any big physical play, pause and ask, "How did that feel in your body?" Builds language around movement and self-regulation.

Week 4: Stretching Bravery & Trying New Things

1. Try a New Route Walk

Take a different path on your usual walk. Ask, "What do you see that's new?"

2. Food Adventure Day

Try a new food together and describe it with all five senses.

3. Brave Breath Pause

Mindful Moment

Before something new, take a big deep breath and say, "I'm ready to try."

Why it matters

Connects courage with regulation.

Try this

Reflect after: "You did it! How did it feel?"

4. Dress-Up Role Game

Put on a costume and try out a new character or job.

5. Upside-Down Challenge

Draw a simple shape or letter upside down and laugh about how it looks.

Parent Hack of the Week – The "Try It Together First" Tip

If your child resists something new, do it first. Then ask, "Want to do it with me?" It lowers anxiety and models bravery.

Life Skill of the Month: Confidence Through Action

Trying new things—even tiny ones—builds:

- Physical courage and balance
- Emotional regulation when things feel hard
- Motor skills and planning abilities
- Resilience to bounce back when things go wrong

You're not just building muscle. You're growing a child who says, "I can do hard things."

Game of the Month: Obstacle Adventure Builder

Let your child create their own obstacle course using cushions, boxes, chairs, or tape. Join them and narrate their plan.

Why it works: Builds creativity, sequencing, motor coordination, and flexible thinking.

Reflect & Recharge Parent Story – The Bravery Spin

"Bhavith used to get scared to jump from a low stool. One day he said, 'I'll just try with one foot.' He did a half-hop and grinned. It wasn't about the jump—it was about the trying. That's when I knew we were building something bigger."

— *Baiju, Dad of 53 month old*

What if my child gives up easily or won't try?

- Start smaller. Even a pretend try counts.

- Say, "You don't have to finish—just try once."

- Celebrate the trying, not the result.

Mindful Reminder

Confidence grows through action. Every time your child tries something new, moves their body, or solves a small problem, they're saying: "I can handle this." Keep cheering that on—it matters more than you know.

Month 54: Everyday Scientists & Explorers

Theme: Discovery, questioning, and experimenting through real-world play

Week 1: Question Everything

1. Why Do You Think? Time

Ask everyday questions like, "Why do you think leaves fall?" Encourage guesses and wondering.

2. Object Detective

Choose a household item. Ask, "What is it for? What else could we use it for?"

3. Curiosity Pause

Mindful Moment

When something unexpected happens, pause and say, "Let's wonder about that."

Why it matters

Builds curiosity and reflective thinking.

Try this

Use in everyday moments: a sound, a spill, a shadow.

4. Invention Box

Give a box of materials (paper rolls, tape, string). Ask, "What could we make?"

5. Guess the Smell Game

Use covered jars with lemon, cinnamon, or soap. Guess by scent only.

Parent Hack of the Week – The "Hmm... I Wonder" Habit

Start asking out loud: "Hmm... I wonder why that happened?" Let your child hear your own curious thinking. It invites them to do the same.

Week 2: Observe, Compare & Test

1. Sink or Float Challenge

Test everyday objects in water. Sort them and talk about why.

2. Shadow Match Play

Make shadow shapes with your hands or toys. Ask, "What do you think that looks like?"

3. Watch it Change

Mindful Moment

Freeze juice, melt ice, or cook eggs together.

Why it matters

Builds understanding of transformation and cause-effect.

Try this

Narrate the changes and invite their observations.

4. Same & Different Sorting

Compare spoons, buttons, or socks. Sort by size, color, use.

5. Animal Movement Match

Watch a video or book. Mimic how animals move. Ask, "What makes them move like that?"

Parent Hack of the Week – The "Let's Test It!" Phrase

When your child makes a guess, respond with: "Let's test it!" Encourages experimentation over just being "right."

Week 3: Build, Create, Innovate

1. Tallest Tower Try

Use blocks, books, or pillows. Ask, "How can we make it taller without it falling?"

2. Nature Tool Builder

Collect leaves, sticks, or stones. Ask, "Can we build something with these?"

3. Try Again Talk

Mindful Moment

When something doesn't work, pause and say, "That was one way. Let's try another!"

Why it matters

Encourages perseverance and flexible thinking.

Try this

Use a warm tone and mirror trying again yourself.

4. Ramp & Roll Race

Create a ramp. Roll different objects and compare speed and distance.

5. Upside Down Challenge

Try building or drawing upside down. Ask, "What feels different?"

Parent Hack of the Week – The "Inventor Voice" Prompt

Say, "Today, we think like inventors!" Shift the mindset to solving and creating, not just completing.

Week 4: Story, Memory & Meaning

1. Retell the Day

Ask your child to tell you what they did that morning. Help add detail.

2. "What Happened Next?" Game

Start a silly story and pause: "Then what happened?"

3. Picture in Your Mind

Mindful Moment

Say, "Let's close our eyes and picture our favourite park. What do you see? Hear?"

Why it matters

Supports visualization, memory, and inner calm.

Try this

Use before bedtime or after a busy day.

4. Memory Tray Game

Place 5 objects on a tray. Cover, remove one. Ask, "What's missing?"

5. Create a Story Map

Draw a simple path with key scenes from a story you read. Let your child walk through it and retell.

Parent Hack of the Week – The "Story Builder" Trick

Start any story with, "Once upon a time there was a..." and let your child build from there. Keeps memory and imagination sharp.

Life Skill + Real-Life Readiness: Thinking Like a Scientist

This month, your child is learning to:

- Ask thoughtful questions and stay curious
- Observe, compare, and experiment
- Try ideas, test them, and revise their thinking
- Build memory, storytelling, and inner reflection

These are the roots of science, innovation, and confident learning. You're teaching them how to think, not just what to know.

Game of the Month: The Sink or Float Game

Set up a tub of water and test household objects - Guess, drop and observe!

Why it works: It builds early hypothesis skills, cause -effect thinking and observational reasoning - all core to scientific thinking.

Reflect & Recharge
Parent Story – The "Why Cloud" Moment

"Vir looked at a dark cloud and said, 'Why is that one sad?' I almost answered with science—but paused and asked, 'What do you think?' He whispered, 'Because it's full.' We both just stood there, watching. I saw his brain and heart growing at once."

— *Kalpana, Mom of 54 month old*

What if my child keeps asking "why?" all day?

- Celebrate it! Curiosity means learning is blooming.
- Answer simply, or turn it around: "What do you think?"
- Don't feel pressure to answer everything. Wonder aloud with them.

> **Mindful Reminder**
>
> Discovery begins with questions. Your patience, pauses, and playful wondering are building a child who doesn't just memorize answers—they build meaning, insight, and lifelong curiosity.

Month 55: Me, You & the World

Theme: Social understanding, empathy, and early citizenship

Week 1: Understanding Others

1. Feelings Through Faces

Look at pictures of different facial expressions. Ask, "What might they be feeling?"

2. Toy Talk Debate

Let two toys "disagree." Help your child practice listening and sharing views.

3. What Would You Do?

Mindful Moment

Describe a simple situation: "If your friend drops their toy, what could you do?"

Why it matters

Builds empathy and decision-making.

Try this

Act it out with stuffed animals.

4. Fair or Not Game

Create pretend scenarios: "You get two cookies and your friend gets none—is that fair?"

5. Reading with Feelings

Choose a storybook. Pause to ask: "How do you think this character feels now?"

Parent Hack of the Week – The "That's One Way to Feel" Phrase

When your child has big feelings, say: "That's one way to feel." It normalizes emotions and opens the door for empathy.

Week 2: Caring in Action

1. Helping Hands Chart

Create a simple chart. Add stars or stickers when your child helps.

2. Kindness Jar

Every time someone in the family does something kind, add a pom-pom.

3. Big Heart Breaths

Mindful Moment

Put hands over your heart and breathe deeply together. Say, "Let's fill our heart with kindness."

Why it matters

Links breath to compassion and calm.

Try this

Use it before playdates or social time.

4. Clean-up for a Cause

Tidy a shared space and say, "We're helping everyone by doing this."

5. Kind Word Echo

Say something kind to your child and have them echo it back to a toy.

Parent Hack of the Week – The "Helper of the Day" Trick

Assign your child a small role each day—plant waterer, snack helper. It builds agency and a caring mindset.

Week 3: Self & Community

1. Neighbourhood Map Drawing

Draw simple shapes to represent home, parks, or shops. Say, "This is where we live!"

2. Local Helpers Roleplay

Pretend to be a mail carrier, cleaner, or shopkeeper. Practice greetings and gratitude.

3. "I Belong Here" Chant

Mindful Moment

Say: "I am safe. I am kind. I belong." Repeat together while placing hands on your chest.

Why it matters

Builds identity and rootedness.

Try this

Use as a morning affirmation.

4. Thank You Walk

Walk around the block and wave to neighbours. Say thank you to a helper if you see one.

5. Our Story Booklet

Fold paper and draw people, places, and routines from your life. "This is our world."

Parent Hack of the Week – The "Belonging Board"

Hang drawings or photos that show your child's place in their community—friends, parks, favourite shop. It strengthens roots.

Week 4: Inclusion & Identity

1. Same & Different Sorting

Use family photos or magazine cut-outs. Group by hair, clothes, or activity—and talk about what makes everyone special.

2. "All Kinds of Friends" Storytime

Read books with characters from different backgrounds. Ask, "What makes a good friend?"

3. Mindful Moment – Respect Hands Game

Hold up hands and say, "These hands are for helping, not hurting."

Why it matters

Builds body awareness and respectful action.

Try this

Trace hands on paper and decorate them with kind actions.

4. Pretend Welcome Party

Pretend a new friend is coming. Ask, "What could we do to make them feel welcome?"

5. Celebrate Me Day

Let your child dress how they want, choose songs and snacks, and talk about what makes them *them.*

Parent Hack of the Week – The "We All Belong" Phrase

Say: "Everyone belongs here—no matter what they look like, play with, or wear." Simple words shape big hearts.

Life Skill of the Month: Social Awareness & Inclusion

Your child is learning how to:

- Recognize and respect feelings in others
- Practice kindness and helpfulness
- Understand fairness, turn-taking, and inclusion
- Feel proud of their identity while appreciating others

This growing awareness builds the foundation for healthy friendships, classroom community, and strong values. You're giving them roots *and* wings.

Game of the Month: Matching Feelings Faces

Use printed emojis, drawn faces, or flashcards. Flip two at a time and find the match. When matched, talk about what might make someone feel that way.

Why it works: Builds memory, emotional vocabulary, and empathy through fun.

Reflect & Recharge
Parent Story – The Neighbour Moment

"My son waved to our elderly neighbour and said, 'You look happy today!' She smiled so wide. He didn't even know her name—but he knew how to connect. That's what I hope he always keeps."

— Hoyame, mom of a 55-month-old

What if my child seems shy or doesn't notice others' feelings?

- That's okay—social awareness takes time.
- Narrate your observations gently: "She looked a little sad—what could we say to help?"
- Celebrate moments of noticing, no matter how small.

> ### Mindful Reminder
>
> Your child is watching how *you* treat others—the warmth in your voice, the care in your words. That's the real lesson. Every kind moment you model becomes a seed they carry into the world.

Month 56: Think Big, Try Brave

Theme: Confidence, perseverance, and flexible thinking

Week 1: Trying New Things

1. Try Something New Day

Choose one new food, game, or activity and explore it together. Ask, "How did it feel to try something new?"

2. Brave Bucket List

Write or draw 3 things your child wants to try. Check them off across the week.

3. Brave Breath Count

Mindful Moment

Breathe in for 4, hold for 2, out for 4. Say: "Brave breath in, calm breath out."

Why it matters

Helps regulate when trying something unfamiliar.

Try this

Use before entering a new place or starting a new task.

4. Story of a First Time

Tell a short story about when *you* tried something new.

5. Play "What If?" Adventure

Ask questions like, "What if you had to meet a new friend today?" Talk through possibilities.

Parent Hack of the Week – The "You Did It Anyway!" Phrase

When your child feels nervous, say: "You were scared, and you did it anyway! That's being brave."

Week 2: Growth Mindset in Action

1. Puzzle Stretch

Try a slightly harder puzzle than usual. Say, "This is a challenge—let's figure it out together!"

2. "Not Yet" Jar

Write things your child is working on. Instead of "can't do," say "not yet."

3. Try Again Tap

Mindful Moment

Tap knees while saying: "Try again, try again, I can try again!"

Why it matters

Builds perseverance through rhythm.

Try this

Use during frustrating moments like dressing or clean-up.

4. Mistake Storytime

Read a book where a character makes a mistake and learns from it. Reflect on what they learned.

5. Sticker for the Struggle

Celebrate effort by giving a sticker not just for results, but for trying something hard.

Parent Hack of the Week – The "Oops Means I'm Learning" Trick

Say: "Oops! That means your brain is growing!" Celebrate mistakes as stepping stones.

Week 3: Flexible Play & Problem-Solving

1. Change the Plan Game

Start playing a game, then change one rule. Ask, "How can we make this work now?"

2. Toy Mix-Up Time

Combine toys in new ways (cars + blocks + animals). See what stories emerge.

3. Pause & Pivot Talk

Mindful Moment

Say: "Plans can change, and that's okay. What can we try now?"

Why it matters

Helps with transitions, change, and flexibility.

Try this

Use when something unexpected happens.

4. Fix-It Challenge

Break part of a block tower or drawing. Ask, "What can we do to fix or improve it?"

5. Opposite Day Decisions

Let your child pretend to do things the opposite way (e.g., silly breakfast for dinner).

Parent Hack of the Week – The "Switch Gears" Phrase

Use when plans change: "Let's switch gears!" It adds fun language to build emotional flexibility.

Week 4: Courage in Conversation

1. Brave Talk Practice

Model phrases like, "Can I play too?" or "I didn't like that."

2. Feel & Speak Cards

Use cards or drawings to practice saying how they feel and what they need.

3. Mirror of Courage

Mindful Moment

Look in a mirror together. Say, "I can do hard things. I can try again."

Why it matters

Builds confidence through self-affirmation.

Try this

Use before school or social outings.

4. Roleplay "Standing Tall"

Pretend someone says something unkind. Practice calm, clear responses.

5. Kind Assertiveness Game

Take turns asking for a toy or a turn with kindness and confidence.

Parent Hack of the Week – The "Say It Strong" Cue

When your child hesitates to speak up, say: "Say it strong, even if it's small."

Life Skill of the Month: Confidence & Flexible Thinking

This month, your child is learning that bravery isn't about being fearless—it's about trying anyway. They're also learning to:

- Take risks and try new things
- Recover from mistakes and keep going
- Adapt when plans change or challenges pop up
- Speak up kindly and clearly

These skills build emotional resilience and real-world readiness for school, relationships, and beyond.

Game of the Month: "Switcheroo Storytelling"

Start a simple story, then say "Switch!" and let your child change the direction. Keep switching every few lines.

Why it works: Boosts imagination, confidence, and quick thinking in a playful way.

Reflect & Recharge
Parent Story – The Brave Voice Surprise

"Yudhir used to hide behind me at playdates. Last week, he walked up to a new kid and said, 'Hi, want to play cars?' I nearly cried. That one sentence took months of courage. And now? He's ready to try more."

— Harshita, mom of a 56-month-old

What if my child gives up easily or avoids new situations?

- Validate their feeling: "Trying new things *can* be hard."
- Model your own effort: "I wasn't sure about that either—but I tried."
- Celebrate tiny brave moments: "You looked even when you didn't touch. That's a step!"

> **Mindful Reminder**
>
> Confidence grows not from perfection, but from trying, wobbling, and trying again. Each brave moment is a seed. You are watering it with love, patience, and belief.

Month 57: Brave Thinkers, Bold Hearts

Theme: Confidence, curiosity, and emotional courage

Week 1: Big Feelings, Brave Choices

1. Emotion Adventure Map

Draw a simple map of places: Happy Hill, Angry Volcano, Calm River. Let your child act out how they'd feel in each place.

2. Feel & Freeze Game

Play music and pause. Name a feeling: "Freeze like you're excited!"

3. Brave Breath Pause

Mindful Moment

Inhale and say, "I can try." Exhale: "Even if it's hard."

Why it matters

Connects breath to emotional resilience.

Try this

Use before new experiences or challenges.

4. Try Again Toy Time

Offer a slightly tricky toy or puzzle. Say, "Let's see what we can figure out together."

5. Courage Crown Craft

Make a paper crown. Write or draw things that made your child proud recently.

Parent Hack of the Week – The "You Did That Hard Thing" Phrase

Instead of just "good job," try: "You were nervous, but you did it anyway." This builds brave self-image.

Week 2: Asking, Exploring & Wondering

1. Why? Box

Set out a box and label it the "Why? Box." Drop in a note when your child asks a big question. Revisit a few each day.

2. Tool Time Exploration

Offer safe kitchen or household tools. Ask, "What do you think this does? Want to test it?"

3. Quiet Wonder Minute

Mindful Moment

Sit together silently. Whisper, "What do you hear? What do you wonder about today?"

Why it matters

Fosters reflection and deeper thinking.

Try this

Use after a walk or storytime.

4. Question Chain Game

Ask a question like, "Why do cats meow?" Let your child answer, then ask another related question.

5. Mystery Bag Game

Place an object in a bag. Ask yes/no questions until they guess what it is.

Parent Hack of the Week – The "Hmm, Let's Find Out Together" Trick

You don't need all the answers. Say, "Let's look it up or test it," and model curiosity alongside your child.

Week 3: Body Bravery & Bold Movement

1. Obstacle Choice Challenge

Set up two short obstacle paths. Let your child choose which one to try.

2. Dance-Your-Name Game

Spell out your child's name in movements: J for Jump, A for Arms up!

3. Shake It Off

Mindful Moment

Shake arms, legs, feet one by one. Say, "Let's shake off the worry!"

Why it matters

Releases tension through physical movement.

Try this

Use before new or tricky tasks.

4. Backward Day Race

Walk backward or try silly crawling patterns. Encourage laughter and confidence.

5. Animal Action Adventure

Act like brave animals: soar like eagles, pounce like lions, balance like flamingos.

Parent Hack of the Week – The "Try It Two Ways" Strategy

If your child hesitates, offer a choice: "Want to try it fast or slow? Alone or together?" This builds autonomy and courage.

Week 4: Courage in Everyday Moments

1. Story of the Brave Bunny

Tell or read a story about a small animal doing something big. Ask, "What would you do if you were Bunny?"

2. My Brave List

Write or draw 3 things your child did this week that felt big or new.

3. Strength Tap

Mindful Moment

Tap shoulders, knees, heart, and say: "Strong arms, strong legs, strong heart."

Why it matters

Reinforces internal strength with physical cues.

Try this

Use before heading out the door.

4. Goodbye Game

Practice saying goodbye to toys, people, or places. Say, "Let's say goodbye with a wave, a bow, or a dance!"

5. Celebration Station

Set up a mini stage or rug. Let your child stand and say, "Today I tried ____!"

Parent Hack of the Week – The "Show Me Brave" Prompt

Ask, "Can you show me your brave face? Brave voice? Brave walk?" Playfully reinforcing inner strength builds real courage.

Life Skill & Real-Life Readiness: Courage & Confidence

Your child is starting to:

- Step into new situations with less hesitation
- Express curiosity and pursue big ideas
- Feel proud after doing something hard or new
- Show resilience after setbacks

These small moments of courage build future confidence, self-starting, and leadership. They learn: "I can do hard things" – and they believe it.

Game of the Month: Brave Bunny Story Dice

Make or buy story dice with characters, places, and emotions. Let your child roll and tell a short story about a brave bunny using what they roll.

Why it works: Supports narrative skills, confidence, and emotional flexibility.

Reflect & Recharge
Parent Story – The Slide Moment

"For weeks, Amira refused to go down the tall slide. Then one day she whispered, 'I want to try.' She climbed slowly, paused, then whooshed down and shouted, 'I DID IT!' I almost cried. She taught herself she could."

— *Ajeera, mom of a 57-month-old*

What if my child avoids anything hard?

- Normalize the feeling: "It's okay to be nervous."
- Reframe bravery: "Brave means doing it *even if* you feel unsure."
- Let them watch you do it first: model your own "first tries."

> ## Mindful Reminder
>
> Courage grows in the trying, not just in the triumph. Every small "yes" to a new experience becomes a building block of bravery. Stand beside them, and soon they'll soar.

Month 58: Ready, Set, Focus!

Theme: Concentration, self-regulation, and mindful engagement

Week 1: Focus Through Movement

1. Body Path Walk

Use tape or string to create a winding path. Let your child walk slowly, balancing on the line.

2. Mirror Me Moves

Take turns making slow body movements. Your child copies you like a mirror.

3. Candle Breathing

Mindful Moment

Pretend to blow out a candle slowly. Repeat a few times.

Why it matters

Builds calm focus through breath control.

Try this

Use it before transitions or new tasks.

4. Slow Snack Sort

Let your child sort snacks by type or color. Count and arrange them mindfully.

5. Drum Pause Game

Beat a slow rhythm with a pot and spoon. When you stop, your child freezes.

Parent Hack of the Week – The "Whisper Start" Trick

When you want to grab your child's attention, start with a whisper instead of a shout. It draws focus like magic.

Week 2: Sticking with a Task

1. Finish the Picture

Draw half a picture. Invite your child to complete it any way they want.

2. Story Puzzle Time

Cut up a favourite book cover or drawing into 4-6 pieces. Let your child reassemble.

3. Noticing Pause

Mindful Moment

Hold up an object. Ask, "What do you see? What colours? What shape?"

Why it matters

Teaches observation and attentional detail.

Try this

Use a flower, toy, or household item.

4. Toy Repair Challenge

Offer a toy with a small issue (missing piece, tangled string). Brainstorm solutions together.

5. Thread & Bead Calm

Use a shoelace and beads or pasta for focused fine motor work.

Parent Hack of the Week – The "Focus Jar"

Fill a small jar with glitter and water. When shaken, it becomes a calm-down tool. Watch the glitter settle as a reset ritual.

Week 3: Mental Flexibility & Focused Fun

1. Rule Switch Game

Play a simple game (like "Simon Says") but change the rules halfway. "Now jump means clap!"

2. Pattern Builder

Use blocks or coloured objects to make and copy patterns.

3. "What Changed?" Game

Mindful Moment

Set out 3-4 objects. Have your child look, then close their eyes while you change one thing.

Why it matters

Strengthens working memory and visual attention.

Try this

Make it harder each time by increasing the number of items.

4. Opposite Action Game

Say, "When I say up, do down!" Practice switching actions.

5. Dance Freeze Story

Pause during dance play to narrate: "You're a sleepy cat now!" and resume.

Parent Hack of the Week – The "Reverse Routine" Trick

Once a week, reverse the bedtime or snack routine. It keeps flexibility fun and thinking sharp.

Week 4: Concentration in Everyday Life

1. Cooking Step Game

Let your child help with one small recipe task: stirring, pouring, or spreading. Focus on one step at a time.

2. Sock Sort Race

Mix socks and ask your child to match pairs. Set a timer for fun, not pressure.

3. "One Sound" Listening

Mindful Moment

Pause and listen: "What's the softest sound you can hear?"

Why it matters

Anchors attention through the auditory sense.

Try this

Use at bedtime or before transitions.

4. Sticker Shape Art

Give a shape outline and small stickers. Ask your child to fill it slowly, carefully.

5. Tidy-Up Challenge

Set a mini-goal: "Let's find all the blue toys!"

Parent Hack of the Week – The "Mini Goal" Strategy

When your child is distracted, break the task down: "Let's just do 5 puzzle pieces." Small wins build focus endurance.

Life Skill of the Month: Concentration & Self-Regulation

Your child is learning to:

- Focus attention for longer periods

- Start and finish short tasks

- Pause, notice, and shift gears with growing independence

- Manage energy through mindful movement

These early focus habits lay the foundation for learning, listening, and classroom readiness. Attention is built through play, repetition, and your patient support.

Game of the Month: Match & Flip Memory Game

Use a set of homemade cards or picture pairs. Flip and match two at a time. Add more pairs as your child's memory grows.

Why it works: Sharpens memory, turn-taking, and sustained attention.

Reflect & Recharge
Parent Story – The Concentration Click

"My daughter was beading a necklace and dropped them all. I expected her to walk away, but she said, 'It's okay, I'll start again.' She sat for 10 more minutes, quietly working. That moment felt like magic."

— *Sia, mom of a 58-month-old*

What if my child still struggles to sit still or finish a task?

- Don't force stillness—focus can happen while moving.

- Break tasks into tiny parts: "Can we just find one more?"

- Celebrate the trying, not just the completion.

Mindful Reminder

Focus isn't about silence or stillness. It's about presence. Every time you pause, wonder, and slow down with your child, you're growing the muscles of attention—together.

Month 59: I Can Do Hard Things

Theme: Resilience, delayed gratification, and developing stamina

Week 1: Trying, Failing & Finishing

1. Almost There Puzzles

Choose a puzzle that is slightly harder than usual. Encourage your child to stick with it and finish.

2. One More Time Game

After an activity (throwing, hopping, writing), say, "Let's try one more time!"

3. Finish Line Visual

Mindful Moment

Close your eyes and say: "Imagine you're at the end of a race... how does it feel to finish something hard?"

Why it matters

Builds mental endurance and emotional closure.

Try this

Ask what they want to finish today.

4. Stack & Crash Challenge

Build a tower. Let it fall. Ask, "Want to rebuild and try a different way?"

5. Time Me, Please

Ask your child to time how long it takes to do a task (buttoning shirt, lining up blocks). Try again to beat their time.

Parent Hack of the Week – The "Try Muscle" Talk

Say, "You're growing your try muscle!" when they keep going after a setback. It reframes failure as effort.

Week 2: Delayed Gratification & Self-Regulation

1. Freeze Before You Eat

Place a snack in front. Say, "Can we count to 10 before taking a bite?"

2. Wait & Wiggle Game

Have them wait a few seconds before starting a game. Add a silly movement while waiting.

3. Candy Choice Talk

Mindful Moment

Ask: "Would you take 1 sweet now or wait for 2 later? Why?"

Why it matters

Begins the concept of impulse control and future thinking.

Try this

Let them create their own "wait or take" game.

4. Helping Before Playing

Ask them to do one small task before play. Praise their patience.

5. Sticker Story Delay

Offer a sticker now or a full storybook of stickers later. Let them decide.

Parent Hack of the Week – The "First, Then" Frame

Use, "First we clean up, then we play!" consistently. It links short wait times with positive outcomes.

Week 3: Moving Through Challenge

1. Obstacle Stamina Course

Add more steps to a movement path: jump, crawl, balance, freeze.

2. Strong Body Countdown

Count backward from 10 with each movement: 10 jumps, 9 hops...

3. Belly Breathe & Whisper

Mindful Moment

Take 3 deep belly breaths. Whisper: "I can do hard things."

Why it matters

Connects breath with self-talk and calmness.

Try this

Do it together after frustration or before a new task.

4. Stamina Stacker Game

See how many blocks or toys they can balance or stack before toppling.

5. Slow-Mo Task Day

Brush teeth, tie shoes, or pour water slowly. Talk about control and staying focused.

Parent Hack of the Week – The "Keep Going Count"

During a tricky task, count aloud each try: "That's your third try! Let's keep going!" It celebrates effort.

Week 4: Grit, Focus & Confidence

1. Story Finish Challenge

Read half a story and ask your child to finish it. Then read the real ending.

2. Spot the Same Mistake

Repeat a mistake in a task (drawing, matching). Ask, "Did we do it again?"

3. Big Breath, Big Task

Mindful Moment

Before a big task, take one strong breath. Say, "Ready, mind and body? Let's go."

Why it matters

Grounds and focuses attention on the process.

Try this

Use when your child says, "I can't."

4. Gratitude Delay Jar

For every time they wait, say thank you and add a stone or sticker to a jar.

5. Memory Match Perseverance

Use a memory card game. Encourage finishing even if mistakes happen.

Parent Hack of the Week – The "I Noticed" Praise

Instead of outcome praise, say, "I noticed you kept trying even when it was tricky." That's what builds grit.

Life Skill of the Month: Resilience in Real Time

This month is about helping your child keep going—mentally and physically—even when things don't come easily.

- Celebrate trying, not just winning
- Pause to name effort: "You worked hard on that!"
- Use waiting and slowing down as practice
- Offer doable challenges and stay nearby
- Remind them: "You're learning how to keep going, even when it's hard."

Game of the Month: Stack, Stop & Restart

Use blocks or books. Build a tower. When it falls, pause and say: "Now what?" Encourage creative solutions or try again with a new strategy.

Why it works: Blends physical movement, problem-solving, emotional regulation, and persistence.

Reflect & Recharge
Parent Story – The Shoe-Tying Moment

"We'd been working on tying shoes for weeks. One morning, Kasvi said, 'Don't help.' She fumbled for nearly five minutes. Then she did it. Her look of pride? It made every moment worth it."

— Swati, mom of a 59-month-old

What if my child gives up too easily?

- Break tasks into smaller pieces
- Use phrases like "Let's figure it out together"
- Celebrate the effort: "You didn't give up!"

> **Mindful Reminder**
>
> You're not just building skills. You're shaping identity. Every time your child tries again, they're learning: "I am someone who doesn't give up." That's a gift they'll carry for life.

Month 60: Growing Strong & Ready

Theme: Confidence, capability, and transition readiness

Week 1: I Can Do It!

1. My Big Kid List

Ask your child what things they can do on their own. Write or draw them together.

2. Dress & Dash Game

Time how fast they can dress, zip, or put on shoes. Celebrate effort, not speed.

3. The "I Can" Mirror

Mindful Moment

Stand together in front of a mirror. Say, "I can..." and name a skill. Let your child try.

Why it matters

Boosts self-efficacy and self-pride.

Try this

Say, "You've learned so much. What's one thing you feel proud of?"

4. Snack Maker Station

Set up a small area where your child can prepare simple snacks with minimal help.

5. Try It Two Ways

Choose a task (e.g., building a block tower) and ask, "What's another way we could do it?"

Parent Hack of the Week – The "From Me to You" Trick

Let your child teach you something they've mastered. Say, "Show me how you do it!" You'll boost their confidence and deepen your connection.

Week 2: Goodbye to Little, Hello to Big

1. Memory Lane Storytime

Look at old pictures or videos and talk about how much your child has grown.

2. Play School Day

Roleplay as if it's the first day of school. Practice saying goodbye, putting on a backpack, and asking for help.

3. "Then & Now" Reflection

Mindful Moment

Say: "You used to say 'ba-ba' for water. Now you ask, 'Can I have a drink, please?'"

Why it matters

Highlights growth and builds self-narrative.

Try this

Do one "Then & Now" at bedtime each night this week.

4. Special Goodbye Circle

Gather family or toys to "say goodbye" to toddler days. Celebrate what's next.

5. All About Me Book

Create a mini-book with drawings or pictures: name, age, favourite toy, best friend, big dream.

Parent Hack of the Week – The "You Grew Into It" Frame

Revisit something your child used to struggle with. Say, "You grew into it. Just like you will with the next new thing."

Week 3: Ready to Meet the World

1. Kind Words Call-Out

Practice greetings, thank yous, and polite requests using puppets or toys.

2. Follow the Day Game

Talk through a pretend school day or group class: "First we put our bags down…"

3. Brave Breath Practice

Mindful Moment

Hold hands and say, "Brave on the inside, calm on the outside." Breathe slowly together.

Why it matters

Encourages emotional regulation and internal strength.

Try this

Use before trying something new or when facing a transition.

4. Backpack Helpers Challenge

Pack a pretend school bag. Talk about what goes inside and why.

5. Roleplay Conflict Fixers

"What if two kids want the same toy?" Act out solutions together.

Parent Hack of the Week – The "What Would You Say?" Prompt

Instead of feeding answers, ask: "What would you say if…?" It strengthens social language and decision-making.

Week 4: Celebration & Connection

1. Party for Me Day

Let your child plan a small celebration—choose decorations, snacks, and music.

2. Family Parade Walk

Go for a walk and cheer for your child: "You're five! You're kind! You're ready!"

3. "I Am, I Can, I Will" Mantra

Mindful Moment

Say: "I am strong. I can try. I will grow." Repeat together.

Why it matters

Anchors self-belief and readiness.

Try this

Use as a bedtime chant the night before school or big transitions.

4. Thank You Notes Time

Help your child draw or dictate a thank you note to someone who's helped them grow.

5. Pass the Memory Circle

Share a memory of your child's early years. Let others (siblings, grandparents) join too.

Parent Hack of the Week – The "You're Not Losing a Baby" Reminder

When nostalgia hits, remind yourself: "I'm not losing my baby—I'm watching them become who they're meant to be."

Life Skill + Readiness: Transition Confidence

This month is about sending your child forward with:

- The pride of what they've already accomplished
- The curiosity to keep learning
- The courage to face new places, people, and routines

You've taught them how to try, how to feel, how to ask, how to care. That's the heart of real readiness.

Game of the Month: "Big Feelings Freeze"

Play music and dance. When the music stops, call out a feeling: "Happy!" "Nervous!" "Excited!" Your child freezes in that face or pose.

Why it works: Builds emotional expression, quick thinking, and fun vocabulary practice.

Reflect & Recharge
Parent Story – The Grown-Up Giggle

"I watched Arnav tie his own shoes, then winked and said, 'I got this, Mom.' I laughed—he still needed help with one loop—but that moment? That was the bridge. He's growing, and I'm growing too."

— *Sonal, mom of a 60-month-old*

What if I'm feeling emotional about this milestone?

- It's not just your child's transition—it's yours too.
- Let yourself feel proud, tender, even a little sad.
- You've done something beautiful. Breathe that in.

> ### Mindful Reminder
>
> This isn't the end. It's a new beginning—with deeper conversations, bolder ideas, and a relationship that keeps evolving. You've walked them through babyhood with presence and love. Now, you walk beside a confident child—ready for the world.

Year 5: A Milestone Year – You Did It!

Congratulations! You and your child have reached an incredible milestone—five whole years of learning, growing, and building the foundation for a lifetime of success. Your little one is now more independent, expressive, and full of curiosity, and **it's all thanks to your love, patience, and dedication. You are doing an amazing job!**

This past year has likely been filled with big emotions, growing confidence, and exciting new discoveries. Your child is developing critical thinking, creativity, and social skills that will prepare them for the next stage of their journey. There may have been challenges, but through every high and low, **your support, encouragement, and belief in them have made all the difference.**

Take a moment to **track and rate your child's progress** using the **Milestone Tracker,** celebrating their achievements and recognizing areas for continued growth.

As you step beyond Year 5, new opportunities and adventures await. Whether it's starting school, making new friends, or exploring new interests, **your love and support will continue to be their greatest strength.** Keep trusting yourself, enjoy the journey, and remember— **every moment you invest in your child's growth is shaping their bright and beautiful future.**

You've got this! Congratulations on completing Year 5! Your dedication has helped shape a confident, capable, and happy child, and the best is yet to come.

Understanding Your Child's Developmental Tracker

Every child develops at their own pace. These trackers are designed to provide a structured way to observe and support your child's growth, but they should not be seen as rigid timelines. It's completely normal for some children to excel in certain areas while taking more time in others.

How to Use the Tracker

- **Rate on a scale of 0-5** based on your child's current abilities in each category.

- **No need to rush or compare!** Some children might be more advanced in speech but take longer with motor skills, and that's completely fine.

- **Use it as a guide**, not a test. If your child isn't yet meeting certain milestones, observe their progress over time instead of worrying.

- **Celebrate small wins!** Any progress, no matter how small, is valuable.

What If My Child is Behind in Some Areas?

- **Variability is normal** – Development is not linear, and children often leap ahead in some skills while taking more time in others.

- **Support their growth** through interactive play, reading, conversations, and hands-on activities that align with their interests.

- **Patience is key** – Keep engaging them in activities without pressure or comparisons.

- **Seek guidance if necessary** – If you have concerns, consulting a paediatrician or child development expert can provide reassurance and strategies for support.

Encouraging a Positive Learning Experience

This tracker is meant to **empower you as a parent** and help you understand your child's unique journey. Focus on their strengths, provide encouragement, and create a nurturing environment where learning feels fun and natural. Every child has their own timeline – trust the process, and enjoy watching them grow!

Remember: Progress over perfection! ❀

Domain	Emerging Milestones	Rating (0-5)
Communication & Language	Speaks in 6–8 word sentences with clear articulation	
	Asks thoughtful "why," "how," and "what if" questions	
	Uses emotion words and expressive language to describe thoughts	
	Follows multi-step directions in sequence	
	Begins experimenting with rhyming, story structure, and simple explanations	
	Recognizes letters, name words, or symbols in books and surroundings	
Social & Emotional Development	Navigates group play with cooperation and leadership	
	Understands turn-taking, fairness, and basic social rules	
	Names and manages a wider range of emotions	
	Shows empathy and awareness of others' needs or moods	
	Attempts simple conflict resolution without adult prompting	

Cognitive & Thinking Skills	Sequences steps for routines and storytelling	
	Plans ahead in pretend play and real tasks (e.g., "First we need plates…")	
	Sorts and classifies using more than one category (e.g., big red cars)	
	Engages in early logic and prediction: "If we forget shoes, our feet get cold"	
	Explores numbers through play: counting, estimating, comparing	
Fine & Gross Motor Skills	Runs, hops, skips, and rides scooters or tricycles confidently	
	Cuts along curves or shapes with scissors; begins writing name	
	Builds tall or detailed structures using blocks or mixed materials	
	Draws figures or symbols with increasing control	
	Manages personal care independently (dressing, cleaning up spills)	
Play, Creativity & Real-Life Readiness	Leads pretend scenarios and invents characters or stories	
	Solves simple real-world problems through trial and error	
	Takes pride in helping with home routines (setting table, folding clothes)	
	Begins to understand time concepts (yesterday, next, soon)	
	Makes simple plans or choices based on logic or preference	

Remember -You don't need worksheets or drills. If your child is telling a made-up story, helping sort laundry, or asking why the moon follows the car—learning is alive.

As early childhood winds down, take a moment to marvel at the confident, curious soul your child is becoming.

Each shared moment laid the foundation for a future full of possibility.

Growth is in the values, voice, and love you've nurtured.

This chapter ends, but your legacy of connection carries forward.

CHAPTER 7

Conclusion

A Journey of Love, Growth, and Endless Possibilities

Congratulations on completing this incredible **five-year journey** with your child! From their very first days to these exciting years of curiosity, learning, and discovery, you have been their greatest guide, cheerleader, and source of love. **Your dedication, patience, and commitment have laid the foundation for a strong, capable, and confident individual. You are an amazing parent!**

The past five years have been filled with milestones - first words, first steps, first friendships, and countless learning moments. There have been joys, challenges, and everything in between, but through it all, **your love and support have made all the difference.** The little moments— the bedtime stories, the giggles, the endless questions - are the ones that shape a child's future in the most profound ways.

As your child continues to grow beyond these first five years, **trust yourself and your parenting instincts.** Every child is unique, and every journey is different, but what remains constant is the impact of a parent's love and guidance. **Keep celebrating small wins, embracing challenges, and enjoying the journey - because the best is yet to come!**

Use the **Milestone Tracker** to reflect on this incredible journey, this will serve as a beautiful reminder of how far you and your child have come - and a guide for the wonderful years ahead.

Stay Connected & Share Your Feedback!

No clutter, no fluff — just thoughtful posts when there's something meaningful to share. Join us on Instagram at **[@mindformindfulparenting]**

Loved this book? Support us by leaving a **rating and review on Amazon** - your feedback helps other parents too!

Have questions or suggestions? Feel free to reach out at mindformindfulparenting@gmail.com - we'd love to hear from you!

Parenting is a journey, not a destination. You have given your child a strong start in life, and your love and support will continue to shape their future.

You're already doing more than enough—by showing up, by being curious, by caring.

Come back to this book whenever you need a little clarity, comfort, or inspiration.

Remember You're not just raising a child — you're raising the future, mindfully

Wishing you and your child a lifetime of learning, joy, and success!

CHAPTER 8

Parent's Toolkit

This final section gathers the most essential resources to support your parenting journey from birth to age five. Inside, you'll find answers to frequently asked questions, developmental red flags to watch for year by year, screen time guidance, stress relief strategies for parents, brain-boosting nutrition tips, and curated resources for when you want to explore more.

It also includes a Quick Reference: Milestones & Activities by Age—a simple, at-a-glance guide to help you track your child's growth, support their learning, and know when to seek additional support if needed.

This toolkit is designed to be your everyday companion—practical, reassuring, and easy to turn to whenever you need it most.

A. Frequently Asked Questions (FAQ)

Parenting comes with many questions, and each stage of a child's development brings new challenges. Here are answers to some common concerns during the first five years.

1. How do I know if my child is developing at a normal pace?

Every child develops at their own pace, but general milestones can help track progress. If your child is consistently behind in multiple areas (e.g., speech, motor skills, or social interaction), refer to the *Red Flags to Watch Out For* section and consult a paediatrician.

2. What if my child isn't talking as much as others their age?

Some children are late talkers and catch up naturally. However, if your child isn't saying single words by 16 months or combining words by 24 months, consult a paediatrician or speech therapist. Reading, singing, and talking regularly help boost language skills.

3. How can I encourage my child to be more independent?

Offer opportunities to do small tasks like dressing, tidying toys, or making simple choices. Praise efforts and allow them to try on their own before stepping in.

4. My child throws frequent tantrums. Is this normal?

Yes. Tantrums are a normal part of early childhood. Stay calm, acknowledge their emotions, and guide them to express themselves. Offer coping strategies such as deep breathing or a quiet space.

5. How can I make learning fun for my child?

Incorporate learning into play. Puzzles, storytelling, pretend play, and sensory activities make learning engaging and enjoyable.

6. My child isn't interested in socializing with other kids. Should I be concerned?

Some children are more reserved. Encourage socialization through playdates or group activities. If your child avoids all interaction or struggles with communication, seek a professional opinion.

7. How much screen time is okay for my child?

Refer to the *Tech & Screen Time Guidelines* section for detailed age-based recommendations. Focus on high-quality, interactive content and avoid passive or unsupervised screen use.

8. What are the best ways to improve my child's attention span?

Start with short, engaging tasks and gradually increase focus time. Minimize background noise and distractions. Storytelling, pretend play, and puzzles work well.

9. How can I discipline my child effectively without being too harsh?

Use positive discipline - clear boundaries, consistent routines, and modelling good behaviour. Redirect misbehaviour, offer choices, and reward good behaviour with praise.

10. How can I track my child's progress over the years?

Use the *Milestone Tracker* provided in this book. Adjust learning approaches based on your observations and your child's unique needs.

11. How can I adapt activities for different learning styles?

Children may be visual, auditory, or kinesthetic learners.

- Visual: Use picture books, flashcards, color-coded tools
- Auditory: Use songs, rhymes, and verbal instructions
- Kinesthetic: Focus on hands-on play, crafts, and movement-based learning

12. What if my child resists certain activities?

It's normal. Try turning the activity into a game, offering choices, or incorporating their interests. Keep sessions short and revisit later if needed.

13. How can I manage sibling dynamics while following the plan?

Balance shared and individual time. Encourage teamwork, set clear rules, and recognize each child's progress without comparison.

Need more help?

For specific concerns, you can reach out via email at:

mindformindfulparenting@gmail.com

B. Year-Wise Red Flags to Watch Out For

Some delays may signal the need for professional support. If several red flags persist, consult a paediatrician or specialist.

Year 1: (0–12 months)

- Not holding head up by 3 months
- Not sitting without support by 9 months
- No babbling, no response to name by 9 months
- No smiling or interest in interaction

Year 2: (12–24 months)

- Not walking by 18 months
- No words by 16 months
- Doesn't point or follow simple directions
- Avoids interaction or lacks curiosity

Year 3: (24–36 months)

- Difficulty with stairs or using hands for simple tasks
- Fewer than 50 words, unclear speech
- Extreme tantrums or repetitive behaviours
- No interest in pretend play

Year 4: (36–48 months)

- Trouble running or using tools like crayons
- Cannot form simple sentences
- Struggles socially or with instructions
- Doesn't recognize shapes or answer basic questions

Year 5: (48–60 months)

- Poor coordination or fine motor delays
- Speech not understandable to strangers
- Difficulty making friends
- Can't recall name, age, or basic concepts

When to Seek Help

If delays persist over time or interfere with daily life, seek support from paediatricians, speech therapists, or developmental experts. Early intervention makes a difference.

C. Tech & Screen Time Guidelines

Technology can enhance learning when used mindfully. Too much passive screen time, however, may disrupt development.

Recommended Limits (Based on AAP Guidelines):

Age	Recommended Time	Best Practices
0–18 months	Avoid (except video calls)	Focus on real-world interaction
18–24 months	Limited, supervised use	Watch together; use high-quality content
2–5 years	Max 1 hour/day	Co-watch and discuss; prioritize learning apps

Healthy Screen Habits:

- Choose interactive over passive content
- Watch and talk together
- Balance with physical, hands-on play

- Use screens as a tool - not a pacifier

- Create screen-free routines for meals and bedtime

Signs of Excessive Screen Time:

- Irritability when screens are turned off

- Avoidance of toys or outdoor play

- Delayed speech or social skills

- Trouble falling asleep

Tip: Gradually replace screen time with books, play, or storytelling.

Final Thought: Screens should support, not replace the real-world exploration and connection.

D. Nutrition and Brain Development

While love, play, and learning shape the brain, nutrition fuels it. The foods your child eats today directly impact their memory, mood, focus, and lifelong habits.

Top Brain-Boosting Nutrients:

Certain nutrients supercharge early brain development:

- **Healthy Fats –** Avocados, nut butters, eggs, and fatty fish build brain cells and improve memory.

- **Iron –** Found in meats, beans, and leafy greens; supports oxygen flow to the brain.

- **Choline –** Eggs and dairy help with memory and brain structure.

- **Zinc –** Whole grains, nuts, and seeds support attention and learning.

- **Omega-3s –** Flaxseeds, chia, and fish improve focus and emotional balance.

Smart Snack Ideas for Growing Minds:

No fancy prep needed—just real, simple food:

- Apple slices with nut butter
- Yogurt with berries
- Veggie sticks with hummus
- Oatmeal with banana and seeds
- Boiled eggs and whole-grain crackers

Hydration = Concentration

Even a little dehydration can affect mood and focus. Keep water handy, especially after play or meals.

Real Life, Not Perfect Plates

It's normal for toddlers to be picky. Your job isn't to control what they eat—it's to keep offering variety. Sit down together, eat the same food, and make mealtimes a calm, pressure-free zone.

Quick Tip: Involve your child in simple kitchen tasks—washing veggies, stirring oats, or choosing between two snack options. When kids help, they're more likely to eat.

E. Stress Management for Parents: Avoiding Burnout

Caring for children is deeply fulfilling, yet emotionally and physically demanding. Your well-being matters too.

Signs of Burnout

- Constant exhaustion
- Irritability or detachment
- Loss of joy in parenting
- Physical symptoms (headaches, sleep trouble)

10 Practical Ways to Manage Stress

Prioritize Small Breaks

1. Take 10 minutes daily for yourself. Breathe, stretch, or get some fresh air.

Set Realistic Expectations

2. Embrace imperfection. "Good enough" is enough.

Ask for Help

3. Share responsibilities or connect with supportive peers.

Simplify Self-Care

4. Eat, hydrate, and rest when you can.

Move Daily

5. Light exercise boosts mood—even a walk counts.

Practice Mindfulness

6. Try breathing exercises like 4-7-8 or focus on one task at a time.

Create a Guilt-Free Ritual

7. Read, journal, or unwind with a simple joy each day.

Build a Support Network

8. Join parenting groups or talk to fellow parents.

Avoid Social Media Comparison

9. Follow pages that uplift you, not pressure you.

Celebrate Small Wins

10. Write down one good moment per day. Small joys add up.

Final Reminder

A happy parent creates a happy home. Taking care of yourself is not a luxury - it's a necessity

F. Additional Sources – Further Reading by Age

If you're the kind of parent who likes to dig a little deeper, this section is for you.

These resources have been carefully selected from some of the most trusted experts around the world. Whether you're looking for research-backed guidance, simple tips, or reassurance that you're on the right track, you'll find something here to support you.

Take what helps, explore what speaks to you, and come back anytime you want to learn more.

Note: All article links and QR codes were active at the time of publishing.

1-Year-Old

Article Title & Link	QR Code
Serve and Return – Harvard https://developingchild.harvard.edu/key-concept/serve-and-return/	
12–24 Months Guide – Zero to Three https://www.zerotothree.org/resource/12-24-months-social-emotional-development/	
Safety for Your Child: 1 to 2 Years – AAP https://www.healthychildren.org/English/ages-stages/toddler/Pages/Safety-for-Your-Child-1-to-2-Years.aspx	
Children and Sleep – Sleep Foundation https://www.sleepfoundation.org/children-and-sleep	
Fostering Curiosity – NAEYC https://www.naeyc.org/resources/pubs/yc/dec2020/fostering-curiosity-infants	

2-Year-Old

Article Title & Link	QR Code
Why Your Toddler's 'No!' Phase Matters – Today's Parent https://www.todaysparent.com/family/parenting/why-your-toddlers-no-phase-is-so-important-and-how-to-survive-it/	
Literacy at Home – Reading Rockets https://www.readingrockets.org/literacy-home	
Milestones at 2 Years – CDC https://www.cdc.gov/ncbddd/actearly/milestones/milestones-2yr.html	
Discipline Tips – CDC https://www.cdc.gov/parenting-toddlers/discipline-consequences/index.html	

3-Year-Old

Article Title & Link	QR Code
Playful Learning – NAEYC https://www.naeyc.org/resources/pubs/yc/ summer2022/power-playful-learning	
Helping Children with Sharing – Zero to Three https://www.zerotothree.org/resource/helping-young-children-with-sharing/	
Teaching Kids Self-Control – Focus on the Family https://www.focusonthefamily.com/parenting/ teaching-kids-self-control/	
Milestones at 3 Years – CDC https://www.cdc.gov/ncbddd/actearly/milestones/ milestones-3yr.html	
Reading Development – Reading Rockets https://www.readingrockets.org/reading-101/how-children-learn-read/typical-reading-development	

4-Year-Old

Article Title & Link	QR Code
10 Things About Play – NAEYC https://www.naeyc.org/our-work/families/10-things-every-parent-play	
Executive Function in Kids – Harvard https://developingchild.harvard.edu/science/key-concepts/executive-function/	
Cognitive Development – AAP https://www.healthychildren.org/English/ages-stages/preschool/Pages/Cognitive-Development-in-Preschool-Children.aspx	
Milestones at 4 Years – CDC https://www.cdc.gov/ncbddd/actearly/milestones/milestones-4yr.html	

5-Year-Old

Article Title & Link	QR Code
Boosting Executive Function – Harvard https://developingchild.harvard.edu/resources/ inbrief-executive-function/	
Milestones at 5 Years – CDC https://www.cdc.gov/ncbddd/actearly/milestones/ milestones-5yr.html	
Positive Parenting Tips – CDC https://www.cdc.gov/child-development/positive- parenting-tips/preschooler-3-5-years.html	
Indoor Games for Child Development – UNICEF https://www.unicef.org/parenting/child-care/games- child-development	

Disclaimer: All linked resources are the intellectual property of their respective organizations. No ownership or affiliation is implied. Links are shared for educational purposes under fair use.

Quick Reference: Milestones & Activities by Age (0–5 Years)

A gentle guide to help you follow your child's growth, support their learning with age-appropriate activities, and notice when a little extra support might be helpful—all in one easy-to-scan place.

Age	Milestones to Watch For	Try This at Home	Keep in Mind
3 Months	Lifts head, makes cooing sounds	Tummy time, mirror faces, tracking toys	Not responding to sounds? Try gentle singing and face time.
6 Months	Rolls, babbles, explores with hands	Peek-a-boo, texture baskets, safe floor play	Not reaching or babbling? Offer varied textures and mimic sounds.
9 Months	Crawls, responds to name, explores surroundings	Crawl chases, stacking toys, sound play	No babble yet? Repeat simple sounds back and forth.
12 Months	Pulls to stand, says a few words	Push toys, pretend phone, naming body parts	Not trying to stand? Offer safe furniture for cruising.
18 Months	Walks confidently, uses basic phrases	Action songs, naming games, water play	No words yet? Talk through routines, name everything aloud.

2 Years	Understands simple directions, shows empathy	Pretend play, sorting games, everyday chores	Trouble following steps? Slow down and show each one clearly.
2.5 Years	Understands opposites, gains balance	Obstacle paths, shape hunts, movement games	Trouble balancing? Try low steps and soft climbing activities.
3 Years	Talks in full thoughts, plays imaginatively	Dress-up, story prompts, role play	Not talking much? Give space, listen deeply, and model phrases.
3.5 Years	Follows 2–3 step routines, asks "why?" often	Puppet shows, pattern games, rhythm claps	Struggles with steps? Use routines with visual prompts.
4 Years	Describes feelings, tries to solve small problems	Nature walks, calm down tools, storytelling	Big emotions? Offer words for feelings and consistent routines.
4.5 Years	Cooperative play grows, notices shapes and letters naturally	Group games, pretend shops, dance & move play	Avoids group play? Start with one-on-one familiar activities.
5 Years	Tells stories, handles more independence, follows rules	Board games, journaling, creative stations	Trouble with rules? Practice through pretend play and modelling.

Tip: Use this table as a progress check, not a pressure checklist. Every child grows at their own pace—support, observe, and enjoy the journey.

Your Parenting Notes

Use these pages to jot down thoughts, questions, ideas, or milestones that matter to you. Whether it's a breakthrough moment, a funny quote, a concern to ask your paediatrician, or simply a reflection from your day—this space is yours.

Your Parenting Notes

Your Parenting Notes

Shradha Maheshwari is a first-time mom who turned her parenting curiosity into a powerful, practical system for raising mindful, connected children in today's fast-paced world.

Her motherhood journey began in the UK, where she explored some of the world's most progressive early childhood practices. Now living in Dubai, she's spent years learning from mothers of many nationalities— listening, observing, and absorbing diverse parenting styles from around the globe.

With a deep passion for structure, science, and soulful connection, Shradha set out to create what she couldn't find: a clear, no-pressure parenting plan she could follow day by day with her own child. She tested every part of it in real life—and after witnessing the transformation in her own home (and hearing the same from friends and fellow moms), she felt called to share it with the world.

Her mission is simple: to make mindful parenting feel doable and empowering for every family, no matter where they are or how busy life gets.

Professionally, Shradha is a Chartered Accountant who has worked with leading FMCG brands and one of the world's most iconic toy companies—LEGO Group—where she discovered the lasting power of learning through play. That insight became a cornerstone of this book.

MIND for Mindful Parenting isn't just a book she wrote—it's the one she needed. And now, it's her gift to parents everywhere: offered with calm, clarity, and compassion.